The EU in Association Agreement Negotiations

C000075944

Through its focus on EU Association Agreement negotiations, this book goes beyond the study of traditional EU trade negotiations and puts the spotlight on the increasing number of negotiations where trade relations are discussed alongside political ones. This setting makes both the negotiations themselves and the definition of the EU's positions more complicated, raising the question as to what ultimately determines the EU's behaviour in such complex negotiations spanning multiple of the EU's policy areas.

Offering a generalizable analytical model to study such complex EU international negotiations, the book illuminates the preferences and interactions between individual parts of the EU's foreign affairs bureaucracy, and those between the lead actors, the Directorate-General for Trade, and the European External Action Service (EEAS), in particular. In doing so, it demonstrates the utility of adapting the concept of bureaucratic politics from Foreign Policy Analysis (FPA) to the EU's foreign policy decision-making apparatus across different stages of EU international negotiations. It also discusses how the institutional changes of the Treaty of Lisbon have altered the institutional set-up of the EU's foreign affairs bureaucracy and thereby changed the foundations of the EU's bureaucratic politics. Finally, the book finds that the EU's behaviour in these negotiations is ultimately shaped, on the one hand, by the presence of diverging positions between its institutional actors, and the difficulty to bridge them through policy coordination mechanisms, on the other. Empirically, it explores these dynamics by considering the EU's Association Agreement negotiations on the Latin American continent over the last twenty years before demonstrating the analytical model's utility in the context of the EU's negotiations with Ukraine and Japan.

This book will be of key interest to scholars, students, and practitioners in EU foreign affairs/external relations, EU public administration and public policy, EU trade policy, and more broadly to Foreign Policy Analysis and International Relations.

Daniel Schade is a Postdoctoral Researcher and Lecturer at the Otto von Guericke University Magdeburg, Germany, and a Visiting Lecturer at Sciences Po Paris, France.

Routledge Advances in European Politics

Lobbying Success in the European Union
The Role of Information and Frames
Daniel Rasch

Muslim Attitudes Towards the European Union
Bernd Schlipphak and Mujtaba Isani

The Populist Radical Left in Europe
Edited by Giorgos Katsambekis and Alexandros Kioupkiolis

External Energy Security in the European Union
Small Member States' Perspective
Matúš Mišík

The Balkans on Trial
Justice vs. Realpolitik
Carole Hodge

Greece and Turkey in Conflict and Cooperation
From Europeanization to De-Europeanization
Edited by Alexis Heraclides and Gizem Alioğlu Çakmak

Diversity of Patchwork Capitalism in Central and Eastern Europe
Edited by Ryszard Rapacki

The EU in Association Agreement Negotiations
Challenges to Complex Policy Coordination
Daniel Schade

For more information about this series, please visit: www.routledge.com/
Routledge-Advances-in-European-Politics/book-series/AEP

The EU in Association Agreement Negotiations

Challenges to Complex Policy Coordination

Daniel Schade

Routledge
Taylor & Francis Group

LONDON AND NEW YORK

First published 2020
by Routledge
2 Park Square, Milton Park, Abingdon, Oxon OX14 4RN

and by Routledge
605 Third Avenue, New York, NY 10017

First issued in paperback 2022

Routledge is an imprint of the Taylor & Francis Group, an informa business

© 2020 Daniel Schade

Publisher's Note
The publisher has gone to great lengths to ensure the quality of this reprint
but points out that some imperfections in the original copies may be apparent.

British Library Cataloging-in-Publication Data
A catalogue record for this book is available from the British Library

Library of Congress Cataloging-in-Publication Data
A catalog record has been requested for this book

ISBN: 978-1-03-240109-6 (pbk)
ISBN: 978-0-367-32116-1 (hbk)
ISBN: 978-0-429-31670-8 (ebk)

DOI: 10.4324/9780429316708

Typeset in Times New Roman
by Scientific Publishing
Services

Contents

List of figures   vii
List of tables   viii
List of abbreviations   ix

PART I
**Analysing the EU's behaviour in complex Association Agreement
negotiations**   1

1 Introduction: The EU in increasingly complex
   international negotiations   3

2 Foreign Policy Analysis and EU foreign policy-making   15

3 EU Association Agreements and institutional decision-
   making complexity over time   49

PART II
Complex EU negotiations in the Latin American region   87

4 Testing the water: Initial attempts for cross-cutting
   negotiations in the Latin American region   89

5 Institutional complexity and the Lisbon transition:
   Negotiating with Central America and the Andean region   123

6 Negotiations in the aftermath of the Lisbon Treaty's
   institutional turmoil   171

PART III
Understanding the wider dynamics of complex EU negotiations   **197**

7   Negotiations with the rest of the world   199

8   Reflections on the drivers of EU behaviour in complex
    international negotiations   210

    Appendix: List of interviews   225
    Index   227

Figures

3.1   EU Free Trade Agreement decision-making   51
3.2   EU Association Agreement decision-making   58

Tables

1.1	Complex EU negotiations in the Latin American region	8
2.1	Indicators for the presence of bureaucratic politics	33
3.1	European Commissioners with External Relations portfolios over time	63
3.2	Relevant Commission Directorates-General and Directorates over time	70
5.1	EU–CAN and EU–SIECA trade in goods	125

Abbreviations

AA	Association Agreement
ACP	African, Caribbean and Pacific Group of States
AFET	European Parliament Foreign Affairs Committee
ASEAN	Association of Southeast Asian Nations
CAN	Andean Community of Nations
CAP	Common Agricultural Policy
CCP	Common Commercial Policy
CELAC	Community of Latin American and Caribbean States
CFSP	Common Foreign and Security Policy
COLAC	Working Party on Latin America and the Caribbean
COPA	Committee of Professional Agricultural Organisations
COREPER	Committee of Permanent Representatives
DDA	Doha Development Agenda
DG	Directorate-General
DG AGRI	Directorate-General for Agriculture and Rural Development
DG DEV	Directorate-General for Development
DG DEVCO	Directorate-General for International Cooperation and Development
DG Trade	Directorate-General for Trade
EDF	European Development Fund
EEAS	European External Action Service
EFTA	European Free Trade Association
ENP	European Neighbourhood Policy
EP	European Parliament
EPA	Economic Partnership Agreement
EPC	European Political Cooperation
EU	European Union

EUFP	European Union Foreign Policy
FAC	Foreign Affairs Council
FCA	Framework Cooperation Agreement
FPA	Foreign Policy Analysis
FTA	Free Trade Agreement
FTAA	Free Trade Area of the Americas
GAC	General Affairs Council
GAERC	General Affairs and External Relations Council
GSP	Generalized System of Preferences
HI	Historical institutionalism
HRVP	High Representative of the Union for Foreign Affairs and Security Policy
INTA	European Parliament Committee on International Trade
IR	International Relations
LA	Latin America
LAC	Latin America and the Caribbean
LAIF	Latin America Investment Facility
MEBF	Mercosur–Europe Business Forum
MEP	Member of the European Parliament
Mercosur	Southern Common Market
MFF	Multiannual Financial Framework
NAFTA	North American Free Trade Agreement
ODA	Official Development Aid
OLP	Ordinary Legislative Procedure
PA	Principal-agent theory
PCA	Partnership and Cooperation Agreement
PDCA	Political Dialogue and Cooperation Agreement
RELEX	External Relations
S&D	Progressive Alliance of Socialists & Democrats in the European Parliament
SEA	Single European Act
SICA	Central American Integration System
SIECA	Central American Economic Integration System
SP	Strategic Partnership
SPA	Strategic Partnership Agreement
TPC	Trade Policy Committee

TTIP	Transatlantic Trade and Investment Partnership
US	United States of America
USMCA	United States–Mexico–Canada Agreement
WTO	World Trade Organization

Part I

Analysing the EU's behaviour in complex Association Agreement negotiations

1 Introduction

The EU in increasingly complex international negotiations

Complex international negotiations as a challenge for the EU

The Common Commercial Policy (CCP) is one of the European Union's (EU) oldest policy areas with an external remit. A core part of this policy today consists in the EU's capacity to conclude Free Trade Agreements (FTAs) with partners in the rest of the world. In this policy area, the EU's member states have relinquished their capacity for independent policy-making and instead transferred these powers to the EU and its institutions following specific decision-making arrangements.

In the case of so-called pure FTAs, which touch only on the EU's exclusive competencies in the realm of trade policy-making, these decision-making mechanisms are relatively simple and allow for agreements to be ratified by majoritarian decision-making in the European Parliament (EP) and the Council of the European Union[1] only. However, in line with the EU's increasing role in other areas of foreign policy-making, FTAs are only one kind of international agreements that the EU can conclude with external partners. Increasingly, attempts to conclude so-called Association Agreements (AAs) which combine negotiations on trade relations with external partners with other elements of an external relationship, such as political ties or development cooperation, have replaced negotiations of traditional FTAs.

Much like negotiations for FTAs, attempts to conclude Association Agreements are not always successful. This may be down to fundamentally differing views of both sides in such negotiations. However, in some of the EU's Association Agreement negotiations, ultimately an international agreement is still found, albeit in the format of an FTA. Given that FTAs touch on fewer of the EU's policy areas with an external remit, negotiations in this area tend to be less complex than those for Association Agreements. In consequence, the process underpinning the latter can therefore be considered as complex EU negotiations. In such negotiations, the EU's policy aims in several of its external policy areas have to be considered and ultimately form part of the EU's negotiation stance.

Not only do such negotiations make for a more complex decision-making process in the EU—as Association Agreements touch not only on issues where the EU has been given exclusive competencies by the member states—but also the discussion of aspects within the remit of distinct EU policy areas makes an internal coordination of the EU's negotiation priorities a key challenge for the successful conclusion of any such negotiations. This is due to the fact that different aspects of the EU's foreign policy system have distinct origins and involve differing institutional actors and decision-making procedures, ultimately making the EU's external relations system a "hybrid" (Smith, 2012), though one in which economic concerns still dominate other aspects of its external relations (Smith, 2018).

While traditional EU trade negotiations have long been studied by scholars and are relatively well-understood (see, for instance, Conceição, 2010; Dür and Zimmermann, 2007; Gastinger, 2016; Woolcock, 2012, 2014; Young and Peterson, 2006), this book concerns itself with the challenge that the increasingly complex nature of the EU's international negotiations poses for its underlying institutional set-up as complex negotiations ultimately involve distinct institutions and follow differing decision-making logics depending on the policy areas involved. While the focus of the analysis is on the challenge posed by the legal instrument of EU Association Agreements, the book also considers the wider context of complex EU negotiations where a more traditional FTA may be negotiated alongside separate other types of political agreements with third parties. The book's aim, in short, therefore is to explore how the dynamics of external treaty negotiations involving multiple distinct policy areas at once are shaped by the set-up of the EU's internal decision-making and policy coordination system.

Determinants of the EU's behaviour in complex negotiations

The challenge of complex negotiations such as for EU Association Agreements is ultimately down to the fact that what today constitutes the EU's behaviour towards third actors, or what can be considered the sum of its external activities forms part of an overall European Union Foreign Policy (EUFP). This cannot be regarded exclusively in terms of individual activities delineated by specific boundaries of individual policy areas. Instead, when exploring the EU's behaviour in complex EU negotiations, the unity of the EU's activities towards third actors needs to be seen as a given, as EUFP is ultimately

> that body of declarations, decisions, and actions, that are made by the use of all the instruments that the EC/EU has at its disposal, that are decided at the EC/EU level, and conducted in its name toward a country or an area outside its borders.
>
> (Bicchi, 2007: 2)

This is similar to other considerations of the existence of a wider "European foreign policy system" (Smith, 2003, 2008; White, 1999), which similarly caution that the EU's activities towards third actors go beyond its narrow Common Foreign and Security Policy (CFSP) and include many aspects of its policy-making.

Association Agreements are a manifestation of this EUFP, as they contain provisions pertaining not only to the EU's CFSP, but also to a multitude of other policy areas, and the CCP in particular. This makes them a yardstick for the EU's capacity to link considerations relating to its different policy areas with an external remit and the varying underlying decision-making mechanisms. Yet, in many instances, a consideration of an ultimate outcome of such negotiations sees this once more reduced to the format of a traditional FTA and thereby limited to an individual area of the external activity. The dynamics of the actual negotiations with the negotiation partners aside, this points to problems related to the EU's capacity to achieve this goal. Ultimately, this book therefore aims to answer the question as to how the EU's behaviour in complex negotiations is shaped by its capacity to (successfully) link different of its policy areas together in the process for such negotiations. This, in turn, requires a consideration of decision-making and coordination mechanisms in the area of its external relations.

After all, this "administrative Holy Grail of co-ordination and 'horizontality'," i.e. the ability to link different policy outputs, "is a perennial quest for the practitioners of government" (Peters, 1998: 295), and this has been no different in the case of the European Union's external relations. Whereas problems of (external) policy coordination are not absent from traditional state-based policy-making, concerns over the coherence of the EU's policy outputs towards third actors have been voiced for many of the EU's activities in the realm of its external relations (see, for instance, Furness and Gänzle, 2017; Portela and Orbie, 2014; Verdonck, 2015).

These observations occur despite repeated attempts to increase the EU's capacity to generate policy outputs which are coordinated between external policy areas, as "each progress towards enhanced coherence was paradoxically increasing internal complexity" (Telò, 2013: 27). This is ultimately due to the fact that the typical response to a lack of external policy coherence due to failures in policy coordination mechanisms has been to reorganize the functioning of the EU's foreign policy bureaucracy in an attempt to foster coordination. This was achieved through treaty changes, portfolio and organizational reforms, or the invention of new roles such as that of the EU's High Representative for its Common Foreign and Security Policy (HRVP). This will make it necessary to consider which broad factors internal to the set-up of the EU's foreign policy bureaucracy affect its capacity to produce coherent foreign policy outputs.

It is here that a consideration of analytical tools developed for the study of the foreign policy of states, namely Foreign Policy Analysis (FPA), can help inform the study of the external relations of the EU, which increasingly resemble those of states in nature, scope, and ambition. Consequently, this book seeks to adapt and apply this framework to the study of the EU's foreign policy with all its peculiarities. In exploring the challenge of complex EU negotiations, it therefore offers a generalizable analytical model to study complex EU international negotiations based on an adaptation of FPA literature.

Latin America as a test case for complex EU negotiations

While the analytical model to understand the internal dynamics of complex EU negotiations developed in this book is of a general nature, its utility is explored and tested in detail primarily through an analysis of the EU's negotiations for Association Agreements with regional organizations in the Latin American (LA) region over time. In doing so, both the utility of the theoretical model itself and its consideration of institutional changes can be outlined. In particular, this allows to point to decision-making complexity and the associated duration of complex Association Agreement negotiations as an important negotiation dynamic in and of itself. This is followed by a brief analysis of other recent EU negotiations so as to demonstrate the general utility of the model.

As one of the largest trading blocs in the world, the EU has concluded a large number of FTAs and other kinds of agreements with both third countries and regional organizations. Simultaneously, it has concluded various kinds of political and cooperation agreements, making it a particularly active player in international agreement negotiations. While Association Agreements represent a more recent addition to the toolbox of international EU negotiations, the EU has nonetheless also concluded or attempted to negotiate a large number of such types of agreements up to this date, including agreements with countries such as Ukraine or Georgia. Even where EU negotiations are ultimately not legally concluded as Association Agreements, the EU may negotiate in parallel on separate but interlinked FTAs and political agreements, as has been the case in the EU's negotiations with Japan. This means that ultimately a variety of negotiations could have been chosen to explore the utility of this book's analytical framework empirically.

Nonetheless, most of these negotiations are embedded in a particular economic or political context which might involve the EU's concerns in a wide array of policy areas. Considering negotiations with Ukraine, for instance, issues such as security or migration become important factors in addition to more traditional trade, political and development considerations. While a wide array of EU policy areas also form part of its negotiations with Japan, the latter country's role as a key global economy makes the trade aspect of such negotiations even more crucial than would be the case elsewhere.

A deliberate choice was therefore made for the empirical analysis in this book to focus on complex EU negotiations in the Latin American context. This is a setting where a more limited set of EU policy areas would be involved, and the region's relatively low economic salience should allow to explore EU policy coordination underpinning these negotiations in a context where concerns related to a single policy area are not too dominant from the outset.

Furthermore, over a little more than twenty years, the EU has ultimately attempted to negotiate Association Agreements with all countries and regional organizations in the region, offering the possibility to analyse a wide array of negotiation processes. These are furthermore all linked by an underlying dynamic which saw the EU invest considerable efforts in improving its ties to this region overall, and to utilize the novel model of Association Agreements, in particular (Dominguez, 2015: 172) in what amounted at first to the EU's application of a "one-size fits all approach" (Börzel and Risse, 2009: 10) to actors in the region. Therefore, unlike for most other individual EU negotiations, the Latin American context also allows to study how individual negotiation processes have interacted with one another over time.

Table 1.1 provides an overview over the relevant negotiations for Association Agreement negotiations which are covered in the main empirical section in this book. These negotiations are in addition to ties that the EU has developed to the entirety of the region in the guise of regular EU–Latin American summits which have taken place since 1999. Today, this is structured on the Latin American side around the Community of Latin American and Caribbean States (CELAC) which regroups all 33 Latin American and Caribbean states.

Considering the specific complex EU negotiations at hand, it is of note that Mexico and Cuba aside, all negotiations listed above began within an interregional setting and were grouped as parallel processes in different waves of negotiations (as marked by the horizontal dividing lines). While the former is one of the most important Latin American economies, it nonetheless differs from the remainder of the region in that it is integrated with North America through the North American Free Trade Agreement (NAFTA)[2] and has until recently not been a member of any of Latin America's substantive subregional integration mechanisms. In contrast, Cuba's distinct political history as a communist country meant that the country has not joined either of the above regional integration mechanisms. The agreement also differs in nature as it does not contain an FTA and has been termed as a Political Dialogue and Cooperation Agreement (PDCA).

When negotiations began for an Association Agreement with Mercosur[3] and Chile, it was hoped that the country would eventually join Mercosur, thus simultaneously supporting the enlargement of an existing regional integration mechanism (García, 2011: 151). The next grouped set of negotiations was that for Association Agreements with the Andean Community and Central America, which passed through the EU's foreign policy decision-making system in parallel up to their eventual ratification by the European Parliament. All of the interregional negotiations were flanked by other policies aimed at ensuring their success, such as through earmarking large parts of the EU's development cooperation funding towards the region for the specific goal of regional integration, including the direct support of the regional integration organizations themselves (European Commission, 2007).

While the initial goal of all negotiations was to reach comprehensive Association Agreements, covering multiple policy areas, the ultimate outcome of the negotiations has only been compatible with this in three cases: The Global Agreement with Mexico, and the Association Agreements with Chile and Central America. In the case of negotiations with Mercosur, the interregional approach was initially abandoned, while politically Brazil was prioritized over the others by concluding a "strategic partnership" (SP) with the country (which is not based on a binding international agreement, but rather defined by ad hoc declarations and fora for cooperation). Only in 2019 was an initial political agreement on an EU–Mercosur Association Agreement finally reached. In the context of negotiations with the Andean Community, the EU's approach shifted towards bilateral trade negotiations with some of the countries in question only and abandoned the political pillars of the proposed Association Agreement entirely. Additionally, even for the

Table 1.1 Complex EU negotiations in the Latin American region

	Type	First discussed	Mandate	Negotiations	Signed	Provisional application	Ratification	Application
Mexico	AA	1994	1995	1995–1997/1999	1997	–	2000	2000
Mercosur	AA	1995	1999	1999–2019 (with interruptions)	–	–	–	–
Brazil	SP	2007	–	2007	2007	–	–	2007
Chile	AA	1995	1999	1999–2002	2002	–	2003	2003
Andean Community	AA	2004	2007	2007–2011	–	–	–	–
Colombia	FTA	–	–	–2011	2012	2013	–	–
Peru	FTA	–	–	–2011	2012	2013	–	–
Ecuador	FTA	–	–	2014–2016	2016	2017	–	–
Central America	AA	2004	2007	2007–2011	2012	2013	–	–
Cuba	PDCA	2009	2014	2014–2016	2016	2017	–	–
Mexico 2	AA	2012	2016	2016–2018	–	–	–	–
Chile 2	AA	2012	2017	2018–	–	–	–	–

Source: Own compilation.

concluded negotiations, the ratification processes have been lengthy in most cases, meaning that with the exception of the earliest agreements, ratification is still not completed for others.

What is of note is the sheer duration of most negotiation processes from their initial informal consideration to their ultimate ratification and then implementation. Of the legal agreements considered in detail in this book, only two have been fully ratified and implemented, with the strategic partnership with Brazil not requiring any formal ratification procedure at all. The lengthy duration of these processes is ultimately down to three distinct periods, all of which are considered in the analysis in this book. Firstly, any complex EU negotiation requires a formal negotiation mandate before the negotiation process with the external partner can go ahead. Secondly, the actual negotiation phase may take a substantial amount of time as the 20-year negotiation period with Mercosur demonstrates. Lastly, depending on the type of legal agreement ultimately found, ratification processes may take a considerable period of time, given the necessity for national ratification in all of the EU's member states.

The focus on Latin America also allows to study a number of innovations and firsts for the EU's complex negotiations. The 1997 Global Agreement with Mexico was at the time "one of the most ambitious pacts ever negotiated by the EU with a state that has absolutely no possibility of joining the EU" (Szymanski and Smith, 2005: 172). Signed in 2002, the Association Agreement with Chile was in turn "the most comprehensive agreement ever signed with a third party," serving as "a model for current EU negotiations and a statement of future intentions" (García, 2011: 501–2). The 2010 Association Agreement with Central America then represented "the first ever region-to-region agreement of the EU covering at the same time political dialogue, cooperation and trade" (Van Rompuy, 2010). Renewed negotiations with Mexico and Chile then mark first attempts to upgrade a first generation of Association Agreements. Lastly, the recent political agreement in principle on an EU–Mercosur Association Agreement indicates the likely successful conclusion of the longest-running EU negotiation and would represent the largest-ever EU FTA (DG Trade, 2019).

When it comes to the scope of the Association Agreement negotiations in this region, this is mostly limited to three kinds of EU policy areas, thus allowing for a consideration of policy coordination between a relatively limited number of policies, yet also ones' which are naturally interlinked. The European Commission has explained these interlinkages for the case of the EU's negotiations with Central America:

> The Association Agreement consists of three pillars: political dialogue, cooperation and trade. The Agreement is a comprehensive tool that provides with [sic] all the means needed for an integrated relation, going from political dialogue to cooperation and trade. The different parts of the Association Agreement complement each other. That is the most important added value of this instrument. It is not only a trade agreement and it goes far beyond traditional agreements as it creates interdependence between the various parts of the Agreement.
>
> (European Commission, 2012)

In addition, the Latin American context also allows to study complex EU negotiations not only in a setting where the EU negotiates with an individual country, but also with other regional integration mechanisms, and Mercosur, the Andean Community, and Central America, in particular. The pursuit of further integration in these regions has, in turn, been one of the EU's political aims for most of these negotiations (García, 2015: 622).

While the core empirical part of this book offers the most in-depth analysis of particular negotiation processes for complex EU Association Agreements, the last part of the book also considers some EU negotiations in other geographic areas: The purpose of analysing the negotiations for the Ukraine–EU Association Agreement, and for the EU's negotiations with Japan, then, is to demonstrate that the book's analytical framework can also be applied successfully to other kinds of settings where EU political concerns over aspects such as security or the potential economic effects play a differing role than was the case in the Latin American negotiations. Both cases chosen here also overlap with some of the Latin American negotiations in terms of the overall negotiation process and some of the underlying institutional dynamics such as the coming into force of the Treaty of Lisbon. Nonetheless, the discussion of the negotiations outside of Latin America is somewhat less detailed, as its purpose is to illustrate how the analytical framework can and should be refined and applied to other complex EU negotiation processes.

Considering the sources used for the empirical analysis in this book, its analysis ultimately relies on triangulation between various kinds of sources such as press coverage, EU primary documents (public and classified), and most importantly elite interviews with individuals involved in complex EU negotiations. In total, around 40 interviews were done with EU officials, EU member state diplomats, partner country diplomats, as well as members of the European Parliament and their staff.

A brief outlook on the contribution of this book

Independently of its specific focus on complex EU negotiations, this book demonstrates the utility and possibility of adapting FPA approaches developed for the study of sovereign states to the context of the EU's foreign policy-making. It thereby follows other attempts to link FPA literature to the European integration process, such as arguments that an analysis of the foreign policy of EU member states needs to be based on a distinct flavour of FPA (Larsen, 2009), or utilizing some concerns prevalent in the FPA literature to explore specific dynamics of EU foreign policy-making (Dijkstra, 2009).

The consideration of bureaucratic processes internal to the EU, as cautioned by this book's adaptation of insights developed in FPA, then helps to augment our understanding of the wider dynamics of complex EU negotiation processes. While this book does not claim that a consideration of bureaucratic politics within the EU can solely explain key developments in EU negotiations nor their ultimate outcomes, it still cautions that this perspective should not be overlooked when faced with the sometimes surprising developments, particularly in long-running EU negotiations. Ultimately, this insight is relevant irrespective of whether a complex EU negotiation under consideration is of a relatively low salience for the EU or to the contrary touches on important economic and security concerns.

Considering the internal dynamics of EU negotiations on a microlevel, the book cautions specifically that complex EU negotiations are shaped by a number of factors. Firstly, institutional conflict needs to be explored not just between distinct EU-level institutions, but also within the complex bureaucracies of these institutions themselves. The possible conflict lines, in turn, are determined by the specific institutional set-up at any given point in time. Irrespective of these bureaucratic constraints, there is also an important scope for individual political leadership or absence of it to influence the presence of intra- and inter-institutional conflict.

Ultimately, the importance of this can be attributed to the prevalence of institutional autonomy which tends to be greater in the EU-level political system than one would expect at the national level in most instances. This is related, in particular, to the EU's treaty changes which tend to alter the institutional set-up relevant for the EU's international negotiations, as well as regular attempts to reform and streamline EU-level institutions regularly. This is then amplified by the long duration of most complex EU negotiations, as electoral cycles alter the composition of the European Parliament and the Commission at regular intervals, but also of the Council in line with national elections. This means that the political composition of all key EU-level institutions may change over the course of a negotiation, all while previous decisions such as on negotiation mandates create a certain path dependence for ongoing negotiation processes. Ultimately speaking, the influence of bureaucratic politics on the dynamics of complex EU negotiations thus observed is a continuous phenomenon, rather than a one-off event.

Lastly, given the focus of the empirical section of this book, it also contributes some important and novel insights into specific EU negotiation processes with partners in the Latin American region. While ultimately always explored through the lens of the book's analytical framework, the analysis is nonetheless dependent on a more profound overview of wider negotiation dynamics, which can be of interest to scholars interested in EU–Latin American affairs, EU (inter)regionalism, or indeed EU trade policy-making.

The structure of the remainder of this book

The book is structured in three parts: The first introduces this book's analytical framework, with the next chapter detailing how an adaptation of FPA and bureaucratic politics approaches to the context of internal EU bargaining can contribute to our understanding of policy coordination and negotiation dynamics in complex EU negotiations. Given that FPA cautions to consider bureaucratic structure as a key factor determining foreign policy decision-making, the following chapter then details changes to the set-up of the EU's foreign policy system over the timeframe relevant for the empirical analysis in the second part of the book. In addition to focusing on changing decision-making mechanisms which upset the EU's institutional balance, it also discusses internal structure of both the Council and the European Parliament. Its core section, however, deals with the changing organization of the European Commission and its Commissioners' portfolios over time, including the set-up and inclusion of some Commission Directorates-General (DG) in the European External Action Service (EEAS) after the Treaty of Lisbon.

Part II of the book then tests its analytical framework in the context of the EU's complex negotiations in the Latin American region. Its first chapter considers initial attempts to conclude Association Agreements with regional organizations and countries there. Specifically, it outlines how the negotiation for the initial EU–Mexico Global Agreement set first precedents for future EU Association Agreements in both complexity and negotiation dynamics. It also considers the dynamics of the EU's negotiations with the Mercosur regional integration mechanism. This has turned out to be the longest-running EU Association Agreement negotiation. Given the duration of these negotiations, the case of the EU's Association Agreement with Chile which emerged out of the original Mercosur negotiations is also explored.

The next empirical chapter then focuses on two parallel negotiations with two other regional organizations, namely the Andean Community and the Central American region. While the EU's initial aim for both negotiations was relatively similar, the ultimate negotiation outcomes diverge considerably. Through a side-by-side analysis of both, the influence of distinct institutional dynamics and bureaucratic politics in the EU is thus explored, including the effects of the transition to the Treaty of Lisbon. The last empirical chapter then explores the internal dynamics of complex EU negotiations after the Lisbon Treaty in greater detail. It considers institutional autonomy in the cases of EU negotiations with Ecuador and Cuba, as well as the negotiation processes for upgrading existing agreements with Chile and Mexico. In so doing, the impact of the creation of the EEAS on the EU's policy coordination processes in complex negotiations can be explored.

The last part of the book then considers its insights in a wider context. Chapter 7 briefly examines the validity of its analytical framework for other kinds of complex EU Association Agreement negotiations. Specifically, it uses the negotiations for the Ukraine–EU Association Agreement to explore the influence of bureaucratic politics on a negotiation where EU integration, geographic proximity, and security concerns were of relevance. Similarly, a consideration of the EU–Japan FTA and the parallel negotiations for a political agreement details negotiations in a case where economic concerns were dominant. The last chapter then brings together the insights from the individual parts of the book and offers a conclusion as to what kinds of insights it has provided for our understanding of the EU's behaviour in complex negotiations.

Notes

1 This book hereafter refers to the Council of the EU simply as the Council.
2 This is supposed to be eventually replaced by its successor USMCA agreement.
3 This is the Spanish-language abbreviation for the Common Market of the South, composed of Argentina, Brazil, Paraguay, and Uruguay and founded in 1991.

Bibliography

Bicchi F (2007) *European Foreign Policy Making Toward the Mediterranean*. 1st ed. Europe in Transition: NYU EU Studies. New York, NY: Palgrave Macmillan.

Börzel T and Risse T (2009) *The Rise of (Inter-)Regionalism: The EU as a Model of Regional Integration*. APSA 2009 Toronto Meeting Paper, 13 August. SSRN. Available at: http://papers.ssrn.com/abstract=1450391 (accessed 15 January 2018).

Conceição ED (2010) Who Controls Whom? Dynamics of Power Delegation and Agency Losses in EU Trade Politics. *JCMS: Journal of Common Market Studies* 48(4): 1107–1126. DOI: 10.1111/j.1468-5965.2010.02086.x.

DG Trade (2019) *EU and Mercosur Reach Agreement on Trade*, 28 June. Brussels: European Commission. Available at: http://trade.ec.europa.eu/doclib/press/index.cfm?id=2039.

Dijkstra H (2009) Commission Versus Council Secretariat: An Analysis of Bureaucratic Rivalry in European Foreign Policy. *European Foreign Affairs Review* 14(3): 431–450.

Dominguez R (2015) *EU Foreign Policy Towards Latin America*. New York, NY: Palgrave MacMillan.

Dür A and Zimmermann H (2007) Introduction: The EU in International Trade Negotiations. *JCMS: Journal of Common Market Studies* 45(4): 771–787. DOI: 10.1111/j.1468-5965.2007.00747.x.

European Commission (2007) *Latin America Regional Programming Document 2007–2013*. E/2007/1417. Brussels: European Commission. Available at: http://eeas.europa.eu/la/rsp/07_13_en.pdf (accessed 17 January 2013).

European Commission (2012) *Comprehensive Association Agreement Between Central America and the European Union*. Memo/12/505. Brussels: European Commission. Available at: http://europa.eu/rapid/press-release_MEMO-12-505_en.htm?locale=en (accessed 12 January 2016).

Furness M and Gänzle S (2017) The Security–Development Nexus in European Union Foreign Relations After Lisbon: Policy Coherence at Last? *Development Policy Review* 35(4): 475–492. DOI: 10.1111/dpr.12191.

García M (2011) Incidents Along the Path: Understanding the Rationale Behind the EU–Chile Association Agreement. *JCMS: Journal of Common Market Studies* 49(3): 501–524. DOI: 10.1111/j.1468-5965.2010.02149.x.

García M (2015) The European Union and Latin America: 'Transformative Power Europe' Versus the Realities of Economic Interests. *Cambridge Review of International Affairs* 28(4): 621–640. DOI: 10.1080/09557571.2011.647762.

Gastinger M (2016) The Tables Have Turned on the European Commission: The Changing Nature of the Pre-negotiation Phase in EU Bilateral Trade Agreements. *Journal of European Public Policy* 23(9): 1367–1385. DOI: 10.1080/13501763.2015.1079233.

Larsen H (2009) A Distinct FPA for Europe? Towards a Comprehensive Framework for Analysing the Foreign Policy of EU Member States. *European Journal of International Relations* 15(3): 537–566. DOI: 10.1177/1354066109388247.

Peters BG (1998) Managing Horizontal Government: The Politics of Co-ordination. *Public Administration* 76(2): 295–311. DOI: 10.1111/1467-9299.00102.

Portela C and Orbie J (2014) Sanctions Under the EU Generalised System of Preferences and Foreign Policy: Coherence by Accident? *Contemporary Politics* 20(1): 63–76. DOI: 10.1080/13569775.2014.881605.

Smith KE (2003) Understanding the European Foreign Policy System. *Contemporary European History* 12(2): 239–254. DOI: 10.1017/S0960777303001176.

Smith M (2012) Still Rooted in Maastricht: EU External Relations as a 'Third-Generation Hybrid'. *Journal of European Integration* 34(7): 699–715. DOI: 10.1080/07036337.2012.726010.

Smith ME (2008) Researching European Foreign Policy: Some Fundamentals. *Politics* 28(3): 177–187. DOI: 10.1111/j.1467-9256.2008.00327.x.

Smith MH (2018) Does the Flag Still Follow Trade? Agency, Politicization and External Opportunity Structures in the Post-Lisbon System of EU Diplomacy. *The Hague Journal of Diplomacy* 13(1): 41–56. DOI: 10.1163/1871191X-13010011.

Szymanski M and Smith ME (2005) Coherence and Conditionality in European Foreign Policy: Negotiating the EU–Mexico Global Agreement. *JCMS: Journal of Common Market Studies* 43(1): 171–192. DOI: 10.1111/j.0021-9886.2005.00551.x.

Telò M (2013) The EU: A Civilian Power's Diplomatic Action After the Lisbon Treaty. Bridging Internal Complexity and International Convergence. In: Telò M and Ponjaert F (eds) *The EU's Foreign Policy: What Kind of Power and Diplomatic Action?* Farnham: Ashgate, pp. 27–63.

Van Rompuy H (2010) *Remarks by Herman Van Rompuy, President of the European Council, at EU–Central America Summit Madrid, 19 May 2010*. PCE 100/10. Madrid: European Council. Available at: www.consilium.europa.eu/uedocs/cms_data/docs/pressdata/en/ec/114563.pdf (accessed 14 January 2016).

Verdonck L (2015) Coherence in the EU's External Human Rights Policy: The Case of the Democratic Republic of the Congo. *European Foreign Affairs Review* 20(3): 379–397.

White B (1999) The European Challenge to Foreign Policy Analysis. *European Journal of International Relations* 5(1): 37–66.

Woolcock S (2012) *European Union Economic Diplomacy: The Role of the EU in External Economic Relations*. Aldershot: Ashgate.

Woolcock S (2014) Differentiation Within Reciprocity: The European Union Approach to Preferential Trade Agreements. *Contemporary Politics* 20(1): 36–48. DOI: 10.1080/13569775.2014.881603.

Young AR and Peterson J (2006) The EU and the New Trade Politics. *Journal of European Public Policy* 13(6): 795–814. DOI: 10.1080/13501760600837104.

2 Foreign Policy Analysis and EU foreign policy-making

Introduction

This chapter outlines the analytical framework adopted in the book, details the research methodology used, and discusses it in the context of relevant literature. In doing so, it outlines why FPA literature was used and adapted to the context of the EU's foreign policy, rather than utilizing other theoretical frameworks. Ultimately this chapter details that despite some differences with the foreign policy decision-making systems of sovereign states for which FPA was originally developed, it is nonetheless ideal to capture the complexity of the EU's foreign policy system.

The remainder of this chapter is structured as follows: The following section develops a formal definition of EU foreign policy coherence which is required for a structured discussion as to the dynamics of the EU's behaviour in complex negotiations. This is followed by the outline of the analytical framework based on FPA and why it was chosen over other theoretical perspectives. The following section then outlines the methods used and methodology adopted and describes the empirical sources that have been consulted in the writing process. Lastly, the book is situated in the wider literature.

Defining EU foreign policy coherence

The EU's capacity to negotiate complex international agreements spanning multiple of its foreign policy areas ultimately depends on its capacity to link its interests which span multiple policy areas coherently. EU policy coherence, at its most basic level, can be described as "the absence of contradiction between policies" (Portela and Raube, 2012: 4). However, such a definition is a minimal one and does not allow for a differentiation between different kinds of policy (in)coherence. Moving away from it, Hertog and Stroß (2013) have instead suggested that a mere absence of contradiction between policies could rather be described by the term of consistency, which in itself would form a subset of policy coherence. In their view, policy coherence is instead a more active process which "refers to *the synergic and systematic support towards the achievement of common objectives within and across individual policies*" (italics in original, Hertog and Stroß, 2013: 377).

However, rather than describing different *kinds* of policy coherence, such a definition offers clues as to the conditions under which it may originate. The definition developed here instead focuses on factors outlining *how* the EU's foreign policy may ultimately be incoherent when spanning multiple policy areas. The evaluation of policy coherence in the context of this book is thus based on "systemic outputs, i.e. the way in which the substance of different policies generated by the EU forms part of a coherent whole" (Christiansen, 2001: 747).

When taking such a perspective, it is then possible to define different *kinds* of coherence that need to be fulfilled for the EU's policy outputs to be coherent overall. In this context, most authors (Gebhard, 2011; Hertog and Stroß, 2013; Mayer, 2013; Portela and Raube, 2012) discuss at least two distinct varieties of policy coherence that need to be fulfilled for the EU's foreign policy to be coherent overall, namely vertical and horizontal policy coherence. While the definitions differ somewhat, *horizontal policy coherence* is described as the necessity for policy outputs to be consistent across various policy areas and different modes of decision-making at the EU level. While Gebhard (2011: 108) adds an additional factor, namely internal policy coherence—described as the absence of contradiction between policies falling under the remit of different former pillars of the EU's structure—this is included in the definition of horizontal policy coherence provided here.

An example for the lack of such horizontal policy coherence would be if different EU policies simultaneously aim to promote trade with a third country through FTA negotiations, all while imposing economic sanctions on it in another. In contrast, *vertical policy coherence* focuses on the necessity for outputs at the EU level to match those of its member states. An example for this would be if the EU decided to halt its development cooperation funding towards a third country, while some EU member states still continue to provide their own development funding.

A third kind of coherence can be found in the EU's interaction with third actors, namely *external policy coherence*, which considers the need for consistency between the EU's outputs in international fora, be it of different internal EU actors towards the same third actor, or in different institutions, such as NATO and the OSCE (Gebhard, 2011: 108–9). In consequence, "external coherence is primarily concerned with functionality and credibility rather than with specific foreign policy contents" (Gebhard, 2011: 109).

Although delineating different elements of foreign policy coherence somewhat differently, two useful additions can be made to the above three types of coherence when looking at Mayer's (2013: 107) conceptualization, as he adds a requirement for narrative and strategic coherence. *Narrative policy coherence* describes the necessity for the EU's foreign policy outputs having to match the rhetoric which legitimizes them. The last type of coherence to be considered is that of *strategic policy coherence* which is concerned with the EU's policies following a broader goal. Mayer sees this as fulfilled when "[s]imilar or overlapping policies would follow the same principles, values and aims" (Mayer, 2013: 107). Diverging somewhat from this definition, it will be used in this book to describe the necessity for policy outputs to be the same in similar situations, and that these should continue to be the same over time in absence of fundamental changes to the underlying situation that prompted such a position in the first place.

These five elements form a list of components of policy coherence necessary for the EU's foreign policy towards a third actor to be coherent overall. Crucially, in line with others' considerations, the components of foreign policy coherence detailed here differ from the concept of policy effectiveness (Thomas, 2012: 460–1), which is instead based on the effect of policy outputs.

For the analysis at hand, at least three different kinds of possible policy incoherence will need to be considered: A lack of horizontal policy coherence between the EU's trade and development policy, a lack of narrative coherence given the disjunction between the EU's discourse and negotiation behaviour, and lastly a lack of strategic coherence given the changes to the format of various negotiations over time.

EU foreign policy through the lens of Foreign Policy Analysis

Given this book's focus on the dynamics of complex EU negotiations, its analysis needs to consider the EU's policy-making processes, and particularly how institutional processes contribute to achieving coherence between different policy areas of the EU' external relations. This is in line with alternative and more process- rather than output-focused definitions of policy coherence. Christiansen argues that on the one hand,

> we can conceive of 'coherence' in terms of the systemic outputs, i.e. the way in which the substance of different policies generated by the EU forms part of a coherent whole. Alternatively, we can regard 'coherence' in terms of the institutional process by which policies are made, i.e. in terms of the degree to which institution(s) operate a coherent and well-coordinated process of deliberation and decision-making [...] which in the following is termed 'institutional coherence'.
>
> (Christiansen, 2001: 747)

Similarly, Smith has argued that research into European Foreign Policy should use "actor-centred analyses where variations among, and linkages between, those actors are explicitly problematised rather than neglected or 'assumed' away" (Smith, 2008: 181).

This view is shared by Duke, a scholar of administrative processes in the EU, who cautioned that

> For those with an interest in public administration and organizational science, coherence is assessed from the perspective of the administrative and bureaucratic bases of the organization, its routines, functioning, and resources. International Relations scholars tend to concentrate on the coherence of the

'end product', assessing the outcome of policies or the uniform treatment of third parties by the EU.

(Duke, 2012: 45–6)

In this view, the determinants of coherence in EU foreign policy outputs can thus be found in internal EU decision-making processes, such as the interaction between the EU's institutions, its member states, and the activity of different administrative units within the institutions themselves (Christiansen, 2001: 748). This resonates with a specific field of enquiry in International Relations (IR) research, namely that of FPA. As Hudson argues,

One hallmark of FPA scholarship is that the subfield views the explanation of foreign policy decisionmaking as of necessity being multifactorial and multi-level. Explanatory variables from all levels of analysis, from the most micro to the most macro, are of interest to the analyst to the extent that they affect decisionmaking.

(Hudson, 2015: 1)

For FPA researchers, there is not a single model to explain foreign policy outcomes and its underlying decision-making processes. Rather, it encourages conceptual pluralism in an attempt to offer multifaceted determinants of foreign policy outcomes. While developed and popularized in the specific context of explaining decisions of both superpowers during the Cuban Missile Crisis (*Essence of Decision* by Allison, first published in 1971, then updated with Zelikow in 1999), it has gained academic attention to explain all kinds of foreign policy choices, such as radical reorientations of states' foreign policy in the aftermath of the Cold War (Carlsnaes, 1993; Hermann, 1990) or determinants of small states' foreign policy choices in the context of NATO (Doeser, 2011).

Initially, FPA was developed to explore national foreign policy decisions in the realm of so-called high politics, having to do with questions directly impacting on national sovereignty, such as defence or the membership of one of the Cold War's two rivalling blocs. This would have made it difficult to apply FPA insights to the context of the EU, given that it is neither a state nor does it deal with most aspects of what has traditionally been considered "high politics." Luckily, FPA has been adapted to contexts of "low politics," such as the ones in which the EU plays an important role in and of itself.

For instance, Odell (1979) has studied the United States' (US) historic decision to move from a system of fixed exchange rates to a flexible one by applying insights from FPA literature. The EU has come to be involved in this realm through its Economic and Monetary Union (EMU) and the associated common currency. Given the importance of trade aspects in complex EU negotiations, one can also consider Welch's (2005) book, which uses Canada–US free trade negotiations as one of his case studies to illustrate his take on policy change in foreign policy-making. In the European context, Gustavsson (1998) has developed a theory of foreign policy change to explain the reorientation of Sweden's position towards membership in the European Union through economic factors. More importantly still, the very creators of FPA have argued in a footnote to a seminal article on bureaucratic determinants of foreign policy that while their arguments were limited to the realm of national security so as to provide for analytical clarity, "[e]xtension of the argument to other issue areas, e.g., foreign trade, is straight-forward" (Allison and Halperin, 1972: 47).

While the problem remains that FPA has been developed to study the foreign policy of states, it is argued here that it can and should readily be applied to the context of complex EU negotiations. After all, the EU can be considered as an entity which disposes of a foreign policy in its own right, if lacking some of the tools at the disposal of most sovereign states. While Hill has provided a useful general definition of foreign policy in a contribution that sees it as the "sum of external relations conducted by an *independent* actor (usually a state) in international relations" (Hill, 2003: 3, emphasis mine), his focus on the activity of an independent actor is particularly relevant, as the EU is solely responsible for some parts of the traditional foreign policy of its member states, and it shares powers with them in others. This is particularly the case for its foreign economic policy, as exemplified through its activity in the realm of trade. Here, Smith has argued that while the "aims and means" of the policy may be principally economic, its under-lying reasoning could still be "implicitly political or concerned with security" (Smith, 1994: 287), thus rendering the EU's external relations politically relevant.

Furthermore, other authors have already used FPA to study foreign policy in the context of the EU, such as Larsen (2009) who has argued that an analysis of the foreign policy of EU member states necessitates an adaptation of FPA literature to take into account the existence of the EU. Conversely, White (1999) has argued that the existence of the EU offers new possibilities for the study of FPA itself. The most systematic attempt to utilize FPA to study the EU is an edited volume on *Contemporary European Foreign Policy* (Carlsnaes et al., 2004), which has argued that the existence of the EU requires a reconsideration of most FPA insights in the European context.

Some authors have also used FPA to study specific institutional dynamics of the EU's foreign policy decision-making process (Dijkstra, 2009). Lastly, some of the insights from FPA research promote a focus on the bureaucratic and institutional determinants of foreign policy which may actually be deployed for an even greater analytical gain in the context of the EU. While most states dispose of some kind of ultimately hierarchical and unitary foreign policy decision-making system that is influenced by institutional and bureaucratic dynamics, bureaucratic factors may actually be even more relevant in the context of the EU:

> In contrast to states, which rely on one single bureaucracy for foreign policy and mostly a unitary source of foreign policy authority – the executive –, EU foreign policy has struggled with differences between the EU level and the member states as well as between the Community and the intergovernmental level.
>
> (Portela and Raube, 2012: 4)

Studying determinants of (in)coherence in complex EU negotiations thus requires a focus on internal EU decision-making processes and the actors involved in them. When taking such a perspective, the use of FPA literature appears logical given that it cautions that foreign policy decisions should be analysed as more than rational decisions by unitary actors in the international system. While some differences exist between the EU and the foreign policy apparatuses of sovereign states, for which FPA was initially developed, this book argues that it can still be usefully deployed to study the EU's foreign policy.

EU-level decision-making as the primary object of analysis

While IR research has historically placed the level of analysis at the systemic level, i.e. where different independent actors interact with one another, FPA literature has cautioned from the very beginning that such a perspective should be supplemented by others which focus on the foreign policy bureaucracies of states themselves (Allison and Zelikow, 1999). This raises the question as to where the equivalent lies when studying the EU's foreign policy given the parallel existence of member state foreign policies and ministries in addition to that of the EU itself.

Smith (2008) has pointed to these challenges for conducting research into what he calls European Foreign Policy. For him, this term encompasses the coordination of European states' foreign policy, either at the national level, or by making use of the EU's institutions and policies, or as a mix of both. While his definition encompasses the object of interest for this project, the view taken in his work is a member state-centric one, which sees the EU's institutions primarily as facilitators for collective action as is the case in classic principal-agent approaches.

Extending on the earlier definition, EUFP is the set of "systematic EU intervention" (Smith, 1998: 168) towards third actors or regions that goes beyond policy boundaries and modes of decision-making in the EU's bureaucracy (Smith, 2002: 9–10). The primary level of analysis is thus the EU's collective foreign policy output in the name of the EU and at the level of the EU's institutions. The analysis in this book therefore spans across the EU's former pillars of decision-making, an approach also favoured by other FPA scholars who have studied the EU (White, 2004: 15–17).

This leaves the question of the continued existence of the foreign policies and related ministries and decision-making processes of the EU's member states and how to integrate these into the perspective taken in this book. This problem of a "Multilevel Foreign Policy" (Foradori et al., 2007), where decisions taken at the national and EU levels—sometimes even by the very same actors—influence the dynamics of the foreign policy of the EU itself has been recognized by others as well. A conceptual solution to this problem lies in an adaptation of Putnam's two-level games approach (Putnam, 1988) to the specific context of the EU. Here, Collinson (1999: 217–20) has suggested that decision-making in the EU's commercial policy should be conceptualized as a three-level game instead, which simultaneously considers the bargaining of the EU's negotiators with third actors at the international level, the bargaining taking place at the EU level, as well as that at the national level. This has been applied and refined in an article on the EU's negotiations for the EU's 1999 Trade, Development and Cooperation Agreement with South Africa. The author cautions that

> [t]he main argument of the article is that the three-level game model needs to place its domestic focus at the level of the Commission, rather than, as is done in most traditional three-level game models, at the level of the Member States.
>
> (Frennhoff Larsén, 2007: 858)

Conceptualizing the main level of analysis as that of the EU's institutions (but not limited to the Commission), and treating these as the main foreign policy bureaucracies that are the subject of most FPA literature, thus allows for overcoming the problem of the continued existence of member state foreign policy decision-making processes. Instead, member state activity will be considered mainly in the context of their actions in the Council, with each member state seen as a part of the internal Council decision-making processes.

Different administrative lenses on complex EU negotiations

In line with existing FPA scholarship, foreign policy decisions can best be understood when analysed through different analytical "lenses." A first analytical lens that can be taken is to consider whether the dynamics of complex EU negotiations are actually the result of rational decision-making within the EU's foreign policy bureaucracy. This perspective ultimately cautions that decisions were taken because EU decision-makers considered external factors and acted accordingly in a process of organized decision-making. This corresponds roughly to the first analytical perspective explored in Allison's and Halperin's work on the Cuban Missile Crisis, which describes it as follows:

> This approach depends primarily on the assumption that events in international politics consist of the more or less purposive acts of unified national governments and that governmental behavior can be understood by analogy with the intelligent, coordinated acts of individual human beings. Following this approach, analysts focus on the interests and goals of a nation, the alternative courses of actions available, and the costs and benefits of each alternative.
>
> (Allison and Halperin, 1972: 41)

In this view, foreign policy decisions are based on rational decision-making. Given this assumption of rationality, the EU would only undertake complex negotiations with a third actor when a cost-benefit analysis of various underlying factors warrants it. A specific part of the FPA literature that is concerned with foreign policy change allows for the identification of different such factors, or "drivers" for new approaches in foreign policy-making as the pursuit of Association Agreement negotiations represents.

Hermann (1990: 10–13) has identified four such factors for the foreign policy of states: 1. leader-driven change, 2. bureaucratic advocacy, 3. domestic restructuring, and 4. external shocks. The first describes the initiation of the process for foreign policy change based on authoritative top-down decisions by political leaders, due to altered opinions at that echelon. The second encompasses instances in which groups of officials lobby for a reorientation of foreign policy in absence of political leadership. The third then describes changes as induced by altered majorities after elections which may bring a party to power that has a different vision as to how foreign policy should be conducted. Lastly, and perhaps most relevantly, external shocks describe the initiation of foreign policy change as warranted by changes to the external environment of a state which is perceived by actors in a state's foreign policy decision-making system.

While leader-driven change by an individual in the context of the EU appears unlikely given the absence of a single foreign policy decision-making hierarchy, any of the other factors relevant for foreign policy change to occur could be of importance in the context of the EU's decision to undertake complex negotiations.

Considering the EU's complex negotiations in the Latin American region, the existing literature has privileged the consideration of external factors, and particularly the effect of US policy towards Latin America (García, 2008: 234, 2015; Grabendorff, 2005; Gratius and Legler, 2009; Meissner, 2018; Roy, 2010; Santander, 2005). García suggests in particular that developments in the realm of international trade have altered the EU's rationale for the negotiation of Association Agreements over time:

> The AAs emphasize continued commitment to, and hopes for, regional integration. However, given changes in other economic powers' trade strategies and setbacks at the WTO, since 2006 the EU has been willing to forgo some of its interregional objectives in favour of perceived improvements in competitiveness.
>
> (García, 2015: 636)

Nonetheless, the presence of external factors that may lead to the launch of complex EU negotiations is only a first step in concluding that rational decision-making in the EU's foreign policy bureaucracy was indeed at play. After all, drivers for foreign policy change are little more than "[e]xternal stimuli [...] that potentially form feedback to the policymakers" (Hermann, 1990: 16). These still need to form the basis for the rational cost-benefit analysis taking place in a foreign policy bureaucracy that ultimately shapes the change of foreign policy. The presence or absence of such rational decision-making processes can only be fully explored when contrasting them with differing analytical angles.

Therefore, a second lens on the EU's complex negotiations needs to be considered, namely seeing bureaucratic processes as determining factors for foreign policy decision-making. This has come to be known as the bureaucratic politics paradigm (Allison and Halperin, 1972). Rosati (1981: 236–8) provides a concise overview of it, summarized in four propositions: Firstly, the bureaucratic politics paradigm assumes that multiple entities and individuals make up the executive branch of any government, that these differ in their assessment of specific issues and that their individual preference structure differs. Secondly, there is no dominant institution or individual in any state's foreign policy decision-making system, although presidents/heads of government hold a particular and privileged position. Thirdly, foreign policy decisions are the outcome of bargaining between the different actors involved in foreign policy decision-making. Lastly, there are gaps between decisions taken and how these are being implemented.

This perspective resonates with the above elaboration on internal determinants of EU foreign policy coherence and provides an analytical lens that contrasts with the one seeing the undertaking of complex EU negotiations as the result of rational decision-making. Where the bureaucratic politics paradigm comments on the activity of the executive branch of national governments, this book instead considers the entities involved in the EU's complex negotiations at the EU level, similarly stipulating that no single actor is in a dominant position to define the EU's conduct in such negotiations. In consequence, the second perspective taken here considers bureaucratic processes and institutional factors that shape the EU's decision-making in complex EU negotiation processes.

In and of itself, this analytical lens cannot be operationalized and needs to be further detailed in individual sub-perspectives, so as to be able to study how the various elements that are parts of bureaucratic politics may have shaped the EU's policies towards the region. While each provides a distinct perspective on internal EU foreign policy decision-making, by definition these perspectives interact and overlap.

Policy inertia

An initial element to consider here is that foreign policy decision-making is a difficult process that is hampered by existing bureaucratic processes and commitments. Even when decision-makers agree on the broad aims of the EU's foreign policy, it will take time to permeate existing bureaucratic structures, as these operate according to specific organizational cultures which develop over time (Beach, 2012: 142). To simplify the functioning of complex bureaucracies, often "standard operating procedures" (Allison and Zelikow, 1999: 169–70) are developed to deal with specific situations.

A major decision such as on undertaking a complex EU negotiation will often require changing such procedures and altering the existing administrative culture before they can get underway. This is particularly important in contexts where an institution is short-staffed and struggles to keep up with the demands placed on it. Notoriously low staffing levels have been a major problem for the EU's development policy bureaucracy in the past (Orbie and Versluys, 2008: 69), and the same can currently be said of the EU's trade policy (see Chapter 6).

There are also material factors limiting the EU's capacity for complex EU negotiations, related to the long timeframes of certain EU programmes and the way in which funding decisions are taken internally. Certain parts of the EU's policy towards a given third actor may be predetermined due to long-term funding commitments and planning periods. This means that particular EU policies can only be altered with great difficulty in the short term, such as its development cooperation funding which is based on seven-year planning periods, in line with the EU's budget.

The capacity of the EU to coherently undertake complex negotiations spanning multiple of its policy areas is also limited by the fact that many actors in the EU's foreign policy system are influenced by existing principles, values and norms that have previously served as its basis for foreign policy action. It is generally assumed that most actors in a foreign policy system share certain underlying values and beliefs:

> Beneath the differences that fuel bureaucratic politics is a foundation of shared assumptions about basic values and facts. These underlying assumptions are reflected in various attitudes and images which are taken for granted by most players.
>
> (Allison and Halperin, 1972: 56)

When it comes to the specific example of the EU, Thomas has pointed out that

> the policy-making behaviour of member states is shaped significantly by shared perceptions regarding which policy options are consistent or inconsistent with pre-existing EU norms and commitments. [...] As a result, once member states have committed themselves to a particular set of norms and/or policy course, they are likely to find themselves entrapped, constrained to take further actions that do not reflect their original intentions and/or current preferences [...]. If this is correct, one would expect EU common and community policies to be consistent with pre-existing EU norms and policy commitments.
>
> (Thomas, 2011: 15–16)

While his argument is limited to the behaviour of member states, it can easily be extended to other institutional actors involved in the EU's foreign policy, such as the European Commission and its various administrative sub-entities.

The presence of such entrapment may lock in specific policy outputs by individual institutional actors, thus increasing the risk of horizontal and rhetorical policy incoherence. This problem can also be fuelled by the power of precedent, as long-standing (public) commitments and resources dedicated to a previous policy goal will make it more unlikely for actors to want to initiate a change of policy (Thomas, 2011: 17), and even less so when the suggested policy change is incompatible with other EU policy goals (Thomas, 2012). The public dimension of this has been described as rhetorical entrapment (Schimmelfennig, 2009; Splidsboel Hansen, 2006), where an alteration of the EU's policy will lead it or its institutional actors to incur a loss of reputation given previous public commitment to a specific policy goal.

The first perspective to be considered here is thus based on the fact that it is difficult to translate an overarching foreign policy aim into a coherent foreign policy output given the existence of previous commitments, the prevalence of established views on an issue, as well as established bureaucratic procedures. This analytical lens is thus ultimately concerned with what can be described as policy inertia.

Diverging interests

Bureaucratic actors may also be naturally inclined to hold diverging views on particular policy issues. While such differing views may simply be based on the fact that certain bureaucratic actors are bound more strongly by previous commitments given their role in past decision-making processes, the factors that can lead to diverging views between various bureaucracies are much larger.

The positions of specific actors within the EU's foreign policy apparatus may also diverge in line with their (perceived) role, their current position in the decision-making process, and the likely effect of any decision on the former two. When considering national foreign policy bureaucracies, this has been summarized as follows:

> Organizational interests are often dominated by the desire to maintain the autonomy of the organization in pursuing what its members view as the essence of the organization's activity.
>
> (Allison and Halperin, 1972: 49)

Relatedly,

> The drawing of organizational boundaries between as well as within ministries tends to bias the allocation of attention and the formation of preferences and identities.
>
> (Egeberg, 1999: 163)

These insights can easily be translated to the specific context of the EU, and existing research points to the fact that disagreements between different EU institutions in the foreign policy process are common (Orbie, 2008: 39), that different institutional actors such as the Commission and the Council Secretariat compete for influence in the EU's foreign policy (Christiansen, 2001; Dijkstra, 2009), that an actor's position in the policy process will have an important impact on its view of any given issue (Stetter, 2007: 139), and that EU policy output is always shaped by the competition of different interests internal to the EU (Carbone, 2008: 330).

While differing views of individual institutional actors are likely to have a negative impact, particularly on the EU's horizontal and vertical policy coherence, the likelihood of this happening depends on how much individual actors care about the issue at hand. The more an actor is invested in a given policy, the less likely it is to want to change the status quo (Kleistra and Mayer, 2001: 392). This will also be determined by the general salience of an issue, with policy questions that will likely have important effects or be heavily scrutinized in public leading to individual actors' wanting to defend their positions more vehemently than otherwise:

> EU foreign policy is the more powerful the less it is in the headlines. Where the policy content is routine and does not provoke rivalry and controversy among member states, it [the EU] is at its most powerful.
>
> (Matlary, 2013: 138)

Once more, this member state-centric perspective can easily be extended to other institutional actors such as the European Commission or the European Parliament. Lastly, taking the specific example of Latin America, it is important to note that policy questions relating to the region will differ greatly in salience between different institutional and intra-institutional actors, for instance with most Eastern European member states typically remaining passive in discussions due to their limited historical or economic ties to the region (Ruano, 2013a: 4).

Overall, diverging interests of the different institutions involved in the EU's foreign policy decision-making are thus likely to negatively impact the coherence of the EU's position in complex negotiations, as actors will be determined to defend their view on specific issues, and in particular if these are politically salient.

Actor autonomy

While the above is seen as an important element behind the relevance of bureaucratic politics in the literature, it is nonetheless key not to overestimate its importance on its own, as

> easy harmony of preferences is rare and this hypothesis leads one to expect failure of agreement except for those few issues where the member states' preferences are identical or where the stakes are so small that nobody cares about the outcome. Moreover, we know this to be false: member states' representatives often argue intensively about issues that nobody considers inconsequential before they reach agreement on a common policy. Nor can we simply dismiss these debates as meaningless rhetorical exercises. The reason that such debates are so intense, it is reasonable to assume, is that even where some preference convergence has occurred, the quest for agreement on an EU policy involves the compromise of policy preferences and adjustment of policy behaviour by member states that otherwise would prefer to avoid such concessions.
>
> (Thomas, 2011: 12)

Additionally, Egeberg has cautioned that

> those who focus on bureaucratic structure do not necessarily figure out in what ways varying administrative arrangements might intervene in policy processes and ultimately shape policy outputs.
>
> (Egeberg, 1999: 155)

It is thus important to also focus on the policy-making process itself, and particularly how much individual actors in the EU's foreign policy system are bound by collective decisions or those taken by individual actors elsewhere. Only when there are no mechanisms in place that ensure an ultimate agreement between different institutional and bureaucratic actors despite their diverging views on particular issues can the above analytical lens influence complex EU negotiations in an important manner. The consideration of individual actor's ability to defend their position and act independently of other actors on it is thus of the essence in this analytical perspective.

It has already been pointed out that despite the various reforms of the EU's treaties, there is no single foreign policy decision-making hierarchy in the EU (Portela and Raube, 2012: 4). Even the Treaty of Lisbon's language was sufficiently vague to leave the implementation of its provisions to those very actors meant to abide by them (Missiroli, 2010: 429), a process which has not been without difficulty in certain policy areas (Schade, 2019a; Tannous, 2013). Yet it is the presence of coordination requirements and mechanisms that can determine the EU's coherence in its complex negotiations even when diverging interests are present. Taking insights from administration research, policy coordination that can help coherent policy outputs is less likely the more individual actors are self-contained in their activity and capable to act on their own, and it will not occur automatically unless actors' share the same views on any given issue (Peters, 1998: 301, 304).

The typical response to a lack of coordination mechanisms or their malfunctioning has been to reorganize the functioning of the EU's foreign policy bureaucracy in an attempt to foster coordination. Yet, it is these very changes that can increase the autonomy of an actor in the EU's foreign policy process and change its position on a given issue, as this can involve the breaking up of functioning established coordination mechanisms, be they formal or informal. This is problematic as

> The changing nature of politics and policy problems raises another issue about co-ordination, having to do with the extent to which co-ordination is a one-off event or a part of an ongoing series of interactions. Everything else being equal I would expect co-ordination processes to be more effective when each event represents one in a continuing series of interactions.
>
> (Peters, 1998: 305)

In consequence, scholars who have studied the reorganization of bureaucracies have cautioned that "most major reorganization efforts have been described by outsiders, and frequently by participants, as substantial failures" (March and Olson, 1983: 288). In the context of the EU, researchers have observed that

> In parallel with efforts to ensure coherence between external relations and the CFSP, the 'Brusselisation' of foreign policy has provoked both rivalries between EU institutions and national foreign ministries and intensified

intra-bureaucratic struggles. [...] Likewise, the reorganised Commission external relations empire has suffered from prolonged internal bickering over turf
and resources.

(Peterson and Sjursen, 1998: 179)

This situation is also rendered worse by the continuing growth of the EU's institutions and their tasks (Christiansen, 2001), thus increasing the autonomy of
individual actors until new coordination mechanisms are established. Overall, in
addition to a focus on the divergence of opinions between individual institutional
actors, it is also important to consider their capacity to act on their own and how
this is curtailed by functioning coordination mechanisms.

Decision-making complexity

It is important to note here that the EU's foreign policy decision-making process
in itself is highly volatile and follows different logics depending on if it is an
exclusive or shared competence of the EU, or whether it is intergovernmental
in nature. In this context, Smith has described the EU's foreign policy decision-
making system as a hybrid with "a political, institutional and legal structure
derived from heterogeneous sources, or composed of elements of different or
incongruous kinds" (Smith, 2012: 700). This has arisen "from the operation of
a 'mixed actor system' and [is] reflecting heterogeneity of political influences"
(Smith, 2012: 700) on the EU's foreign policy system. These different institutional
structures have then evolved in parallel, perpetuating this heterogeneity over time
(Elgström and Pilegaard, 2008).

Even where requirements and mechanisms for policy coordination are in place,
reducing actor autonomy overall, the complexity of decision-making mechanisms,
the duration of decision-making processes and the number of actors involved
in different capacities can help individual bureaucratic actors to increase their
overall decision-making autonomy through an exploitation of these complexities
to escape control and coordination mechanisms. Particularly when placed at key
positions within the EU's foreign policy decision-making hierarchy, such as DG
Trade for the EU's CCP, this and other institutional actors have utilized information asymmetries arising in this set-up to increase their decision-making autonomy
over other institutions meant to control them. While in the EU's trade negotiations the member states were meant to control DG Trade's negotiation efforts,
in the past no mechanisms were put in place to do so in pre-negotiation phases
(Gastinger, 2016), which is one of many steps necessary for the EU to conclude
trade agreements. This allowed DG Trade to sometimes bargain strategically with
third actors to overrule certain member state concerns.

If the complexity of decision-making within one policy area such as trade
already allows individual actors to gain more decision-making autonomy than
foreseen, then this is likely to increase when considering coordination across
different policy areas. This is facilitated by the fact that depending on the policy
area under consideration the same actors at the EU level may take up different

roles and decision-making may require differing majorities or even unanimity voting. These difficulties extend beyond a consideration of CFSP and policies that used to be part of the EU's first pillar, as varying provisions may guide decision-making in different areas even within the former pillars (Portela and Orbie, 2014).

Rather than reducing the number of actors involved in EU-level decision-making over time, the creation of the HRVP and the EEAS with the Treaty of Lisbon has only increased the number of actors involved, thereby raising the complexity of the system overall, and further increasing the risk associated with each one defending its own interests due its unique position in EU decision-making (Lequesne, 2013: 81–3). Furthermore, established institutions are likely going to want to defend their established position within the system in line with the analytical lens based on diverging interests and will dispose of more knowledge of the process to act independently than newly created institutional actors, or those which have been reshaped in important ways.

The complexity of the EU's foreign policy decision-making system poses two additional risks to its coherence in complex negotiations, one related to the sheer number of actors involved and the different roles that these fulfil, the other to the duration of the decision-making process. Foreign policy decision-making has, for a long time, been conceptualized as a process, rather than individual decisions taken at specific points in time. This duration in turn introduces risks related to different discount rates between the various actors involved (Allison and Halperin, 1972: 50, 53).

In essence, the longer the time period that it takes for foreign policy decisions to be taken and implemented, the more likely it will become that the positions of individual actors involved in the process will start to diverge, possibly contributing to the incoherence of the EU's negotiations stance. This risk is further aggravated by the number of actors involved in the process and the requirements for individual decisions taken by these at different points in time.

Alternative analytical perspectives

While this book uses insights from FPA to analyse factors internal to the EU that contribute to the dynamics of its complex AA negotiations, some alternative analytical perspectives such as new institutionalism(s) or principal-agent theory could also have been used to structure the analysis undertaken here. All these theories

> have in common that they do not consider the EU as a unitary actor in international politics, but rather as a complex political system that consists of more than merely member states and in which Brussels-based actors matter.
>
> (Delreux, 2015: 152)

This section outlines why despite certain advantages of such analytical frameworks FPA was ultimately chosen over these, all while outlining that some of their assumptions are shared with the analytical framework outlined above.

Starting with new institutionalism, theories falling under this heading examine the role of institutional actors in foreign policy decision-making processes and consider under what conditions and for what purposes they are created, and how they subsequently shape decision-making processes. A large body of the literature on new institutionalism revolves around rational choice institutionalism. Principal-agent theory (PA) itself can be considered as a subset of this variety of new institutionalism (Delreux, 2015: 159).

Rational choice institutionalism assumes that actors in the international realm, or member states in the context of the EU, attempt to maximize their interests based on cost-benefit analyses. Under this perspective, the creation of institutions, defined as rules constraining the behaviour of individual actors, can help overcome collective action problems and thereby reduce transaction costs hampering cooperation.

Principal-agent theory then expands these basic insights to discuss the dynamics that can unfold once an institution—or an agent in the language of principal-agent theory—has been created by so-called principals. When applied to the context of the EU, the latter are most often its member states. PA then assumes that despite the intentions of the principals the newly created agent will develop its own interests and given its privileged access to resources such as information will, under certain conditions, be able to take decisions against the preferences of its principals. The latter in turn are then incentivized to set up certain control mechanisms, such as "police-patrol," meaning an active and regular oversight of the actions of the principal, or less resource-incentive "fire-alarm" oversight, where principals will set up mechanisms to control only important and large deviations by an agent from its assigned role (Pollack, 1997: 111).

Pollack (1997, 2003) has outlined the advantages of using PA to conceptualize the independent role of the EU's supranational institutions on its decision-making processes, and particularly that of the European Commission and the European Court of Justice. However, his work was primarily concerned with the EU's single market, leaving aside a possible application of PA to the EU's foreign policy.

Considering PA's application to the EU's foreign policy, most of the literature uses it to analyse the dynamics of decision-making in specific policy areas, such as the EU's trade policy or its behaviour in international organizations (Delreux, 2015: 160). A special issue of the *Journal of European Public Policy* considers the value of principal-agent analysis for the study of the EU's foreign economic policies in particular (see the introduction by Dür and Elsig, 2011) and thereby offers a good overview of the utility of PA for such policy-specific analyses where the positions of principals and a single agent are clearly delineated.

However, applying PA to the EU's external relations more broadly is challenging as the set-up of principals and agents varies between different policy areas and does not help to conceptualize how agents may interact in more complex decision-making settings. If one considers decision-making in two distinct policy areas relevant for this book, trade and the CFSP, for instance, it is possible to note that principals, agents, and control mechanisms differ between both policy areas. While theoretically the member states mandate the EU's supranational institutions to perform certain tasks, the member states themselves should not be considered as unitary actors. When it comes to the delegation and control of powers for trade negotiations to the European Commission, or more specifically DG Trade, different national ministers and officials are involved than when delegating powers to the EEAS to negotiate external agreements under the EU's CFSP.

Not only are there thus two different delegation chains for distinct foreign policy areas, but there are implicitly separate sets of principals and explicitly distinct agents in both cases. Given this book's interest in the dynamics of negotiations spanning multiple EU policy areas, the interaction between these distinct principals and agents needs to be considered alongside the dynamics of delegation processes themselves. As outlined above, FPA can help structure such analyses that take into account the existence of parallel decision-making hierarchies and bodies whose competencies are sometimes distinct and may overlap.

Another variety of new institutionalism, namely sociological institutionalism, also considers the socializing effect of institutions on the actors that created them in the first place and thus allows to take into account that EU member state officials will develop an "esprit de corps," or coordination and cooperation reflex, once socialized into the institutions within which they operate on a regular basis (Delreux, 2015: 157). While it can explain why representatives of the EU's member states may sometimes act against the preferences of the member states themselves, as determined by rationalist approaches, this perspective does not allow to take into account all the dynamics that may arise between different institutional actors at the EU level. Nonetheless, it cautions to think about the social identity of officials involved in decision-making processes and how this may transcend the formal roles assigned to them, something which also forms part of FPA literature when considering the role of individuals in policy processes.

Historical institutionalism (HI) is another variety of new institutionalism that needs to be considered. This theory emphasizes the importance of past decisions on future policy choices, underlining that past events restrict the number of future policy options available in a process called path dependency. Under HI, it is hypothesized that past decisions make it more and more costly to deviate from the direction of past decisions taken, thereby contributing to unforeseen effects of the creation of institutions and past choices. While this theory offers a relevant additional perspective on the dynamics of decision-making processes, it is nonetheless important to note that "a pure HI account is rarely sufficient to explain institutional change and design and that it needs to be complemented" (Delreux, 2015: 159).

Nonetheless, HI has been used to study the EU's foreign policy and has generated some important insights. For instance, it has also been pointed out that the distinct evolution and history of EU foreign policy decision-making processes by policy area make it difficult for the EU to reach coherence in external negotiations (Elgström and Pilegaard, 2008). Furthermore, García (2008) has used historical institutionalism to study the dynamics leading to the conclusion of the EU–Chile Association Agreement.

While not explicitly using HI in this book, some of analytical angles outlined above share common assumptions with this theoretical perspective. For instance, the exploration of policy inertia is based on the assumption that within the EU's institutions it is possible to find differing administrative cultures that have developed over time, and which cannot be readily altered in the short term. Similarly, the long duration of complex EU negotiations requires a significant commitment, thus reducing the incentives to letting them fail once they have begun.

While new institutionalism and principal-agent theory would have offered alternative bases for an analytical framework interested in the dynamics of complex EU negotiations, ultimately FPA literature was chosen given that it allows to consider more complex and different dynamics in decision-making processes that could not be sufficiently captured by either of the other approaches.

Methods and methodology

Given that the analytical framework is based on assumptions from the realm of bureaucratic politics, a suitable methodology needs to be adopted to unearth relevant administrative processes underlying complex EU negotiations. A research method suited to unearth causality in political processes is *process tracing*, which can be defined as "the systematic examination of diagnostic evidence selected and analysed in light of research questions and hypotheses posed by the investigator" (Collier, 2011: 823). Process tracing is specifically used to draw causal inferences from empirical data, "often times understood as part of a temporal sequence of events or phenomena" (Collier, 2011: 824).

In order to be able to draw causal conclusion from process tracing in one's research, Collier (2011) emphasizes that the researcher must be familiar with the case at hand and be able to offer sufficient descriptions of phenomena, before being able to analyse them. When using process tracing as a tool to draw causal inferences from empirical data in particular, it is crucial to be able to place empirical evidence in a chronological chain of events.

Process tracing is thus particularly apt as a research method for cases in which a plethora of empirical data is available, so as to be able to provide detailed or "thick" descriptions of phenomena and ultimately identify causal pathways through a temporal analysis and how these have been shaped by other variables. While research into policy-making for recent periods is always limited by problems of access to internal documents given moratoria on archival access and the secrecy surrounding decisions in the realm of foreign policy, the data gathered for this book is nonetheless sufficiently detailed to enable process tracing for the detailed empirical cases under consideration here.

The pursuit of negotiations requires specific decisions to be taken within the EU's foreign policy bureaucracy, such as the granting of negotiation mandates to the European Commission, and therefore offers starting points to unearth causal pathways leading to the success or failure of complex EU negotiations. The analysis in this book is thus structured chronologically and focuses on different rounds in the EU's negotiations for AAs. Each chapter discusses specific grouped negotiations that occurred at that point in time, further breaking down the process into the separate steps necessary before negotiations could begin, the negotiations themselves, and the ratification process where these succeeded. Consequently, this permits an exploration of how foreign policy coordination mechanisms have played a role in the process.

On this basis, different aspects of bureaucratic politics can be explored for each negotiation. Table 2.1 provides an overview over possible indicators that may point to the relevance of any of these analytical lenses in the specific negotiations considered later on. Consequentially, these consider factors such as pre-existing and long-standing policy commitments (policy inertia), the salience of an issue for individual actors (diverging interests), the weakness of coordination mechanisms (actor autonomy), or the presence of different modes of decision-making (decision-making complexity).

When considering the broader insights that this book can contribute to the literature discussing the EU's behaviour in international negotiations, then its empirical scope offers to tests the analytical model in a "standard" setting, where only a relatively limited set of interests on the EU's side is involved. After all, countries in the Latin American region have no EU accession perspective, are not present in concerns over the EU's security, and the EU's economic interests in the region are more limited than is the case for negotiations in other world regions. Furthermore:

> Despite nuances and differences, the gaps between the European and Latin American worldviews are considerably smaller in comparison to the diplomatic clashes between the European Union and other regions or countries.
>
> (Dominguez, 2015: 2)

Table 2.1 Indicators for the presence of bureaucratic politics

Policy inertia	• Long-standing public commitments
	• Established policy principles
	• Long timeframes of existing policies
	• Sunk costs
	  ◦ Previous development funding
	  ◦ Human resources

Diverging interests	• Competence overlap • Salience of an issue • Policy-centred organisation of the European Commission • Established policy-based communities of interest
Actor autonomy	• Weakness of decision-making hierarchies and horizontal coordination mechanisms • Geography-centred organization of the European Commission • Continued validity of previous principles/mandates for activity • Disruption of established coordination mechanisms
Decision-making complexity	• Number of actors involved in decisions • Varying modes of decision-making • Duration of administrative processes

Therefore, the EU's ties to the region ultimately emanate in the domain of "low politics" (Santander, 2005: 286) and should thus allow for important insights into policy areas such as the CCP and development policy-making where the role of the EU's institutions is more pronounced than in the field of the CFSP.

Sources

Given the difficulty of gaining insights into internal EU decision-making processes through any one particular source, the research for this book is ultimately based on a variety of data. These are notably semi-structured interviews, internal documents made available to the author, publicly available documents, leaked diplomatic cables, secondary sources, and media coverage.

Any one kind of source utilized to gather data comes with problems. While for interviews, for instance, the researcher needs to be able to separate an interviewee's opinion from underlying facts (Rathburn, 2008: 686–90), public documents may represent a mere narrative separate from an underlying rationale. Official minutes of internal discussions on the other hand may omit important elements, and their content is shaped by the officials producing such documents.[1] Whenever possible, the analysis for this book is thus based on the triangulation of information gathered from different sources, so as to corroborate information contained in others.

Interviews

Given that concerns related to the practice of the formulation of the EU's foreign policy are at the core of this book, interviews with persons involved in complex EU negotiations, and particularly those in the Latin American context, are a logical choice to generate empirical data. As Rathburn (2008: 689–95) cautions, interviews can be particularly useful in revealing information on motivations, preferences, and personal thoughts of interviewees when they are conducted carefully and thoroughly fact-checked. Thus, gathering data in this way has only been undertaken as one of the last steps in the data collection process, as this allowed to ask questions related to specific pieces of information contained in other primary sources.

In total, 40 individuals were interviewed in 35 separate interviews (see Appendix). While most of these were with a single person, some involved groups of interviewees. Where necessary, some interviewees have also been contacted again for follow-up interviews. Interviews were conducted with EU officials working in the Council, the European Commission and the EEAS, member state officials, members of the European Parliament, as well as Latin American diplomats. Interviewees were selected based on their previous or current role related to complex negotiations in the EU–Latin American context, while some individuals previously active in the field were recommended to me during prior interviews. Caution was taken to preserve interviewees' anonymity. Consequently, references to interviews do not contain interviewees' names and only provide some information on them, such as a broad description of their role, and the location of the interview.

Each interview began with a set of open-ended questions depending on the position and background of the individual concerned. These were then followed by further questions depending on the initial answers given. This made it possible to react flexibly to the viewpoint or expertise of individual interviewees. Over the course of conducting different interviews, the focus changed more and more from general questions to those attempting to situate particular pieces of information or corroborate elements learned in a different context beforehand.

The core problem revealed itself to be the high turnover of staff in the institutions targeted, making it difficult to gain insights into developments dating back more than a few years. While this could be compensated for partially by asking interviewees for contact details of previous personnel holding their posts, often these individuals were not available to be interviewed or did not remember details from their previous postings. Consequently, empirical insights gained from the interviews have proven to be the most valuable for general conceptual insights, as well as the chapters on the EU's negotiations with the Andean Community and EU–Latin American relations after the Lisbon Treaty.

Documents

Significant empirical insights for this project also emanated from a large range of official documents generated by the EU institutions, its member states, and Latin American countries. Many relevant documents can be accessed through the EEAS website or the Council's online database. While the most recent documents are typically classified, some formerly secret documents from the relevant time period for this have been declassified fully or in parts. The online *Archive of European Integration* hosted at the University of Pittsburgh similarly contains many significant documents, including some that are not listed in the Council's database. The online repository *Foreign Trade Information System* hosted by the *Organisation of American States* (OAS) has been particularly helpful in tracking developments for individual trade negotiations rounds between the EU and its Latin American partners. Lastly, specific keyword Google searches limited to the backend of the EU's official websites have also revealed some relevant documents that are not linked in a publicly accessible manner. These are regularly referred to in the bibliography by providing the full hyperlink to access the document in question.

At times, classified documents have been made available by interviewees and others. It was only possible to consult some of these documents under the condition that I do not publicly refer to them. Others are referenced with some identifying information in footnotes, though not fully identified and referenced as this could contribute to the identification of the sources who have made them available.

Diplomatic cables

EU diplomatic correspondence, that of its member states and of most of its Latin American partner organizations for the time period relevant for this book, remains inaccessible at present due to archival embargo periods typically spanning thirty years. Nonetheless, certain types of diplomatic communication have been used extensively.

The so-called Cablegate leak of the US diplomatic cables by the organization WikiLeaks has created an important and easily accessible database of diplomatic communication significantly ahead of the lapse of embargo periods. In total, the database contains 251,287 diplomatic cables, from the period between 2003 and 2010. While not emanating from a state actor directly involved in EU–Latin American relations, these cables have nonetheless proven to be a useful contribution for a number of reasons. On the one hand, the extensive diplomatic network of the US and its significant interests in the Latin American region mean that American diplomats have followed developments in the EU's relations with the region closely and hence reported on it. On the other hand, American diplomats appear to regularly consult with EU and member state officials on Latin American issues, offering some insights into the positions and opinions of key EU officials on certain issues. Lastly, some EU member state foreign offices have regularly shared internal EU documents and position papers with their American counterparts, hence making either their text or detailed summaries publicly available. An example of this is the provision of a summary of an internal discussion on the EU's Cuba policy provided by the Czech Ministry of Foreign Affairs (US Embassy Czech Republic Prague, 2005).

While researchers should be cautious as to the authenticity of the documents given their non-official source and publication, there remains little doubt at present as to the database's accuracy. Not only have official US sources acknowledged the authenticity of these documents and issued restrictions for US civil servants on using them, but also numerous newspapers have researched the context of some of the cables and published stories based on key insights from the archive.

Consequently, keyword searches pertaining to EU–Latin American relations were conducted, as well as searches based on the origin and destination of cables on the database that is available and indexed on the WikiLeaks website. Further cables were then discovered by following cross-references contained in those provided as a result from the keyword searches. In total, around 150 diplomatic cables of relevance were identified, with references to individual cables provided when these have been used in the body of this book. Lastly, a number of other diplomatic cables emanating from smaller leaks have also been sued, such as cables exchanged between the Ecuadorean embassy in Brussels and the country's foreign ministry on EU–Ecuador Free Trade negotiations.

Secondary sources and media coverage

Where empirical work of an academic nature on specific elements of the EU's relations with Latin America is in existence, this has also been used. This has proven to be particularly valuable for the chapters concerned with the pre-Lisbon situation where interview data could not easily be gathered or would have duplicated previous empirical research.

Furthermore, media reports of developments in EU–Latin American relations from a large range of different sources available through online database services such as *Factiva* were consulted. Regular news bulletins produced by the news agency *Agence Europe*, which is focused on reporting on EU politics, have proven the most helpful. Given that many developments in EU–Latin American relations are relatively more important for the Latin American partners concerned, reporting by national media outlets in those countries was used to track smaller developments that may go unnoticed in reporting in Europe. The website *Bilaterals. org*, which follows developments in trade policy from a critical perspective by providing links to reporting on the matters, has also proven to be particularly helpful in this regard. Whenever possible, the information contained in secondary sources has been triangulated with other kinds of data.

A brief literature review: Complex EU negotiations with Latin America in context

The existing literature that considers the EU's relations with Latin America is relatively limited, both in its empirical detail and in the analytical perspectives taken. This section outlines the state of the literature on the EU's ties with the region before arguing that one needs to look at a different kind of literature that uses the EU's policies targeted at third actors to analyse EU foreign policy decision-making in itself, as is the focus of this book.

While comparatively little has been written on EU–Latin American relations in English (Dominguez, 2015: 3–4), there is nonetheless an established body of literature that considers the ties between the two regions from different perspectives. The first detailed and structured elaboration on the relationship is Smith's (1995) seminal contribution which outlines how different aspects of the EU's foreign policy have interacted to support the Central American peace process up to the early 1990s. Her theoretical argument focuses on the fact that the EU was able to play a central role in the region due to the activity of the European Commission, and the relative absence of the member states from the overall policy process. The author then expanded her empirical contribution somewhat in a book chapter (Smith, 1998), which extended the analysis through most of the 1990s and considered the evolution of the EU's ties with Latin America as a whole.

Amidst growing EU foreign policy activity towards the region from the 1990s onwards, a volume edited by Grabendorff and Seidelmann (2005) discussed the evolution of the EU's ties with Latin America's different regional integration mechanisms, focusing on Mercosur in particular. Conceptually, the ties are elaborated on by using the concept of biregionalism, i.e. the development of ties between two geographical regions and how these are shaped by factors internal and external to the dyad under consideration. Crucially, the book also considers how EU–Latin American biregionalism has been shaped by a triangular relationship including the US, be it with the latter conceptualized as a partner or a competitor. A similar perspective is taken by Meissner (2018) who discusses the EU's negotiations with Latin America and Asia in the context of economic competition with the US and China.

The latest detailed account of the state of EU–Latin American relations over time is a book by Dominguez (2015), which categorizes the EU's ties with the region according to the degree to which it is based on interregional relations. Overall, the book outlines a varied picture of the relationship as having been shaped primarily by a number of EU strategies and disagreements between actors on both sides of the Atlantic. In consequence, the book describes the EU abandonment of some of the Association Agreement negotiations primarily as the result of Latin America's unwillingness to proceed with its own regional integration (Dominguez, 2015: 173–4).

Leaving aside the consideration of regional and subregional factors of the two volumes introduced above, an edited volume on *The Europeanization of National Foreign Policies towards Latin America* (Ruano, 2013b) applies the concept of Europeanization to study the linkage between national policies and EU policies towards the region. Through its consideration of various national foreign policies, its main contribution is that the history of member states' ties with Latin America is an important explanatory factor for whether a member state tends to want to shape the EU's policy towards the region (such as Spain), or rather tends to accept an existing consensus (such as Poland) (Ruano, 2013a: 4–5).

Other works have focused on the evolution of the EU's ties with individual actors on the Latin American continent. For instance, García has described the EU's negotiations for an Association Agreement with Chile in detail, using historical institutionalism to structure her analysis (García, 2008, 2011). She focuses on a number of critical junctures that have shaped the negotiations with the country, thus explaining how the EU came to conclude an agreement despite important odds against it from the outset. The same author has written on the evolution of the EU's ties with Latin America's regional integration organizations (García, 2015), emphasizing how these have been shaped by the EU's structural power towards the countries concerned and the primordial importance of EU trade interests to elaborate on the different fate of negotiations with Mercosur, the Andean region, and Central America.

The EU's ties with various countries and regional organizations in the region have also been the focus of specific strands of research: The EU–Mexico Global Agreement (Szymanski and Smith, 2005), the EU's strategic partnership with Brazil and Mexico (Schade, 2019b; Whitman and Rodt, 2012), the 2010 EU–Central America Association Agreement (Arana, 2015), and the EU's FTA with Ecuador (Schade, 2016) have all been the focus of detailed analysis.

For the most part, however, the EU's Latin America policy has not been seen as an object of analysis in its own right, but rather as one expression of a nascent phenomenon of interregionalism in IR, in which the EU has played a central role. The body of literature, to which some of the works cited above have also contributed, revolves around the conceptual terms of *interregionalism* (Aggarwal and Fogarty, 2004; Börzel and Risse, 2009; Doctor, 2015; Grisanti, 2004; Hänggi et al., 2006; Söderbaum et al., 2005; Telò et al., 2015), *new regionalism* (Grugel, 2004), or *biregionalism* (Grabendorff and Seidelmann, 2005). This literature offers extensive accounts of the EU's motivations for promoting interregional ties, evaluates its prospects, and comments on what conclusions can be drawn from it for the study of IR.

In reality, there are different kinds of interregional ties that need to be considered, ranging from relations based purely on direct ties between two regional organizations with a capacity to enter into direct agreements, to hybrid regionalism where one regional organization such as the EU enters into ties with multiple states in another region (De Lombaerde et al., 2015: 754), sometimes with a goal of influencing ties between states in the region targeted to develop regional ties on their own.

The authors working on this phenomenon claim that "Interregionalism is deeply rooted in the foreign policies and external relations of the EU" (De Lombaerde et al., 2015: 750). The officially stated aim of the EU's interregionalism policies is to expand and formalize its ties to other regional integration organizations and thereby strengthen them. Börzel and Risse (2009, 2015) discuss the EU's motivation to promote regional integration through interregionalism as an attempt "to diffuse its own model of democracy, social welfare and regional integration through partnership agreements and political dialogue" (2009: 22).

Exercising somewhat more caution as to the overall importance of the phenomenon, Söderbaum et al. (2005) have argued that in an attempt to develop its distinct identity as an international actor, the EU has aimed to spread its own model of regional integration. In this sense, the EU has aimed to legitimize its own existence by bolstering similar organizations in Africa, Asia, and Latin America through engagement with them (De Lombaerde et al., 2015: 751). In reality, however, this has proven to be difficult across the board (De Lombaerde et al., 2015: 750), leading to an assessment that interregionalism has recently declined, to be replaced by a renewed focus on bilateralism (De Lombaerde et al., 2015: 752). Yet looking at one particular such interaction, Valladão asserts that with regard to the EU's policy towards one of Latin America's regional blocs, Mercosur, the "EU had an almost missionary drive to diffuse its own 'unique experience'" (2015: 121).

The analysis of the EU's ties with Latin America serves as a core empirical portion of works concerned with the EU's interregionalism (Franck et al., 2009; Söderbaum and Stålgren, 2010; Telò et al., 2015). Often, the EU's interregional ties with Latin America will also be used as a point of comparison to its activity towards other regions, such as with the Southern African region (Lenz, 2012; Robles, 2008a), or the Association of Southeast Asian Nations (ASEAN) (Meissner, 2018; Robles, 2008b). It is important to note, however, that studying the EU's ties with Latin America is only one strand of the literature on the EU and interregionalism.

While the initial literature concerned with interregionalism often portrayed it as a trend that could have an important impact on the international system, the authors have come to be more critical of interregionalism, once more using the EU's ties with Latin America to caution that it may have important limitations. Santander (2009, 2010a, 2010b) has argued that EU interregionalism appears to have come to an end given the EU's negotiation experience with Mercosur. This is also reflected in work which attempts to reconcile the continuation of some interregional EU negotiations with an increasing use of bilateral ties (Hardacre, 2008; Hardacre and Smith, 2009; Meissner, 2019). Nonetheless, the existing literature has yet to engage fully with the phenomenon of the EU beginning complex negotiations in an interregional context, only to revert to bilateral negotiations later on.

Given this book's focus on determinants internal to the EU which influence its behaviour in complex negotiations, work on the EU's foreign policy coherence also needs to be considered. Smith (1995) discusses the particular role of the European Commission in determining the EU's policy activity towards Central America. While also using interregionalism to frame her case study, Allison has studied the EU's ties with ASEAN to gain insights into the EU's actorness in international relations. When studying EU foreign policy, she cautions that

> [a]ctorness is only realized [...] if the actor and its interlocutors both perceive it to have the responsibility and ability to do so, and once this is determined, the actor utilises its resources effectively to ensure that its aims are achieved.
>
> (Allison, 2015: 3)

While conceptually different from foreign policy coherence, her approach nonetheless demonstrates that important insights into EU foreign policy-making can be gained from studying the EU's ties with specific third actors, and regional organizations in particular.

Similarly, in studying the EU's policy towards the Mediterranean, Bicchi (2007) analyses which conditions internal to the EU contribute to the formulation of new initiatives in the EU's foreign policy, thus elaborating on the importance of policy windows, ideational concerns, and the role of policy entrepreneurs. An edited volume on the EU's ties with the Mediterranean after the Arab Spring (Horst et al., 2013) in turn uses this case study to argue that its foreign policy can best be understood by a framework entitled Logics of Action, which focuses on an interaction between the legal framework and the activity of the actors active in its decision-making, collectively reinforcing the weakness of the EU's foreign policy.

In addition to a literature focused on using the EU's ties with third actors to further our understanding of EU foreign policy, there is also a dedicated body of research that studies the EU's foreign policy coherence and how it relates to the EU's actorness towards third actors:

The importance of speaking and acting as one is a prominent theme, both explicitly and implicitly, in the scholarly literature on EU foreign policy and especially EU 'actorness' in world affairs [...] Yet contributors to this literature disagree on how to define and measure the concept. Some scholars focus on the activities of Member States while others focus on EU institutions; some focus on policy-makers' values, some on policy-makers' rhetoric, some on the policy-making process, and still others on policy choices or outcomes.

(Thomas, 2012: 458)

When focusing on the sources of EU foreign policy (in)coherence, researchers have often been concerned with the large number of actors involved in European foreign policy decision-making processes (Allen, 1998). When considering the EU's foreign policy output, one frequent theme in the literature is the problem of foreign policy coherence due to multiple parallel EU policies that target the same third actors in different ways. This can be witnessed when analysing how the EU's development policy goals diverge from those in some other policy areas (Carbone, 2008, 2009; Matthews, 2008).

Others still have focused on problems of policy coherence arising out of the EU's former pillar structure, a problem that has remained important even after the Treaty of Lisbon. For instance, Smith cautions that

while the EU is what some might describe as a 'commercial superpower', in other areas of its external action it is decidedly stunted. For the EU, this creates a problem of coherence and consistency, which is underlined by the interinstitutional problems that persist even after (or because of ?) Lisbon.

(Smith, 2013: 657)

Such problems have also been observed within specific policies spanning multiple modes of decision-making, such as the EU's conflict prevention policies in general (Stewart, 2008) or those aimed at the promotion of democracy and human rights (Verdonck, 2015).

Others have also pointed out that where the EU simultaneously pursues economic and political goals (Algieri, 1999; Szymanski and Smith, 2005), these may ultimately contradict one another with one typically winning out (Dandashly, 2015). Coherence difficulties can be observed when considering two policy areas that have the same objectives, yet originated in different modes of the EU's decision-making system, such as the possibility to grant or withdraw trade access under the EU's Generalised System of Preferences (GSP) (former first pillar), or CFSP sanctions (Portela and Orbie, 2014). Lastly, conflicts of interest between internal EU actors are often cited as a source for incoherence, such as amongst member states when responding to the events of the Arab Spring (Noutcheva, 2015), or the Libyan crisis in particular (Koenig, 2011).

Note

1 A former EU official cautioned that researchers should always attempt to identify the note-taker for official summaries of meetings held in the Council of the EU before analysing the content of said document (Brussels, Interview 17).

Bibliography

Aggarwal VK and Fogarty EA (2004) *EU Trade Strategies: Between Regionalism and Globalism*. New York, NY: Palgrave Macmillan.

Algieri F (1999) The Coherence Dilemma of EU External Relations: The European Asia Policy. *Journal of the Asia Pacific Economy* 4(1): 81–99.

Allen D (1998) 'Who Speaks for Europe?' The Search for an Effective and Coherent External Policy. In: Peterson J and Sjursen H (eds) *A Common Foreign Policy for Europe?: Competing Visions of the CFSP*. London: Routledge, pp. 44–60.

Allison GT and Halperin MH (1972) Bureaucratic Politics: A Paradigm and Some Policy Implications. *World Politics* 24(Supplement: Theory and Policy in International Relations): 40–79. DOI: 10.2307/2010559.

Allison GT and Zelikow P (1999) *Essence of Decision: Explaining the Cuban Missile Crisis*. 2nd ed. New York, NY: Longman.

Allison L (2015) *The EU, ASEAN and Interregionalism: Regionalism Support and Norm Diffusion Between the EU and ASEAN*. Houndmills, Basingstoke: Palgrave Macmillan.

Arana AG (2015). The European Union and the Central American Common Market Sign an Association Agreement: Pragmatism Versus Values? *European Foreign Affairs Review* 20(1): 43–63.

Beach D (2012) *Analyzing Foreign Policy*. Basingstoke: Palgrave Macmillan.

Bicchi F (2007) *European Foreign Policy Making Toward the Mediterranean*. 1st ed. Europe in Transition : NYU EU Studies. New York, NY: Palgrave Macmillan.

Börzel T and Risse T (2009) *The Rise of (Inter-)Regionalism: The EU as a Model of Regional Integration*. APSA 2009 Toronto Meeting Paper, 13 August. SSRN. Available at: http://papers.ssrn.com/abstract=1450391 (accessed 15 January 2018).

Börzel TA and Risse T (2015) The EU and the Diffusion of Regionalism. In Telò M, Fawcett L, and Ponjaert F (eds) *Interregionalism and the European Union: A Post-Revisionist Approach to Europe's Place in a Changing World*. Farnham: Ashgate, pp. 51–65.

Carbone M (2008) Mission Impossible: The European Union and Policy Coherence for Development. *Journal of European Integration* 30(3): 323–342. DOI: 10.1080/07036330802144992.

Carbone M (ed.) (2009) *Policy Coherence and EU Development Policy*. London: Routledge. Available at: https://catalogue.lse.ac.uk/Record/1207793.

Carlsnaes W (1993) On Analysing the Dynamics of Foreign Policy Change: A Critique and Reconceptualization. *Cooperation and Conflict* 28(3): 5–30.

Carlsnaes W, Sjursen H, and White B (eds) (2004) *Contemporary European Foreign Policy*. London: SAGE.

Christiansen T (2001) Intra-Institutional Politics and Inter-Institutional Relations in the EU: Towards Coherent Governance? *Journal of European Public Policy* 8(5): 747–769. Doi:10.1080/13501760110083491.

Collier D (2011) Understanding Process Tracing. *PS: Political Science & Politics* 44(4): 823–830. DOI: 10.1017/S1049096511001429.

Collinson S (1999) 'Issue-Systems', 'Multi-Level Games' and the Analysis of the EU's External Commercial and Associated Policies: A Research Agenda. *Journal of European Public Policy* 6(2): 206–224. DOI: 10.1080/135017699343685.

Dandashly A (2015) The EU Response to Regime Change in the Wake of the Arab Revolt: Differential Implementation. *Journal of European Integration* 37(1), 37–56. DOI: 10.1080/07036337.2014.975988.

De Lombaerde P, Söderbaum F, and Wunderlich J-U (2015) Interregionalism. In: Jørgensen KE, Aarstad ÅK, Drieskens E, et al. (eds) *The SAGE Handbook of European Foreign Policy*. London: SAGE, pp. 750–765.

Delreux T (2015) Bureaucratic Politics, New Institutionalism and Principal-Agent Models. In: Jørgensen KE, Aarstad ÅK, Drieskens E, et al. (eds) *The SAGE Handbook of European Foreign Policy*. London: SAGE, pp. 152–165.

Dijkstra H (2009) Commission Versus Council Secretariat: An Analysis of Bureaucratic Rivalry in European Foreign Policy. *European Foreign Affairs Review* 14(3), 431–450.

Doctor M (2015). Interregionalism's Impact on Regional Integration in Developing Countries: The Case of Mercosur. *Journal of European Public Policy* 22(7), 967–984. DOI: 10.1080/13501763.2014.992932.

Doeser F (2011) Domestic Politics and Foreign Policy Change in Small States: The Fall of the Danish 'Footnote Policy'. *Cooperation and Conflict* 46(2): 222–241. DOI: 10.1177/0010836711406417.

Dominguez R (2015) *EU Foreign Policy Towards Latin America*. New York, NY: Palgrave MacMillan.

Duke S (2012) The European External Action Service: Antidote Against Incoherence? *European Foreign Affairs Review* 17(1): 45–68.

Dür A and Elsig M (2011) Principals, Agents, and the European Union's Foreign Economic Policies. *Journal of European Public Policy* 18(3): 323–338. DOI: 10.1080/13501763.2011.551066.

Egeberg M (1999) The Impact of Bureaucratic Structure on Policy Making. *Public Administration* 77(1): 155–170. DOI: 10.1111/1467-9299.00148.

Elgström O and Pilegaard J (2008) Imposed Coherence: Negotiating Economic Partnership Agreements. *Journal of European Integration* 30(3): 363–380. DOI: 10.1080/07036330802141949.

Foradori P, Rosa P, and Scartezzini R (2007) Introduction: The System of European Foreign Policy. In: Foradori P, Rosa P, and Scartezzini R (eds) *Managing a Multilevel Foreign Policy: The EU in International Affairs*. Plymouth: Lexington Books, pp. vii–xxi.

Franck C, Defraigne J-C, and de Moriamé V (eds) (2009) *L'Union Européenne et La Montée Du Régionalisme: Exemplarité et Partenariats*. Louvain-La-Neuve: Academia Bruylant.

Frennhoff Larsén MF (2007) Trade Negotiations Between the EU and South Africa: A Three-Level Game. *JCMS: Journal of Common Market Studies* 45(4): 857–881. DOI: 10.1111/j.1468-5965.2007.00751.x.

García M (2008) *The Path to the 2002 Association Agreement Between the European Union and Chile: A Case Study in Successful Political Negotiation*. Lewiston, NY: Edwin Mellen.

García M (2011) Incidents Along the Path: Understanding the Rationale Behind the EU–Chile Association Agreement. *JCMS: Journal of Common Market Studies* 49(3): 501–524. DOI: 10.1111/j.1468-5965.2010.02149.x.

44   *The EU's behaviour in complex negotiations*

García M (2015) The European Union and Latin America: 'Transformative Power Europe' Versus the Realities of Economic Interests. *Cambridge Review of International Affairs* 28(4): 621–640. DOI: 10.1080/09557571.2011.647762.

Gastinger M (2016) The Tables Have Turned on the European Commission: The Changing Nature of the Pre-Negotiation Phase in EU Bilateral Trade Agreements. *Journal of European Public Policy* 23(9): 1367–1385. DOI: 10.1080/13501763.2015.1079233.

Gebhard C (2011) Coherence. In Hill C and Smith M (eds) *International Relations and the European Union*. Oxford: Oxford University Press, pp. 101–127.

Grabendorff W (2005) Triangular Relations in a Unipolar World: North America, South America and the EU. In: Grabendorff W and Seidelmann R (eds) *Relations Between the European Union and Latin America: Biregionalism in a Changing Global System*. Baden-Baden: Nomos, pp. 43–69.

Grabendorff W and Seidelmann R (eds) (2005) *Relations Between the European Union and Latin America: Biregionalism in a Changing Global System*. Baden-Baden: Nomos.

Gratius S and Legler T (2009) Latin America Is Different: Transatlantic Discord on How to Promote Democracy in 'Problematic' Countries. In: Magen A, Risse T, and McFaul MA (eds) *Promoting Democracy and the Rule of Law: American and European Strategies*. New York, NY: Palgrave Macmillan, pp. 185–215.

Grisanti LX (2004) *El nuevo interregionalismo trasatlántico: La asociación estratégica Unión Europea-América Latina*. Documento de Divulgación -IECI- 04, March. Buenos Aires: BID-INTAL.

Grugel JB (2004) New Regionalism and Modes of Governance—Comparing US and EU Strategies in Latin America. *European Journal of International Relations* 10(4): 603–626. DOI: 10.1177/1354066104047850.

Gustavsson J (1998) *The Politics of Foreign Policy Change: Explaining the Swedish Reorientation on EC Membership*. PhD Dissertation. Lund University, Lund. Available at: www.svet.lu.se/Fulltext/Jakob_G.pdf.

Hänggi H, Roloff R, and Rüland J (2006) *Interregionalism and International Relations*. Routledge Advances in International Relations and Global Politics 38. New York, NY: Routledge.

Hardacre A (2008) *The EU and Complex Interregionalism: The Case of Latin America*. PhD Dissertation. Loughborough University, Loughborough. Available at: https://dspace.lboro.ac.uk/dspace-jspui/handle/2134/8105 (accessed 18 January 2013).

Hardacre A and Smith M (2009) The EU and the Diplomacy of Complex Interregionalism. *The Hague Journal of Diplomacy* 4(2): 167–188. DOI: 10.1163/187119109X440898.

Hermann CF (1990) Changing Course: When Governments Choose to Redirect Foreign Policy. *International Studies Quarterly* 34(1): 3–21. DOI: 10.2307/2600403.

Hertog L den and Stroß S (2013) Coherence in EU External Relations: Concepts and Legal Rooting of an Ambiguous Term. *European Foreign Affairs Review* 18(3): 373–388.

Hill C (2003) *The Changing Politics of Foreign Policy*. Basingstoke: Palgrave MacMillan.

Horst J, Jünemann A, and Rothe D (eds) (2013) *Euro-Mediterranean Relations After the Arab Spring: Persistence in Times of Change*. Farnham, Surrey: Ashgate.

Hudson VM (2015) Foreign Policy Analysis Beyond North America. In: Brummer K and Hudson VM (eds) *Foreign Policy Analysis Beyond North America*. London: Lynne Rienner, pp. 1–14.

Kleistra Y and Mayer I (2001) Stability and Flux in Foreign Affairs Modelling Policy and Organizational Change. *Cooperation and Conflict* 36(4): 381–414. DOI: 10.1177/00108360121962515.

Koenig N (2011) The EU and the Libyan Crisis–In Quest of Coherence? *The International Spectator* 46(4): 11–30. DOI: 10.1080/03932729.2011.628089.

Larsen H (2009) A Distinct FPA for Europe? Towards a Comprehensive Framework for Analysing the Foreign Policy of EU Member States. *European Journal of International Relations* 15(3): 537–566. DOI: 10.1177/1354066109388247.

Lenz T (2012) Spurred Emulation: The EU and Regional Integration in Mercosur and SADC. *West European Politics* 35(1): 155–173. DOI: 10.1080/01402382.2012.631319.

Lequesne C (2013) The European External Action Service: Can a New Institution Improve the Coherence of the EU Foreign Policy? In: Telò M and Ponjaert F (eds) *The EU's Foreign Policy: What Kind of Power and Diplomatic Action.* Farnham: Ashgate, pp. 79–86.

March JG and Olson JP (1983) Organizing Political Life: What Administrative Reorganization Tells Us About Government. *American Political Science Review* 77(2): 281–296. DOI: 10.2307/1958916.

Matlary JH (2013) EU Foreign Policy: 'High Politics', Low Impact—And Vice Versa? In: Bynander F and Guzzini S (eds) *Rethinking Foreign Policy.* Abingdon: Routledge, pp. 137–149.

Matthews A (2008) The European Union's Common Agricultural Policy and Developing Countries: The Struggle for Coherence. *Journal of European Integration* 30(3), 381–399. DOI: 10.1080/07036330802141998.

Mayer H (2013) The Challenge of Coherence and Consistency in EU Foreign Policy. In: Telò M and Ponjaert F (eds) *The EU's Foreign Policy: What Kind of Power and Diplomatic Action?* Globalisation, Europe, Multilateralism Series. Farnham: Ashgate, pp. 105–117.

Meissner KL (2018) *Commercial Realism and EU Trade Policy: Competing for Economic Power in Asia and the Americas.* Abingdon: Routledge.

Meissner KL (2019) Cherry Picking in the Design of Trade Policy: Why Regional Organizations Shift Between Inter-Regional and Bilateral Negotiations. *Review of International Political Economy*: 1–25. DOI: 10.1080/09692290.2019.1625421.

Missiroli A (2010) The New EU 'Foreign Policy' System After Lisbon: A Work in Progress. *European Foreign Affairs Review* 15(4): 427–452.

Noutcheva G (2015) Institutional Governance of European Neighbourhood Policy in the Wake of the Arab Spring. *Journal of European Integration* 37(1): 19–36. DOI: 10.1080/07036337.2014.975987.

Odell JS (1979) The U.S. and the Emergence of Flexible Exchange Rates: An Analysis of Foreign Policy Change. *International Organization* 33(1): 57–81. DOI: 10.1017/S0020818300000667.

Orbie J (2008) The European Union's Role in World Trade: Harnessing Globalisation? In: Orbie J (ed.) *Europe's Global Role: External Policies of the European Union.* Burlington, VT: Ashgate, pp. 35–66.

Orbie J and Versluys H (2008) The European Union's International Development Policy: Leading and Benevolent? In: Orbie J (ed.) *Europe's Global Role: External Policies of the European Union.* Aldershot: Ashgate, pp. 67–90.

Peters BG (1998) Managing Horizontal Government: The Politics of Co-ordination. *Public Administration* 76(2): 295–311. DOI: 10.1111/1467-9299.00102.

Peterson J and Sjursen H (1998) Conclusion: The Myth of the CFSP? In: Peterson J and Sjursen H (eds) *A Common Foreign Policy for Europe? Competing Visions of the CFSP.* London: Routledge, pp. 169–184.

Pollack MA (1997) Delegation, Agency, and Agenda Setting in the European Community. *International Organization* 51(1): 99–134.

Pollack MA (2003) *The Engines of European Integration: Delegation, Agency, and Agenda Setting in the EU*. Oxford: OUP.

Portela C and Orbie J (2014) Sanctions Under the EU Generalised System of Preferences and Foreign Policy: Coherence by Accident? *Contemporary Politics* 20(1): 63–76. DOI: 10.1080/13569775.2014.881605.

Portela C and Raube K (2012) The EU Polity and Foreign Policy Coherence. *Journal of Contemporary European Research* 8(1): 3–20.

Putnam RD (1988) Diplomacy and Domestic Politics: The Logic of Two-Level Games. *International Organization* 42(3): 427–460.

Rathbun B (2008) Interviewing and Qualitative Field Methods: Pragmatism and Practicalities. In: Box-Steffensmeier JM, Brady HE, and Collier D (eds) *The Oxford Handbook of Political Methodology*. New York, NY: Oxford University Press.

Robles AC (2008a) EU FTA Negotiations with SADC and Mercosur: Integration into the World Economy or Market Access for EU Firms? *Third World Quarterly* 29(1): 181–197. DOI: 10.1080/01436590701726608.

Robles AC (2008b) The EU and ASEAN: Learning from the Failed EU–Mercosur FTA Negotiations. *ASEAN Economic Bulletin* 25(3): 334–344.

Rosati JA (1981) Developing a Systematic Decision-Making Framework: Bureaucratic Politics in Perspective. *World Politics* 33(2): 234–252. DOI: 10.2307/2010371.

Roy J (2010) Relations Between the EU and Latin America and the Caribbean: Competition or Cooperation with the United States? In: Bindi F (ed.) *The Foreign Policy of the European Union: Assessing Europe's Role in the World*. Washington, DC: Brookings Institution Press.

Ruano L (2013a) Introduction: Europeanization of National Foreign Policies Towards Latin America. In: Ruano L (ed.) *The Europeanization of National Foreign Policies towards Latin America*. New York, NY: Routledge, pp. 1–11.

Ruano L (2013b) *The Europeanization of National Foreign Policies Towards Latin America*. New York, NY: Routledge.

Santander S (2005) The European Partnership with Mercosur: A Relationship Based on Strategic and Neo-Liberal Principles. *Journal of European Integration* 27(3): 285–306. DOI: 10.1080/07036330500190156.

Santander S (2009) EU–LA Relations: From Interregionalism to Selective Bilateralism? In: Franck C, Defraigne J-C, and de Moriamé V (eds) *L'Union Européenne et La Montée Du Régionalisme: Exemplarité et Partenariats*. Louvain-La-Neuve: Academia Bruylant, pp. 263–272.

Santander S (2010a) *EU–LA Relations: From Interregionalism to Bilateralism?* Working Paper # 29 Programa de América Latina. Buenos Aires: Centro Argentino de Estudios Internacionales. Available at: http://497caei.truelogic.com.ar/sites/default/files/al-29.pdf (accessed 17 January 2013).

Santander S (2010b) The Ups and Downs of Interregionalism in Latin America. In: Söderbaum F and Stålgren P (eds) *The European Union and the Global South*. Boulder, CO: Lynne Rienner, pp. 89–114.

Schade D (2016) Coercion Through Graduation: Explaining the EU–Ecuador Free Trade Agreement. *Journal für Entwicklungspolitik* 32(3): 71–90.

Schade D (2019a) Fuzzy Roles in EU External Relations Governance: The Difficult Construction of Informal Policy Coordination Frameworks. In: van Heumen L and Roos M (eds) *The Informal Construction of Europe*. Routledge, pp. 199–216.

Schade D (2019b) Of Insiders and Outsiders: Assessing EU Strategic Partnerships in Their Regional Context. *International Politics* 56(3): 375–394. DOI: 10.1057/s41311-017-0132-y.

Schimmelfennig F (2009) Entrapped Again: The Way to EU Membership Negotiations with Turkey. *International Politics* 46(4): 413–431. DOI: 10.1057/ip.2009.5.

Smith H (1995) *European Union Foreign Policy and Central America.* Houndmills, Basingstoke: Macmillan.

Smith H (1998) Actually Existing Foreign Policy—Or Not? The EU in Latin America and Central Europe. In: Peterson J and Sjursen H (eds) *A Common Foreign Policy for Europe? Competing Visions of the CFSP.* London: Routledge, pp. 152–168.

Smith H (2002) *European Union Foreign Policy: What It Is and What It Does.* London: Pluto Press.

Smith M (1994) The European Union, Foreign Economic Policy and the Changing World Arena. *Journal of European Public Policy* 1(2): 283–302. DOI: 10.1080/13501769408406959.

Smith M (2012) Still Rooted in Maastricht: EU External Relations as a 'Third-Generation Hybrid'. *Journal of European Integration* 34(7): 699–715. DOI: 10.1080/07036337.2012.726010.

Smith M (2013) Beyond the Comfort Zone: Internal Crisis and External Challenge in the European Union's Response to Rising Powers. *International Affairs* 89(3): 653–671. DOI: 10.1111/1468-2346.12038.

Smith ME (2008) Researching European Foreign Policy: Some Fundamentals. *Politics* 28(3): 177–187. DOI: 10.1111/j.1467-9256.2008.00327.x.

Söderbaum F and Stålgren P (eds) (2010) *The European Union and the Global South.* Boulder, CO: Lynne Rienner.

Söderbaum F, Stålgren P, and Van Langenhove L (2005) The EU as a Global Actor and the Dynamics of Interregionalism: A Comparative Analysis. *Journal of European Integration* 27(3): 365–380. DOI: 10.1080/07036330500190297.

Splidsboel Hansen F (2006) The EU and Ukraine: Rhetorical Entrapment? *European Security* 15(2): 115–135.

Stetter S (2007) *EU Foreign and Interior Policies: Cross-Pillar Politics and the Social Construction of Sovereignty.* Routledge Advances in European Politics 43. New York, NY: Routledge.

Stewart EJ (2008) Capabilities and Coherence? The Evolution of European Union Conflict Prevention. *European Foreign Affairs Review* 13(2): 229–253.

Szymanski M and Smith ME (2005) Coherence and Conditionality in European Foreign Policy: Negotiating the EU–Mexico Global Agreement. *JCMS: Journal of Common Market Studies* 43(1): 171–192. DOI: 10.1111/j.0021-9886.2005.00551.x.

Tannous I (2013) The Programming of EU's External Assistance and Development Aid and the Fragile Balance of Power Between EEAS and DG DEVCO. *European Foreign Affairs Review* 18(3): 329–354.

Telò M, Fawcett L, and Ponjaert F (eds) (2015) *Interregionalism and the European Union: A Post-Revisionist Approach to Europe's Place in a Changing World.* Farnham: Ashgate.

Thomas DC (2011) Explaining EU Foreign Policy: Normative Institutionalism and Alternative Approaches. In: Thomas DC (ed.) *Making EU Foreign Policy: National Preferences, European Norms and Common Policies.* Palgrave Macmillan, pp. 10–28.

Thomas DC (2012) Still Punching Below Its Weight? Coherence and Effectiveness in European Union Foreign Policy. *JCMS: Journal of Common Market Studies* 50(3): 457–474. DOI: 10.1111/j.1468-5965.2011.02244.x.

US Embassy Czech Republic Prague (2005) *In-Depth Readout of EU's Cuba Compromise.* Available at: https://search.wikileaks.org/plusd/cables/05PRAGUE1006_a.html (accessed 20 March 2019).

Valladão AGA (2015) Europe and Latin America: Differing Routes for Regional Integration. In: Telò M, Fawcett L, and Ponjaert F (eds) *Interregionalism and the European Union: A Post-Revisionist Approach to Europe's Place in a Changing World*. Farnham: Ashgate, pp. 109–126.

Verdonck L (2015) Coherence in the EU's External Human Rights Policy: The Case of the Democratic Republic of the Congo. *European Foreign Affairs Review* 20(3): 379–397.

Welch DA (2005) *Painful Choices: A Theory of Foreign Policy Change*. Princeton, NJ: Princeton University Press.

White B (1999) The European Challenge to Foreign Policy Analysis. *European Journal of International Relations* 5(1): 37–66. DOI: 10.1177/1354066199005001002.

White B (2004) Foreign Policy Analysis and the New Europe. In: Carlsnaes W, Sjursen H, and White B (eds), *Contemporary European Foreign Policy*. London: SAGE, pp. 11–31.

Whitman RG and Rodt AP (2012) EU–Brazil Relations: A Strategic Partnership? *European Foreign Affairs Review* 17(1): 27–44.

3 EU Association Agreements and institutional decision-making complexity over time

Introduction

EU foreign policy decision-making involves a large number of actors in differing roles. This is no different for complex EU negotiations. While decision-making in any given EU policy area with an external remit is complex, this is rendered more acute here by the fact that these necessarily include provisions affecting individual EU policy areas. This, in turn, means that different institutional actors play a leading role in each of these policies, all while being subject to varying modes of decision-making.

Unlike decision-making in national contexts, which is the subject of most of the FPA literature, the very foundations of the EU's foreign policy system have been volatile given the EU's frequent treaty reforms, its enlargement processes, and changes to internal bureaucratic structures. This chapter takes stock of the relevant actors in the EU's foreign policy system active in complex Association Agreement negotiations. It further discusses the various decision-making rules and associated practice relevant for the policy areas under consideration. As all of these are subject to change over time, the chapter then specifically considers the possible influence of these changes on the bureaucratic politics underpinning such negotiations.

Reiterating a previously stated claim about the evolution of the EU's foreign policy decision-making, "each progress towards enhanced coherence was para-doxically increasing internal complexity" (Telò, 2013: 27). While there is some truth to this statement, it is important to caution that the full effects of the changes introduced through the Treaty of Lisbon can only be felt in the long term (Holland and Doidge, 2012: 125). In particular, the role of the EEAS as a key institution in the EU's foreign policy in the aftermath of the Lisbon Treaty is likely to continue to evolve given diverging views on its ultimate purpose (Morgenstern-Pomorski, 2018: 196).

The increase in complexity in the EU's foreign policy is related to issues such as the continuous growth of the powers of the European Parliament, or the rising use of qualified majority voting in the Council. With the creation of new institutional actors like the High Representative of the Union for Foreign Affairs and Security Policy (HRVP) and the EEAS, the overall number of stakeholders in the EU's foreign policy has increased even further. While research on EU decision-making in this realm has often focused primarily on the interactions between institutional actors in the EU, it is also necessary to consider decision-making within them, as an entity like the European Commission is composed of different administrative sub-entities. Only a consideration of both inter-institutional and intra-institutional decision-making processes can reveal the full picture of bureaucratic politics influencing the EU's foreign policy decision-making (Christiansen, 2001). After all,

> Contradictory views and policies within as important an institution as the Commission are every bit as damaging to external perceptions of the European Union as is disunity between the Commission and the Council, or among the member states.
>
> (Donnelly, 2010: 21)

While the account below offers insights into most aspects of EU foreign policy decision-making, its focus is on the policy areas most relevant for EU Association Agreement negotiations in the time period relevant for the empirical analysis in this book. Consequently, aspects like trade policy decision-making or that for the EU's development policy are elaborated on in detail, with others featuring less prominently. Thus, this chapter should not be seen as an exhaustive list of all actors and decision-making procedures in the EU's foreign policy.

The remainder of this chapter is structured as follows: It first offers an overview over decision-making in the different policy areas relevant for most Association Agreement negotiations. These are notably trade, development/cooperation, as well as political dialogue. It then focuses on the internal organization of the Commission and the Council over time and how this has influenced the bureaucratic processes underlying complex EU negotiations. Lastly, the chapter details how the wide-ranging changes of the Treaty of Lisbon have attempted to eliminate some of the bureaucratic hurdles to the EU's capacity to undertake complex international negotiations spanning multiple of its (foreign) policy areas.

EU trade policy-making: The heart of Association Agreement negotiations

The CCP is one of the most important and visible policy areas of the EU's external relations as the EU and its predecessors have been active in trade policy-making for a long period of time, and given the potential economic repercussions for both the EU and its negotiation partners. While only one out of three key policy areas discussed in negotiations for Association Agreements in the Latin American region, "[t]he common element in all these [external] agreements is trade" (Bretherton and Vogler, 1999: 61).

While the EU conducts trade policy through its representation in the World Trade Organization (WTO) as a full member, the most relevant aspects of the EU's trade policy-making in ties to individual third countries are its capacity

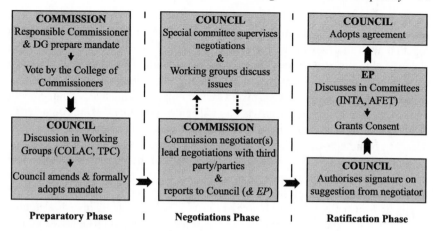

Figure 3.1 EU Free Trade Agreement decision-making.
Source: Own compilation based on different sources.

to negotiate plurilateral and bilateral trade agreements. As Figure 3.1 outlines, the process under which this occurs is divided into three distinct phases, namely the approval of a negotiation mandate, which is an internal EU process, the actual negotiations with a third actor, and finally the ratification process (Meunier and Nicolaïdis, 2011: 283–6). Only once the latter is complete in the EU and the third actor(s) concerned can a trade agreement be applied.

Given that this policy area is one which has originated within the EU's former first pillar, the role of EU-level institutions is particularly pronounced (Orbie, 2008: 37), attributing clear roles to the Commission, the Council, and the European Parliament in the policy-making process. Nonetheless, the process itself is lengthy and highly complex, necessitating an analysis of different factors of bureaucratic politics at various of the decision-making stages.

When describing the overall process in a simplified manner, it is the European Commission that proposes the opening of negotiations to the Council, which in turn provides the Commission with a negotiation mandate after extensive deliberations within its preparatory bodies. With the granting of a mandate, the Commission, led by its Directorate-General for Trade (DG Trade), disposes of a right to negotiate on behalf of the Union with the third actor concerned, which is constantly supervised by a special committee of the Council. Once negotiations conclude successfully, the EP has to give its consent, and the Council has to approve of the outcome with a qualified majority vote. Prior to the Treaty of Lisbon, the European Parliament was merely consulted before FTAs could be ratified, rendering today's ratification phase more complex. It is only once all of these steps are completed that a trade agreement is adopted and enters into its application phase.

While the above considerations are true for trade agreements that relate to the exclusive remit of the EU, some agreements are also considered mixed agreements, which follow a different ratification procedure. These may contain measures relating to the exclusive competencies of the EU, but may also comprise provisions for which the member states are responsible either exclusively or together with the EU. In the latter case, unanimity is required and all member states need to ratify the agreement in question individually and according to their own domestic constitutional provisions (Diedrichs and Wessels, 2006: 231).

The exact delineation between mixed agreements and exclusive EU agreements, as well as which agreement provisions fall under various areas of competency, is often left open so as to avoid inter-institutional conflict (Van der Loo, 2017: 338–42). Nonetheless, even before member states ratify agreements, but after the EP's consent and the Council's final decision, parts of the agreement falling under the EU's exclusive (former first pillar) competence may be provisionally applied, as is the case, for instance, in the liberalization of tariffs on the trade of goods.

Taking a closer look at the practice of EU trade policy-making reveals a number of intra-institutional actors involved in the process. Within the Commission, it is DG Trade led by the EU's Trade Commissioner that undertakes the EU's negotiations today. This structure has been relatively stable over time, though the supervisory role of individual Commissioners has been split according to geographical portfolios from time to time (see below). Before the Commission can ask the Council for a negotiation mandate, a vote by the College of Commissioners is also required.

While the Council does not dispose of a specific trade composition, it was the General Affairs and External Relations Council (GAERC) that dealt with the EU's trade policy (Bretherton and Vogler, 1999: 51) until the Treaty of Lisbon. Since then, this Council composition has been split in two, with the Foreign Affairs Council (FAC) now holding the overall responsibility for the EU's trade policy. This is assisted by a specific Trade Policy Committee (TPC, formerly known as the Article 113 or Article 133 Committee), which is one of the few Council working groups created directly through the EU's treaties, rather than being set up as member states see fit. As one of the oldest Council bodies in continued existence, it is responsible for recommending its views on negotiation mandates to the FAC and follows the Commission's work during actual negotiations in the form of a special committee (Hayes-Renshaw and Wallace, 2006: 91).

The body itself has two main compositions, with one being staffed by the most senior member state trade officials. It furthermore has an official secretary and is attended by DG Trade's Director-General. This composition is responsible for reflecting on the overall direction of the EU's trade policy, while lower-level meetings are there to discuss the actual content of mandates and negotiations (Hayes-Renshaw and Wallace, 2006: 91–2). Lastly, while no formal voting takes place in the TPC given its advisory role, recommendations and discussions will nonetheless informally take member states' voting weights into account (Hayes-Renshaw and Wallace, 2006: 93).

The role of the EP on EU trade agreements was relatively limited in the past. While the Council was regularly kept updated on DG Trade's work, the Parliament did not dispose of similar information rights. Regular oversight of the EU's CCP within the European Parliament is conducted through its Committee on

International Trade (INTA). While some informal contacts between the Commission and the EP have always existed, its influence was relatively limited overall as its legislative role was constrained for most FTAs prior to Lisbon.[1]

While the Amsterdam and Nice treaties made some minor changes to the scope of the EU's CCP and the related voting procedures in the Council (Dominguez, 2008: 128), major changes were only introduced with the Treaty of Lisbon, expanding the scope of the CCP to include investment treaties and altering the underlying institutional set-up. In particular, the Parliament's information rights in ongoing negotiations were significantly increased to be technically on par with those of the Council (Woolcock, 2010: 23). Even in the post-Lisbon context, its consent is only required at the very end of the process though (Hillman and Kleimann, 2010: 5; Woolcock, 2010: 23), and the use of this specific legislative procedure means that it can only vote for an agreement in full, or wholly reject it without being able to introduce amendments.

Researchers disagree as to which institutional actors ultimately have the most influence on the EU's trade policy under this set-up, though the focus was on the Commission and the Council prior to Lisbon (Orbie, 2008: 39–41). Some have claimed that the Commission's powers ultimately depend on the member states' agreement for receiving a negotiation mandate and the approval of a finished agreement (Meunier, 2007). This also extends to the actual negotiation period. While the underlying mandates are often vague, the presence of member state representatives to provide advice nevertheless allows them to control the process to an important degree (Meunier and Nicolaïdis, 2011: 286).

Others have stressed that the multi-level nature of the EU's trade policy plays into the hands of the Commission as the central actor (Billiet, 2009; Elsig, 2007), which is able to exploit different preferences of individual member states and the associated vague mandates provided (Conceição-Heldt, 2011). Its formal role as the initiator of a process leading towards trade negotiations also means that "Member States tend to *respond* to, rather than be part of, the initial development of the agenda" (emphasis in the original, Frennhoff Larsén, 2007: 861).

Further research has emphasized the key role that the Commission plays in choosing the venue in which negotiations are undertaken, be it in the multilateral, regional, or bilateral realm (Dür and Elsig, 2011: 334; Elsig, 2007). Bretherton and Vogler attribute this to the long-lasting experience of DG Trade, which allows for it to defend a generally pro free trade position—sometimes even against the specific wishes of some member states (Bretherton and Vogler, 1999: 65). However, once more, the Commission should not be seen as a single bureaucratic actor either, as, for instance, internal differences between DG Trade officials and those of the Directorate-General for Agriculture and Rural Development (DG AGRI), responsible for the EU's Common Agricultural Policy (CAP), have reduced the internal cohesion of the Commission's position ever since the WTO Uruguay round negotiations (Bretherton and Vogler, 1999: 54). While DG Trade's institutional role is to defend the EU's trade interests, DG AGRI's is to ensure the functioning of the EU's system of agricultural subsidies, which makes for a natural source of diverging views on trade matters.

It is important to note also that one cannot necessarily conceptualize the relationship between the Commission and the Council as one of antagonists. Rather, the latter's TPC is composed of officials who tend to stay in their posts for long periods of time and are socialized into the logic of the EU's trade policy, including the defence of the Union's underlying interests (Hayes-Renshaw and Wallace, 2006: 94), sometime against the preferences of the member states that they represent. In consequence, the relationship between the TPC and DG Trade has been described as one of collaboration, rather than control (Bretherton and Vogler, 1999: 52). Some researchers have even pointed out that specific interest coalitions between the Council and the Commission exist,which represent the EU's trade interests on the one hand, and agricultural interests on the other (van den Hoven, 2007: 62–4), mirroring the opposition within the Commission itself. Lastly, the very complexity of the EU's internal trade policy decision-making can actually strengthen the Commission's position in external negotiations as its room for manoeuvre tends to be regarded as relatively limited by third actor representatives (Bretherton and Vogler, 1999: 41).

Development cooperation

While not a regular feature of all EU Association Agreement negotiations, the differing levels of development between the EU and that of many of its negotiation partners make provisions on development cooperation another subject to be addressed in most negotiations. While this may entail discussions on funding related to the European Neighbourhood Policy (ENP) for countries in the EU's vicinity, this may also involve discussions on more traditional development cooperation funding in negotiations with countries in the Global South. In the latter cases, discussions on development cooperation will typically be of a high salience as the EU's development policy towards such countries is often the most relevant policy area before the consideration of closer trade ties through Association Agreements.

This policy area makes the EU and its member states unique as international players as they are collectively the largest donors of Official Development Aid (ODA) overall, providing more than 50% of the global total according to the EU's own estimates (DG DEVCO, 2019). Nonetheless, as development cooperation is a shared competence between the EU and its member states, it is important to note that the largest budgets remain under the exclusive control of the member states (Dür and Elsig, 2011: 327). Given these facts, it comes as no surprise that the importance of development cooperation concerns for the EU's foreign policy has been noted in the past:

> Achieving coordination, coherence and complementarity between and across [...] [different aspects of foreign policy] is a mammoth task; but it is also an essential one [...]. In such a scenario development policy cannot be an optional extra, but constitutes a core component of Europe's external relations and CFSP.
>
> (Holland and Doidge, 2012: 19)

Under the Lisbon Treaty, the EU's development policy falls under the Ordinary Legislative Procedure (OLP). This gives both the EP and the Council a relevant role in its regular decision-making process. The underlying set-up of legislative decision-making has furthermore remained largely the same, as co-decision—the OLP's predecessor—has applied to it since the Treaty of Maastricht. Nonetheless, the underlying bureaucracy responsible for initially formulating the EU's development policy and lastly implementing it has undergone radical changes over time (Holland and Doidge, 2012: 102–33). Today, this bureaucratic process involves not just the European Commission but also the EEAS.

The overall budget allocations for the EU's development policy depend on the Multiannual Financial Framework (MFF), which determines the overall size of the EU's budget for seven-year periods, while already allocating proportions to very broad policy areas. It is only within this overall frame that decisions on how to allocate the EU's development money are taken, and in consequence, the OLP only applies to this. The implementation of the policy, done largely through the administration of development cooperation instruments, such as the European Development Fund (EDF), was originally mainly delegated to the Commission.

In turn, an analysis of how the Commission's development bureaucracy was structured at different points in time can provide insights into its capacity for coordinating the EU's development policy with other policy areas, including at the time of Association Agreement negotiations. Given the dual nature of EU and member state development funding, the Council's role as the institution representing the member states needs to be considered somewhat more closely than the activity of the EP for the day-to-day business of this policy area. It is formally involved in the oversight of the policy area through its FAC composition and more informal meetings of national development ministers (Holland and Doidge, 2012: 97–8). Much like most Council activity, such meetings are in turn prepared by specialized Council working groups.

Considering the EU's capacity to bring development political aspects into complex Association Agreement negotiations, one has to think of bureaucratic sources of inconsistency which may hinder using EU development policy as an effective bargaining chip. A first and long-lasting difficulty for this policy area has been the different priorities of EU-level and member state bilateral development cooperation activity (Bretherton and Vogler, 1999: 132–3). Major problems also arise out of the previous division of development-related competencies within the Commission itself (Bretherton and Vogler, 1999: 132)—and now within the Commission and the EEAS—and consistently low staffing levels in the policy's administration compared to the relatively large budgets administrated (Holland and Doidge, 2012: 102; Orbie and Versluys, 2008: 69).

While the definition and implementation of the EU's development policy were initially handled within the same bureaucratic structure of the Commission, the Prodi Commission's reorganization in 1999 saw the responsibility for the bulk of the definition of the EU's development policy being attributed to External Relations (RELEX) Commissioner Chris Patten (Holland and Doidge, 2012: 104). In consequence, a separate body, which came to be known as EuropeAid, was set up to handle the policy's implementation (Holland and Doidge, 2012: 120–3). This created the potential for tension between DG RELEX, which would set the policy's overall goals, and officials within EuropeAid, which enjoyed considerable leeway over how to implement the policy on a day-to-day basis.

While the system had remained relatively stable over the intervening years, the Treaty of Lisbon then once more introduced significant administrative changes for this policy area. An effective implementation of these provisions has furthermore been difficult, as many of the treaty's provisions pertaining to the functioning of the EU's development policy have remained somewhat vague (see Tannous, 2013). The complexity and uncertain nature of the changes introduced with Lisbon have been noted by Commission development policy officials as a major source for frustration in their work in the initial years after the introduction of the new treaty.[2]

The most relevant change pertains to the responsibility for defining the EU's development policy having been moved out of the Commission entirely as its former DG RELEX has been integrated into the newly formed EEAS. Additionally, some of the staff from the Commission's DG Development (DG DEV) who had worked on geographical desks have been moved into the EEAS alongside DG RELEX officials. The remnants of DG Development were then fused with EuropeAid to form the new Directorate-General for International Cooperation and Development (DG DEVCO), which once more united some policy definition with the bulk of the EU's development cooperation implementation. As a further important change from the pre-Lisbon set-up, DG DEVCO has gained powers over the annual programming of development cooperation budgets (Holland and Doidge, 2012: 126), making it difficult to discern a clear decision-making hierarchy and creating potential for competence overlap between the different institutions.

The duality of the roles of the EEAS and DG DEVCO in this realm has created problems of policy ownership and double structures that make policy coordination difficult and raise the prospect of conflict between the two institutions (Duke, 2012: 58; Holland and Doidge, 2012: 126–7). Taking stock of the Lisbon-induced changes, Holland and Doidge conclude:

> With the above changes in mind, what remains unclear is precisely who speaks for Europe on development – the exact opposite of what the Lisbon reforms had originally promised.
>
> (Holland and Doidge, 2012: 128)

Decision-making in the EU's development policy thus involves a large number of actors in different capacities that cannot all be discerned by analysing the functioning of the EU's OLP only. In consequence, it is possible to identify a potential for diverging views of different institutional actors to emerge. Where this was formerly situated entirely within the Commission, this now occurs between the Commission and the EEAS, and between the EU's institutions and the development policy administrations of the EU's member states. This potential for diverging views influencing the EU's foreign policy in this area is rendered even more prominent when it has to be coordinated with other policy areas, as is the case for the EU's Association Agreements (Holland and Doidge, 2012: 96–7).

Managing political relations with third parties

Association Agreements aim to structure not only the EU's economic ties with its partners, but are also meant to provide a framework for political relations. Therefore, negotiations on political provisions and any matters which do not directly fit the trade and development chapters are a third area to be considered. Unlike decision-making under the two policy areas discussed above, external political relations of the EU remain largely intergovernmental in nature (Radtke, 2012: 50–1). This is due to the fact that the EU's CFSP evolved out of a purely intergovernmental format, the European Political Cooperation (EPC) in the pre-Maastricht period.

As a consequence, even if CFSP matters have gradually been normalized within the EU's institutional framework, the EU's member states still have a role to play in their own right, rather than as simple members of the Council. This is particularly the case in moments of crisis when member states take matters into their own hands (Devuyst, 2012). Considering an example relevant from the empirical part of this book, the formation of the San José Dialogue, one of the oldest formats of structured cooperation with Latin American countries, was set up at the outset of a meeting between member state ministers and those of their Latin American counterparts. While the Commission has always taken part in such meetings, the member states—or their formal Council representation through, for instance, the rotating Council presidency—can nonetheless claim an equal footing in this and similar dialogue formats set up with the region and elsewhere.

The continued prominent role of the member states in discussions on political matters can also be seen in high-level meetings taking place between the EU and important partners or world regions, such as the EU–League of Arab States summit (European Council, 2019) which are attended by EU heads of state and government alongside key EU officials. A similar meeting format exists for most world regions, including biennial EU–Latin America and the Caribbean summits. Given that many of the issues discussed at such gatherings pertain to policy areas where the member states have retained important competencies, such as peace processes, the fight against terrorism, or non-proliferation (see, for instance, EU–CELAC Summit, 2015), an active participation of the member states in the political aspects of Association Agreement negotiations is therefore logical.

In consequence, as an important difference from the policy areas discussed above, decision-making rules under the CFSP largely exclude the Commission and require unanimous decision-making in the Council instead. While the Treaty of Lisbon has introduced some changes to this end, with the HRVP and the EEAS taking over some of the tasks of the rotating Council presidency and the Council's CFSP staff, this rule has remained largely unchanged (Radtke, 2012: 51).

In the context of the political aspects of Association Agreement negotiations, the degree to which member state positions cohere on particular issues is therefore of considerable relevance. While this may be more problematic for negotiations in the EU's near-abroad given linkages to security or migration concerns, aspects such as prior colonial ties may instead impact negotiations with partners in the Global South.

Overall, the political side of the EU's ties to outside partners operates in a radically different manner from those outlined above, relegating the Commission to an actor of a secondary importance, as well as putting an emphasis on the role of the Council (and now the HRVP and the EEAS) and the member states themselves. These different modes of decision-making are likely to have an impact on the overall dynamics of complex Association Agreement negotiations.

EU Association Agreements: Combining modes of decision-making

Having summarized the decision-making on the most relevant policy areas underpinning complex EU Association Agreement negotiations, this section provides a brief overview over how this relates to the specific context of such negotiations with third actors. Crucially, negotiations for Association Agreements require the parallel use of decision-making mechanisms for the different policy areas concerned, rendering the process more complex than the one for "pure" EU trade agreements, as Figure 3.2 shows.

The complexity arises out of two elements: Firstly, the initial preparation of a negotiation mandate is done by multiple institutional actors and requires coordination between them. This duality then survives in the actual negotiation phase. Secondly, given the inclusion of political clauses, Association Agreements are

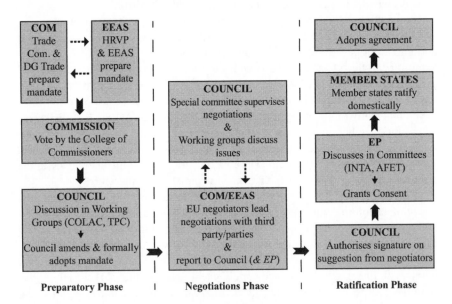

Figure 3.2 EU Association Agreement decision-making.
Source: Own compilation based on different sources.

always almost necessarily mixed in nature, requiring the ratification in all of the EU's 28 member states. Whereas, prior to the Treaty of Lisbon, internal coordination for the preparation of a mandate and between the EU's negotiators was limited to administrative entities within the Commission, and typically DG Trade and DG RELEX (holding the responsibility for the political components and development policy goals), this now requires coordination between administrative units within the Commission and the EEAS, raising the possibility for these to hold diverging views on any given issue.

The structure of Association Agreements puts their trade, development, and political components on a formally equal footing. It should nonetheless be noted that the process is often driven by developments in the realm of trade as

> EU representatives (but also member states' representatives) often prioritize trade and cooperation issues and do not want to disturb negotiations on these issues by tough talks on problematic [political] foreign policy issues. The result is that political dialogue is not exercised to its full foreign policy potential, and cases are limited where it is used as leverage to promote and obtain concrete EU foreign policy goals.
>
> (Keukeleire and Delreux, 2014: 207)

Even when Association Agreements ultimately contain political clauses on regular meetings between officials on specific issues, these are rarely used to their fullest potential as these put further strain on the agenda of already overburdened civil servants (Keukeleire and Delreux, 2014: 207). This has occurred despite the fact that in the pre-Lisbon period, DG RELEX most often held the formal leadership role on Association Agreement negotiations, with the exception of the Prodi Commission when this resided with DG Trade (García, 2008: 135). Since Lisbon, as elaborated on above, this responsibility has moved to the EEAS. No matter the formal institutional responsibilities, however, an informal coalition between Commission Trade officials and members of the TPC (Orbie, 2008: 40) has often led to trade issues being perceived as more important than others.

The mixity and requirement for unanimity in the Council and national ratification aside (Dominguez, 2008: 72), the dynamics of negotiations for Association Agreements are then mainly shaped by procedures for the conclusion of EU trade agreements. While the European Parliament still has to give its consent, it is its Foreign Affairs Committee (AFET) which takes the lead on Association Agreements, while the opinion of INTA is being taken into account. Nonetheless, even here, trade policy elements will be important as its information rights on the progress of negotiations are largely based on those that it has gained in the realm of trade policy since the Treaty of Lisbon.

Given the primacy of trade concerns amongst the three most relevant policies outlined here, negotiations for Association Agreements are shaped by decision-making procedures and dynamics emanating from the EU's trade policy. While this does not represent a problem for EU negotiations in itself, it nonetheless risks emphasizing the divergence of views between different institutional actors responsible for the definition of various areas of the EU's foreign policy, and the EU's approach in such negotiations is likely going to depend on the coordination between these institutional actors in the process.

The European Commission and foreign policy decision-making complexity over time

The brief overview over decision-making mechanisms in the policy areas relevant for the EU's Association Agreement negotiations has revealed that the EU's institutional actors, and particularly the European Commission, cannot be considered as unitary actors in the process. As a consequence, possible sources of bureaucratic conflict which may hinder the EU's negotiation capacity within the set-up of individual institutional actors need to be explored (Donnelly, 2010: 21). This primarily concerns the allocation of portfolios within the Commission, as this may affect the sense of ownership over particular policy areas.

While the general role and functioning of the Commission in the EU's foreign policy system have remained relatively constant over the period under consideration (with the exception of the changes introduced by the Treaty of Lisbon discussed below), there have nonetheless been important alterations to its internal functioning that need to be considered here. These have influenced its capacity to define, coordinate, and implement important elements of the EU's foreign policy and could thus contribute to our understanding of bureaucratic factors shaping complex EU negotiations.

One main problem identified in the literature is that of the autonomy of different administrative units within the Commission vis-à-vis others. Christiansen points out that this is a defining feature of the Commission:

> the very nature of the Commission – a single institution encompassing large and relatively self-contained Directorates-General (DGs) – is a recipe for fragmentation and internal tension. Owing to the internal divisions running through it, authors have for some time regarded it as a 'multi-organization' in which the policy-making of different administrative units creates different bureaucratic and organizational logics.
>
> (Christiansen, 2001: 751)

This underlying complexity of the Commission's structure and operational logics has been rendered more acute by many organizational changes it has undergone, thus weakening established coordination mechanisms and increasing the autonomy of individual DGs and Commissioners. Such mechanisms can then only be rebuilt gradually over time (Schade, 2019). The most important changes impacting the Commission in such a way were fundamental alterations to the EU's treaties and membership, such as through an increase in the EU's foreign policy competencies, the creation of the EEAS, or in line with the EU's various enlargement rounds. Nonetheless, individual factors like portfolio allocation and the personalities of Commissioners also need to be considered. This is even more relevant as:

Although the Commission is in general – beyond foreign policy – probably the most studied EU bureaucracy [...], the bureaucratic entities in the Commission that deal with foreign policy or external relations [...] have largely escaped the attention of bureaucratic politics.

(Delreux, 2015: 155)

While the EU's treaties define the Commissioners' role as neutral defenders of the EU's interests, it would be too simplistic to believe that, once appointed, Commissioners lose their national and party loyalties. The interplay between Commissioners' formal role and their personal background should thus not be underestimated (Lequesne, 2000: 47–8). Given this and the appointment procedure which gives each member state a significant say, cohesion between the Commissioners has historically been very low and the Commission's central administration typically takes a hands-off approach (Kassim et al., 2013: 184–6).

Furthermore, the decision-making style of the Commission has been shaped by a desire to reach a consensus from the lowest to the highest administrative level, including the College of Commissioners. This means that even when no consensus can be reached at that level, a secret vote may take place, with information on voting patterns only occasionally becoming publicly available (Spence, 2006b: 48).

The consensus-driven decision-making is particularly relevant given that historically the Commission president did not play a preponderant role in the College of Commissioners. While the Treaty of Amsterdam ultimately strengthened the president's role, the influence of this institutional memory should not be underestimated (Lequesne, 2000: 46). Ultimately, the strength of the Commission president's authority that could lead to more policy coordination within the Commission is largely dependent on the president's leadership style given important constraints on his or her powers (Spence, 2006b: 28–9). In sum,

A strong President can have his own way. A weak President is perforce obliged to preside over dissent, occasional incoherence among his team and, in the case of Santer, over outright censurable practice or at the very least inappropriate behaviour.

(Spence, 2006b: 27)

Given that individual Commissioners thus possess significant individual powers, a consideration of the distribution of portfolios and its holders is important. Here, again, the particular nature of the European Commission has influenced the way in which Commission portfolios have been assigned, as member states used to hold considerable sway over portfolio responsibilities and allocation.

This was particularly down to member states' desire to ensure that their designated Commissioners would receive positions of responsibility, rather than more symbolic portfolios. As Cameron argues, the necessity to find a suitable number of significant Commission portfolios has hindered the creation of a functioning European Commission foreign policy apparatus ever since the Treaty of

Maastricht (Cameron, 2007: 53). It was only through changes introduced with the Treaty of Amsterdam in 1999 that the designated Commission president was able to influence the division of portfolios in his Commission more actively (Nugent and Saurugger, 2002: 349). While President Romano Prodi made extensive use of this new right, his successor José Manuel Barroso initially faced some difficulties in exercising this power over the preferences of the member states (Spence, 2006b: 37).

The EU's enlargement rounds in the mid-2000s counteracted the effects of this change, as a sufficient number of portfolios had to be found for the acceding member states. While this problem has been addressed today by the use of a number of vice-presidents with coordination responsibilities, member states initially resisted instating a hierarchy between Commissioners as was floated by different Commission presidents.

There has been a long-lasting emphasis on the Commissioner holding the External Relations portfolio as having a coordination role for other Commission portfolios dealing with issues touching on the EU's foreign policy (Spence, 2006b: 50), with RELEX Commissioners also attending meetings of the former General Affairs and External Relations Council composition (Spence, 2006b: 49). Nonetheless, this coordination system has never worked particularly well as individual Commissioners often preferred pursuing their own policies (Cameron, 2007: 54) and is now rendered more difficult by the existence of the hybrid HRVP position.

Commission portfolios over time

The allocation of Commission portfolios has changed considerably over time, in line with the factors outlined above. Aside from these, two opposing paradigms as to the organization of the portfolios with an external remit have shaped various Commission reorganizations. One would see different Commissioners holding responsibilities for relations with different regions or countries (largely based on a country's state of development and geographical region), which should maximize the capacity for cross-policy coordination. The other paradigm holds that portfolios should rather be organized according to policy areas, with each Commissioner being responsible for at least one policy with an external remit, thus increasing intra-policy coordination.

Table 3.1 provides an overview over the evolution of the Commission portfolios with a significant external remit. So as not to render the overview too complex, this has been limited to portfolios relevant for policy areas touched by Association Agreement negotiations and the geographical region that forms the basis of the following empirical chapters. In consequence, it is not a complete overview over Commission portfolios with an external remit where a geographical logic is concerned, but does include Commissioners responsible for internal policy areas such as agriculture, which—at times—play an important role in complex EU negotiations. It is important to remember, however, that as far as a geographic distribution of portfolios beyond the Americas is concerned, similar issues of policy overlap and redistribution could be observed.

Table 3.1 European Commissioners with External Relations portfolios over time

Delors III (1993–1994)

Vice-President: External Economic Affairs and Trade Policy	Leon Brittan	UK
Vice-President: Cooperation, Development and Humanitarian Aid	Manuel Marín	Spain
External Relations and Enlargement	Hans van den Broek	Netherlands
Agriculture and Rural Development	René Steichen	Luxembourg
Environment, Fisheries	Ioannis Paleokrassas	Greece

Santer (1995–1999)

Common Commercial Policy; Relations with North America, Japan, China, South Korea, Hong Kong, Macao, and Taiwan	Leon Brittan	UK
CFSP; Delegations to third countries; Relations with Turkey, Cyprus, Malta, CEEC, and NIS countries	Hans van den Broek	Netherlands
Relations with the Southern Mediterranean, Latin America, Near and Middle East, developing countries in Asia	Manuel Marín	Spain
Lomé Convention; Relations with South Africa, ACP countries, and NGOs	João de Deus Pinheiro	Portugal
Consumer Policy, Fisheries, Humanitarian Assistance, and Emergency Aid	Emma Bonino	Italy
Agriculture and Rural Development	Franz Fischler	Austria

Prodi (1999–2004)

Trade	Pascal Lamy	France
External Relations	Chris Patten	UK
Development & Humanitarian Aid	Poul Nielson	Denmark
Agriculture & Fisheries	Franz Fischler	Austria
Environment	Margot Wallström	Sweden

Barroso I (2004–2009)

Trade	Peter Mandelson	UK
External Relations & ENP	Benita Ferrero-Waldner	Austria
Development & Humanitarian Aid	Louis Michel	Belgium
Agriculture & Rural Development	Mariann Fischer Boel	Denmark
Fisheries & Maritime Affairs	Joe Borg	Malta

Barroso II (2010–2014)

First Vice-President: Foreign Affairs & Security Policy	Catherine Ashton	UK
Trade	Karel De Gucht	Belgium
Development	Andris Piebalgs	Latvia
Agriculture & Rural Development	Dacian Cioloş	Romania
Enlargement & ENP	Štefan Füle	Czech Republic
Maritime Affairs & Fisheries	Maria Damanaki	Greece
Climate Action	Connie Hedegaard	Denmark

Juncker (2014–2019)

Vice-President: Foreign Affairs & Security Policy	Federica Mogherini	Italy
Trade	Cecilia Malmström	Sweden
International Cooperation & Development	Nevem Mimica	Croatia

(*Continued*)

Table 3.1 (Continued)

Humanitarian Aid & Crisis Management	Christos Stylianides	Cyprus
Enlargement & ENP	Johannes Hahn	Austria
Agriculture & Rural Development	Phil Hogan	Ireland
Environment, Maritime Affairs & Fisheries	Karmenu Vella	Malta
Climate Action & Energy	Miguel Arias Cañete	Spain

Source: Own compilation from multiple sources.

Prior to the entry into force of the Treaty of Maastricht, during the Delors II Commission, the portfolios most relevant for the EU's Latin America policy were divided between two Spanish Commissioners,[3] Abel Matutes, the Commissioner for Mediterranean and Latin America policy, as well as Manuel Marín, the Commissioner responsible for Development, Cooperation and Fisheries policy. However, the overall responsibility for trade policy and external relations lay with the German Commissioner Frans Andriessen.

The January 1993 reorganization of the Commission in line with the Treaty of Maastricht then did away with a geographical logic and created largely policy-based portfolios. Leon Brittan was made a vice-president of the Commission and held responsibility for the trade portfolio and external economic relations. An additional portfolio with an external remit was created under the heading of External (Political) Relations and Enlargement under Commissioner Hans van den Broek. The portfolio for Cooperation, Development and Humanitarian Aid, however, was unified under Manuel Marín's portfolio (Lister, 1997: 14). It appears that in addition to questions as to the exact distinction between the different portfolios, foreign policy coordination in the Commission was hindered by personal issues as the "frequently public disputes between van den Broek and Brittan were hardly conducive to efficient delivery of policy" (Cameron, 2007: 53).

This change of organization was short-lived, however, and a geographical logic returned under the following Santer Commission. Under this Commission, the number of portfolios with an external remit increased overall, with some foreign policy coordination responsibilities remaining with the Commission president himself. This increase of portfolios with an external outlook was mainly due to disputes between member state governments as to who would hold the influential External Relations portfolio, with the responsibilities ultimately having been split (Lequesne, 2000: 47; Nugent and Saurugger, 2002: 354).

This reorganization thus emphasized the regional aspects of the EU's external relations and created a portfolio for relations with Latin America, the Mediterranean, the Middle East, as well as the coordination of development policy, which was given to Manuel Marín. Other regional portfolios were also created, such as one focusing on relations with the African, Caribbean and Pacific Group of States (ACP).

While Leon Brittan remained responsible for what had become the CCP, the coordination of the EU's Latin America policy did not fall within his policy remit. In addition to these changes, an External Relations Group of the Commission was created, bringing the Commission president together with the different

Commissioners responsible for external relations (Lister, 1997: 14–15). This entity was meant to introduce greater overall coordination into the Commission aspects of the EU's external relations. However, observers at the time pointed out:

> The Relex Commissioners meet on a monthly basis in an attempt to coordinate vertical and horizontal issues, but there is no doubt that the overlaps between their areas of responsibility generate antagonisms; and that these tensions are also evident within the DGs.
>
> (Bretherton and Vogler, 1999: 182)

The geographical division of portfolios between 1995 and 1999 had two opposing effects on the coordination of the EU's foreign policy. On the one hand, it decreased the Commission's coordination capacity within different EU policy areas (Dominguez, 2008: 132), as for instance international trade agreements were negotiated mostly on an ad hoc basis by different Commissioners at the time (Peterson, 1999: 104), as "[e]ach Commissioner defended each subsequent FTA as a means to strengthen the Union's hand in their 'patch' of the globe" (Peterson, 1999: 105). On the other hand, this focus on geography (Holland and Doidge, 2012: 102) helped the European Commission identify and coordinate all policy areas relevant for its relations with Latin America (Orbie and Versluys, 2008: 69).

Table 3.1 does not take into account a brief interregnum between the collective resignation of the Santer Commission on 15 March 1999 and the Prodi Commission's inauguration in September of that year. In the meantime, a caretaker Commission headed by Commissioner Marín remained in office. This drastic step had occurred over fraud allegations, thus widely weakening confidence in the Commission itself, as well as its organization at that point in time.

Overall, the role of the Commission in the EU's external relations was weakened throughout the 1990s due to the multiplicity of External Relations portfolios, the Commission's reticence to become involved in the intergovernmental CFSP, and ongoing differences between different Commissioners (Cameron and Spence, 2004: 127). While RELEX Commissioners did meet at least monthly during this period in an attempt to coordinate different aspects of the Commission's foreign policy (Bretherton and Vogler, 1999: 182), the roadblocks for this were nonetheless sufficiently large. Bretherton and Vogler summarized the state of Commission-internal policy coordination as follows:

> There are tensions and jealousies between officials of Relex DGs at all levels; and these are reflected in the College of Commissioners. This problem is exacerbated, at present, by the absence of a satisfactory mechanism for resolving disputes between Commissioners.
>
> (Bretherton and Vogler, 1999: 39)

While the Commissioners with responsibilities for a specific region or partner were thus theoretically able to coordinate the policies, this was not necessarily the case when competencies overlapped, or for policy areas in which member state governments would have a more active role.

Against this backdrop, the Treaty of Amsterdam and the Prodi Commission were then seen as a fresh start for the institution. Through a declaration annexed to the treaty, an attempt was made to overhaul the way in which the Commission dealt with its External Relations competencies (Bretherton and Vogler, 1999: 40–1). Specifically, Declaration 32 in the Annex of the treaty read as follows:

> The Conference notes the Commission's intention to prepare a reorganization of tasks within the college in good time for the Commission which will take up office in 2000, in order to ensure an optimum division between conventional portfolios and specific tasks.
>
> In this context, it considers that the President of the Commission must enjoy broad discretion in the allocation of tasks within the college, as well as in any reshuffling of those tasks during a Commission's term of office.
>
> The Conference also notes the Commission's intention to undertake in parallel a corresponding reorganisation of its departments. It notes in particular the desirability of bringing external relations under the responsibility of a Vice-President.
>
> (European Union, 1997, Annex, Declaration 32)

While nominally giving the president of the Commission more decision-making powers on the allocation of portfolios and underlying services, it nonetheless carried instructions as to how to organize the portfolio dealing with External Relations. Under this guidance, an organization along policy areas rather than regions ultimately prevailed. Alongside important administrative reforms, Prodi's appointment of Pascal Lamy as the EU's Trade Commissioner and that of Patten as External Relations Commissioner demonstrate the Commission president's focus on external relations (Dimitrakopoulos, 2004: 5–6).

Despite Prodi's streamlining efforts for EU foreign policy, overall responsibility for Latin America shifted to the Trade Commissioner, while development aid to the region was now Patten's responsibility (Holland and Doidge, 2012: 104). Nonetheless, other attempts were undertaken to strengthen the coordination of the EU's external relations. This is particularly relevant as the very aim of the administrative reform in the realm of external relations was to "define a coherent global approach that combined trade, aid and political dialogues" (Holland and Doidge, 2012: 105).

This manifested itself in the creation of different coordination mechanisms amongst the four Commissioners most centrally involved: Trade, External Relations, Enlargement, and Development (Dominguez, 2008: 121–2). A high-level coordination mechanism for external policy, called the RELEX Group, was also created, uniting the responsible Commissioners and senior officials (Dominguez, 2008: 132). Nonetheless, a potentially even more significant attempt to ensure coordination through the use of Commission vice-presidents was at the time met with scepticism by member states over a fear of competition with the newly created post of the High Representative for CFSP, and small member states particularly feared that their Commissioners would be relegated to a "junior" position (Kassim and Menon, 2004: 101; Nugent and Saurugger, 2002: 354).

The biggest challenge for the Commission's next President, José Manuel Barroso, was to find a sufficient number of portfolios after the EU's 2004 enlargement round and once more after the enlargement to include Bulgaria and Romania in 2007. Despite this, the portfolios with an external relations remit remained very constant, as Barroso did not return to the geographical allocation of the Santer Commission. Nonetheless, the Commissioners holding these portfolios changed, with Benita Ferrero-Waldner receiving the External Relations portfolio and Peter Mandelson the trade brief.

Furthermore, Ferrero-Waldner was made Deputy-Chair of the RELEX Group of Commissioners, thus officially holding the coordination role in absence of Barroso (Cameron, 2007: 54). Shortly before the end of the tenure of Barroso I in October 2009, Mandelson was replaced by Catherine Ashton, who then remained in the post until the inauguration of Barroso II. Similarly, Karel De Gucht took over Louis Michel's portfolio after he joined the European Parliament in July 2009.

Adapting the previous coordination practice during his first tenure as president, Barroso decided to preside over the group of Commissioners with external relations portfolios (Dominguez, 2008: 121). This could have given him the possibility to weigh significantly into the Commissioners' separate portfolios. However, as a former member of Mr. Barroso's cabinet pointed out, the Commission president "picked his fights" and did not want to micromanage the work of any of the important external relations Commission portfolios,[4] allowing individual Commissioners significant leeway in their specific policy domains.[5]

The most significant change to the powers and composition of the Commission occurred with the creation of the HRVP and the EEAS under the Treaty of Lisbon. Its entry into force almost coincided with the beginning of Barroso's second term in office and meant that the Commission would be stripped of its External Relations portfolio and certain other competencies which would become part of the new EEAS together with the existing staff. At the same time, the post of the External Relations Commissioner was fused with that of the new High Representative for the CFSP to form the new HRVP who would now be a permanent vice-president of the Commission (similar to the role of the RELEX Commissioner mandated since Amsterdam). Like most bureaucracies, the European Commission accepted these changes only reluctantly, as it

> was not very eager to give up its competences in external policy areas outside the domain of CFSP/CSDP such as Trade, Development, Neighborhood, or Humanitarian Aid. Development policy in particular was vehemently defended as a competence of the Commission, with the support of the EP.
>
> (Blom and Vanhoonacker, 2015: 214)

While some external relations competencies thus ultimately remained within the Commission, what used to be the External Relations portfolio was entirely moved out of the Commission and incorporated into the EEAS. Catherine Ashton was made the first HRVP of the Union in November 2009, which led to Ferrero-Waldner taking over the Trade portfolio until the inauguration of the second Barroso Commission. While the composition of the Trade portfolio then remained unchanged with Karel De Gucht as its new Commissioner, most other external relations portfolios saw a change of the make-up of portfolios and the Commissioners holding the posts.

It was intended that the newly created HRVP would continue in her role as a coordinating factor for the Commission's External Relations policies in the RELEX Commissioners' Group. However, Catherine Ashton hardly ever chaired these meetings (thus privileging her role within the Council), with Barroso often taking over the role himself during his second mandate (Vanhoonacker and Pomorska, 2016: 54–5).

In 2014, with the inauguration of the Juncker Commission, a number of portfolios and Commissioner changes occurred. Most notably is Federica Mogherini's appointment as HRVP, as well as that of Cecilia Malmström as EU Trade Commissioner. The key innovation within the Commission, however, was the creation of a number of vice-presidents whose role it is to coordinate the Commission's action in a number of different policy areas, and thus creating a hierarchy between individual Commissioners. While this represents the very kind of streamlining effort that Prodi initially advocated, its usefulness in the realm of the EU's external relations is not immediately clear. This is due to the fact that responsibilities for the activities of most of the Commission's vice-presidents touch on the EU's external relations in one way or another, including across different Commission portfolios.

For instance, while Cecilia Malmström is responsible for the EU's trade policy overall, Vice-President Frans Timmerman's responsibility is to ensure that EU's trade policy is transparent as part of the Commission's "Better Regulation" agenda. Additionally, Vice-President Jyrki Katainen's Jobs, Growth, Investment and Competitiveness mandate has obvious links with the EU's CCP. At least on paper, this creates a risk for competence overlap and the divergence of positions between different Commissioners. As a change from the Ashton period, HRVP Federica Mogherini has also taken a more active role within the Commission.[6]

Overall, the necessary division of portfolios as well as the lack or malfunctioning of coordination mechanisms between different Commissioners has remained a prominent feature of any kind of portfolio organization of the Commission. While many of these aspects are rather technical in nature, personal factors, such as Catherine Ashton's focus on her duties outside of the Commission, have further contributed to this picture, thus making for important elements to consider when studying the bureaucratic politics of EU Association Agreement negotiations.

The organization of the Commission Directorates-General over time

Alongside the changes to the Commission's portfolio structure, its bureaucracy has also been reorganized a number of times. Paying attention to this is important as "the position of the Commission in international negotiations, is often affected by turf wars between competing DGs" (Delreux, 2015: 155). These problems have been particularly accentuated where policy formulation and policy implementation are split between different administrative entities, as was and is the case for the EU's development policy (Vanhoonacker and Pomorska, 2016: 55). The alterations to the structure of the underlying DGs were either in the realm of functional mergers or separations of different Directorates-General, or changes to their internal functioning. While these changes have often accompanied reorganizations of the Commission's portfolio structure, this wasn't always the case, and at times, the set-up of Directorates-General has not matched the broader portfolio structure (Spence, 2006a: 135).

These mismatches were often related to the fact that the different Commissioners needed to receive sufficiently important portfolios, with their competencies often spanning the work of multiple DGs, or parts of specific ones (Kassim and Menon, 2004: 98). Much as the absence of a hierarchy amongst the Commissioners rendered coordination difficult at the highest level, this set-up has often led to infighting between DGs and a lack of oversight of their work, particularly when one DG reports to multiple Commissioners at once (Spence, 2006a: 136). This was also influenced by different logics as to how to integrate the Commissioners and their cabinets on the one hand, and the staff of their DGs on the other. For a long time, Commissioners and their cabinets were located centrally in the Berlaymont building so as to facilitate interaction amongst them, which changed towards locating them within their DGs during the Prodi Commission and has reverted to the previous logic ever since (Spence, 2006a: 135).

Table 3.2 provides an overview of relevant changes to Commission DGs over time, as well as their internal division. The 1990s can be seen as a period of fragmentation in this regard. While prior to the Delors III Commission, both external economic and political relations were being dealt with by DG I (Nugent, 2001: 301), the necessity to allocate important tasks to different Commissioners led to the split-off of DG IA.

In the Santer Commission, the portfolio shift towards geographical responsibilities was then partially reproduced in the Commission DGs (García, 2008: 225; Nugent, 2001: 301), leading to the creation of a further DG responsible for external relations. Strikingly though, while geographic responsibilities were now allocated across DG I, DG IA, and DG IB, the former two also kept their previous responsibility for economic and political relations, respectively, thus increasing the number of actors involved in policy coordination. To render this picture even more complex, the role for policy coordination of the Commission's policies in Latin America was given to DG VIII (Development).

Table 3.2 Relevant Commission Directorates-General and Directorates over time

Delors III (1993–1994)

DG I (External Economic Relations)
- External Economic Relations and Commercial Policy
- Relations with North America, South Africa, Australia, and New Zealand
- Relations with the Newly Independent States
- Relations with the Countries of the Far East
- GATT, OECD, Commercial Questions in the areas of Agriculture and Fisheries
- Mediterranean, Near and Middle East
- Latin America

DG IA (External Political Relations)
- Multilateral Political Relations
- Political Relations with European and CIS Countries
- Political Relations with North America, Asia, Australia, and New Zealand
- Political Relations with the Countries of Latin America, Africa, and the Middle East
- Administration of the External Service

DG VI (Agriculture)
- International Affairs Concerning Agriculture

DG VIII (Development)
- Development Policy

Santer (1995–1999)

DG I (External Relations: Commercial Policy and Relations with North America, the far East, Australia, and New Zealand)
- Relations with North America, Australia, New Zealand, NAFTA, and APEC
- Relations with Far East Countries
- WTO, OECD, Commercial Questions with Respect to Agriculture and Fisheries

DG IA (External Relations: Europe and the New Independent States, Common Foreign and Security Policy and External Missions)
- Multilateral Relations
- Management of External Missions

DG IB (External Relations: Southern Mediterranean, Middle East, Latin America, South and Southeast Asia, and North-South Cooperation)
- Southern Mediterranean, Middle East, and Near East
- Latin America
- South and Southeast Asia
- North-South Relations

DG VI (Agriculture)
- International Affairs Relating to Agriculture

DG VIII (Development: External relations and development cooperation with Africa, Caribbean, and Pacific; Lomé convention)
- Projects in the Southern Mediterranean, Middle East, Latin America, South and Southeast Asia, Forests and Environment, Gender Issues

European Community Humanitarian Office (ECHO)

Prodi (1999–2004)

DG Agriculture (DG AGRI)
- International Affairs I, WTO negotiations in particular
- International Affairs II, Enlargement in particular

DG External Relations (RELEX)
- CFSP
- Multilateral Relations and Human Rights
- North America, East Asia, Australia, New Zealand, EEA, EFTA, San Marino, Andorra, Monaco
- Latin America
- External Services

DG Trade
- General Affairs, Resources, Bilateral Trade Relations I
- Free Trade Agreements, Agricultural Trade Questions, ACP, Bilateral Trade Relations II
- Coordination of WTO and OECD Matters, Services, Dispute Settlement, and Trade Barriers Regulation
- Sectoral Trade Questions and Market Access, Bilateral Relations III

DG Development (DEV)
- General Affairs and Operational Support
- Development Policy and Sectoral Questions

Humanitarian Aid Office (ECHO)

Common Service for External Relations

Barroso I (2004–2009)

DG Agriculture & Rural Development (AGRI)

Development and Relations with African, Caribbean, and Pacific States (DEV)

DG External Relations (RELEX)
- International Affairs I, in particular Multilateral Negotiations
- EU Development Policy: Horizontal Issues
- Development Policy: Thematic Issues
- Crisis Platform—Policy Co-ordination in Common Foreign and Security Policy (CFSP)
- Multilateral relations and Human rights
- North America, East Asia, Australia, New Zealand, EEA, EFTA, San Marino, Andorra, Monaco
- Latin America

(Continued)

Table 3.2 (Continued)

DG Trade	• Services and Investment, Bilateral Trade and Relations • Sustainable Development, Bilateral Trade Relations • Development and Economic Partnership Agreements • Public Procurement and Intellectual Property, Bilateral Trade Relations • WTO Affairs, OECD and Food-related Sectors
Barroso II (2010–2014) *European External Action Service (EEAS)*	• Americas • Latin America • Mexico, Central America • Andean countries • Mercosur countries • North America and Caribbean • US, Canada • Caribbean
DG Development and Cooperation—EuropeAid (DEVCO)	• Latin America • Horizontal Questions • Thematic Questions
DG Maritime Affairs and Fisheries (MARE)	• International Affairs & Markets
DG Agriculture and Rural Development (AGRI)	• International Bilateral Relations
DG Trade	• Resources, Information and Policy Coordination • Asia and Latin America • Sustainable Development; Economic Partnership Agreements, Africa-Caribbean and Pacific, Agri-food and Fisheries
Service for Foreign Policy Instruments	• Partnership Instrument

Juncker (2014–2019)

European External Action Service (EEAS)
- Americas
  - United States, Canada
  - Mexico, Central America, Caribbean
  - South America
  - Regional Affairs

Service for Foreign Policy Instruments
- Partnership Instrument

DG Trade
- *See 2010–2014*

DG Development and Cooperation—EuropeAid (DG DEVCO)
- Policy and Thematic Coordination
- Geographic Coordination

DG Maritime Affairs and Fisheries (MARE)
- International Affairs & Markets

DG Agriculture and Rural Development (AGRI)
- International Bilateral Relations

Source: WZB (2014); own compilation from various sources.

When assessing the functioning of the Commission's external relations bureaucracy in the pre-Prodi period, most point to important problems that arose out of this increasing fragmentation:

> The choice of the creation of DG IA and the bureaucratic rivalry seemingly caused by the need to find Commissioners and Directors-General adequate portfolios did much to keep the Commission from becoming the streamlined foreign service to which it might have aspired.
>
> (Cameron and Spence, 2004: 128)

While the European Commission already disposed of offices in third countries at the time, which have turned into EU Delegations since the Treaty of Lisbon, the functioning of these during the 1990s illustrates some of the difficulties that the Commission faced in becoming an actor which focused on foreign policy coordination across individual policy areas. While Commission personnel were on the ground in many Commission offices around the globe, which could have provided country-based insights into the EU's policies, the plethora of Commissioners with various External Relations-related portfolios in reality meant that there was very little interaction with officials posted abroad. This only changed slowly when DG Trade officials began to join the Commission offices in the mid to late 1990s.[7]

Bretherton and Vogler furthermore point out that these "tensions and jealousies between officials of Relex DGs at all levels [...] are reflected in the College of Commissioners" (1999: 39). In their opinion, this problem was further exacerbated by the lack of coordination mechanisms pointed to in the section above. When it comes to the organization of DGs in the Santer period, the same authors have also outlined natural tensions between geographically organized horizontal external relations DGs, as well as those administering individual policies vertically (Bretherton and Vogler, 1999: 132).

With the Prodi Commission's administrative changes, the set-up of Commission DGs was also overhauled significantly. Not only did DGs return to a functional, rather than geographical logic, but the old nomenclature was also abandoned in favour of names designating their functions that remain large intact to this date. The newly created DG External Relations (DG RELEX) after the Treaty of Amsterdam was furthermore designed specifically to address previous policy coordination problems by creating a central administration meant to coordinate the external relations policies of the Commission, including through being put in charge of the Commission's delegations in third countries (Cameron and Spence, 2004: 129–30).

These new administrative divisions together with more fundamental changes to the functioning of Commission cabinets and the way in which the work of DGs is being overseen have indeed had some effect. This was further helped by a system in which DG RELEX did take leadership on many policies under the guidance of Commissioner Patten, as well as a new way for distributing the Commission's development aid. Nonetheless, this emerging shift between the EU's policy definition and implementation did create new room for administrative rivalries (Cameron and Spence, 2004: 128).

Not much changed in this system during the first presidency of Barroso between 2004 and 2009. While the EU's enlargement rounds necessitated the creation of new Commission portfolios, the administrative services supporting the Commission's external relations remained largely intact. It was only with the changes of the Treaty of Lisbon that coincided with the beginning of Barroso's second mandate that the Commission's services were once more significantly overhauled.

With the Lisbon changes, both DG RELEX's geographical units and those of DG DEV were moved to the newly created EEAS, thus doing away with this division that first emerged in the Santer period (Holland and Doidge, 2012: 125). Nonetheless, the continued division between the EEAS and DG DEVCO has once more created a complex balance of competences between what is now two different institutions (Holland and Doidge, 2012: 126–8). Internally, how-ever, the historically fragmented administration of different parts of the EU's development policy has now been streamlined within DG DEVCO. The system that ensued once more brings together policy definition and implementation and looks much more like one that can be observed in states (Holland and Doidge, 2012: 121–3).

While the creation of the EEAS was meant to address some of the previous problems of policy coordination, a new fundamental problem for the coordina-tion of the EU's foreign policy is that the oversight role is now attributed to a new actor which is no longer a part of the European Commission's bureaucracy, with the exception of the Foreign Policy Instruments Service (though part of the Commission, it is housed within the EEAS). While Vanhoonacker and Pomorska have argued that EEAS and DGs now appear to work better together as the EEAS has been included in intra-Commission coordination meetings (Vanhoonacker and Pomorska, 2016: 55), interviews with officials did not confirm this relatively positive outlook across the board. Equally important, a fundamental problem remains with the functional division of the different external relations DGs that have persisted in the Commission even after the Treaty of Lisbon. As Keukeleire and Delreux argue:

> They each have their own working culture, set of objectives, legal bases for policy initiatives, and different type of instruments. This explains why, beyond the normal turf battles, coherent action is not always straightforward.
>
> (2014: 73)

Overall, while the Commission's services have seen a major overhaul over the period under consideration here, issues of administrative divisions have remained relevant up to this day and thus form a key part for the analysis of bureaucratic politics underpinning the EU's Association Agreement negotiations.

The Council's changing internal organization

While, given its size and competencies, the European Commission is responsible for the bulk of the activity underpinning Association Agreement negotiations and the implementation of the relevant parts of the EU's foreign policy, the Council nonetheless has a role to play in all of the policy areas concerned, be it as a co-legislator, the granter of negotiation mandates, or the primary institution which serves as an interlocutor for political dialogues. Just like the Commission, however, the Council needs to be seen not as a unitary actor in decision-making processes, but rather as a multifaceted institution. In turn, not only are changes of government in individual member states significant, but bureaucratic politics can also play out between different Council preparatory bodies and may include its permanent independent bureaucracy in the Council Secretariat.

Much as is the case for the European Commission, the Council's preparatory bodies taking part in its internal decision-making process (ultimately culminating in the meetings of the actual Council of Ministers in its different compositions) have been shaped by functional logics arising out of the European Union's former pillar structure. While its internal decision-making process is hierarchical, the presence of different preparatory bodies with various and overlapping policy competencies—often staffed by different member state officials according to policy areas—can nonetheless provide a backdrop for bureaucratic politics in complex EU Association Agreement negotiations.

Once more using the geographic area relevant for the empirical section of this book as an illustration for the period under consideration here, Latin American issues have been dealt with inside the Council by working groups operating on a policy-oriented logic on the one hand, and those holding a geographical coordination role on the other. While the set-up of the former is the result of decision-making in what used to be the EU's first pillar, the latter have emerged out of EPC and later on CFSP. Over time, some reform efforts were made to better integrate bodies which have originated within the different pillars of the EU's superstructure (Smith, 2004: 223–4). Nonetheless, the overall set-up of bodies within the Council remains largely untouched. Post-Lisbon the TPC, the Working Party on Latin America and the Caribbean (COLAC), and the Working Party on Development Cooperation are the most relevant Council preparatory bodies for the EU's Latin America policy at the initial stage.

While the TPC has always existed per the EU's foundational treaties, its name has nonetheless varied over time and used to be known as the Article 133 and Article 113 Committee in reference to the treaty articles outlining the EU's powers in the realm of trade policy-making. Considering the explicitly political side of relations with Latin America, the responsible Council preparatory bodies have undergone a few changes. Where there was formally a relatively senior and infrequent COLAT staffed by diplomats based in national capitals and a lower-level Brussels-based body named AMLAT, both have now been folded into a renamed COLAC which also discusses the EU's ties to the Caribbean region.[8]

Formerly, all of these bodies were chaired by a representative of the rotating Council presidency. This has been altered somewhat since the Treaty of Lisbon, with most bodies relating to the EU's External Action being chaired by a representative from the EEAS in the name of the HRVP. For the three bodies mentioned above, both COLAC and the Working Party on Development Cooperation are permanently chaired by the EEAS, while the TPC retains the rotating Council presidency (General Secretariat of the Council, 2019).

The organization of most Permanent Representations of member states to the EU also follows this functional logic, with officials from different ministries holding responsibilities for individual policy areas and only attending the meetings of the relevant Council preparatory bodies. Only some Permanent Representations, such as those of France or Spain[9] integrate their officials or attribute competencies based on external partners, thus making it easier to link political concerns with those arising in other EU policy areas.

The role and structure of the Council Secretariat—the Council's underlying bureaucracy that provides administrative support—also need to be explored. While it employs comparatively few civil servants in relation to the European Commission, its central and permanent role within the Council puts its officials into privileged positions. Its formal role is limited to that of administrators of the Council's activity, and supporting the presidency (be it the rotating one or the permanent chairmanship of the European Council introduced with the Treaty of Lisbon), but its autonomous influence on the EU's policy-making should not be underestimated (Stetter, 2007: 153–9).

Ultimately, this actor is central in advising the presidency, is crucial for finding compromise solutions between the positions of different member states, and provides the official record of the Council's meetings (Hayes-Renshaw and Wallace, 2006: 114, 117). The latter is particularly important, as Council officials are present at every Council Working Group session, and can influence future discussions through emphasizing certain aspects in the minutes of previous meetings and the structure of meeting agendas,[10] something which has also been recognized for the EU's Association Agreement negotiations.[11]

While the Council Secretariat was originally split between officials dealing with issues arising out of the former EPC in the pre-Maastricht days, since then the administrative structures have been integrated, originally creating some tensions within the Secretariat itself given the presence of different administrative cultures and roles (Bretherton and Vogler, 1999: 181).

Overall, the structure of the Council's preparatory bodies closely resembles the functional policy-based logic that has come to be the norm for portfolio attribution within the European Commission. This creates similar coordination problems as are present in the latter actor. While the representatives of the member states attending such meetings all ultimately serve in the name of the same member state government, the fact that attendance at various working groups differs makes it more challenging to coordinate views across policy areas.

The quest for coordination in EU foreign policy-making

The above has outlined potential sources for bureaucratic politics affecting the EU's complex negotiations for Association Agreements. The following section instead deals with attempts to improve coordination mechanisms between individual parts of the EU's bureaucracy over time that could have contributed to increasing the EU's capacity to link concerns from individual policy areas in its complex negotiations.

Attempts to address problems of policy coordination in the EU's foreign policy have regularly featured on the agenda of EU treaty reforms and in more informal discussions between the various actors involved. Despite continuous efforts to increase the coordination and ultimately the coherence of the EU's foreign policy, the underlying issues have not been resolved up to this day. This can be attributed primarily to the continued existence of different modes of decision-making on various aspects of the EU's foreign policy, which is in turn related to member states' reluctance to give up parts of their control over certain EU policy areas.

The first treaty-based provisions on the necessity for foreign policy coherence in the context of what today is called the Union's External Action go back to the period of the Single European Act (SEA) (Gauttier, 2004: 25). These were extended with the Treaty of Maastricht, which introduced a specific Article C on the coherence of the EU's foreign policy, which reads as follows:

The Union shall be served by a single institutional framework which shall ensure the consistency and the continuity of the activities carried out in order to attain its objectives while respecting and building upon the 'acquis communautaire'.

The Union shall in particular ensure the consistency of its external activities as a whole in the context of its external relations, security, economic and development policies. The Council and the Commission shall be responsible for ensuring such consistency. They shall ensure the implementation of these policies, each in accordance with its respective powers.

(Official Journal of the European Communities, 1992, Article C)

The treaty thus sets out a list of policy areas that needed to be consistent with one another and distributed the responsibility for this to the Commission and the Council. In reality, however, the treaty did not set up "a single institutional framework" as it claimed, but structured the functioning of the EU's policy-making according to the three different pillars, which varied greatly in the underlying decision-making provisions and functioned largely separately from one another. Furthermore, the above article in the treaty concerned with policy coherence provides a coordinating role for both the Commission and the Council, without clearly delineating when each should take a leadership role. This led to significant conflict potential as to the competencies of each. After all, both actors could adopt a reading of the article in question that would best suit their preferences (Gauttier, 2004: 27–8).

Gauttier also cautions that the Treaty of Maastricht set up a number of overlapping competencies for certain parts of the EU's foreign policy (Gauttier, 2004: 28–32), such as the fact that concerns over rule of law, human rights and democracy in partner countries would need to be reflected not only in its CFSP, but also in the policies administered under the first pillar (Bretherton and Vogler, 1999: 132). Such overlapping competencies made it particularly hard to identify decision-making hierarchies or leadership roles between them. While coordination mechanisms between CFSP officials and those in the Commission have been in place since the Treaty of Maastricht (Smith, 2004: 223), these ultimately fuelled misunderstanding and administrative rivalry (Bretherton and Vogler, 1999: 182).

Such problems occurred not only between the Commission and the Council, the main institutional actors involved here, but also in their internal organizational structure. While some member states suggested that the Treaty of Amsterdam should address some of these problems by uniting the former treaty's provisions on the EU's foreign policy under a single heading, this did not come about due to a lack of consensus between the member states (Bretherton and Vogler, 1999: 191). Ultimately, the Treaty of Amsterdam did little to resolve the fundamental issues that the Treaty of Maastricht introduced to the coordination of the EU's foreign policy (Gauttier, 2004: 27). As some authors have outlined, while many informal and ad hoc attempts were made to overcome such difficulties, ultimately the structural elements and the different preferences of the institutions trumped such efforts (Gauttier, 2004: 33–7; Smith, 2001), and an institutional answer to the issue of foreign policy coordination remained absent even beyond the Treaty of Amsterdam.

Literature on what this meant for the coordination of the EU's foreign policy at the time has cautioned that this set-up was particularly problematic for relations between staff charged with the management of the EU's new CFSP and DG RELEX staff in the Commission, creating large potential for rivalry and mutual misunderstanding (Bretherton and Vogler, 1999: 182). Others have pointed out that the overlapping competencies that the Commission holds in the different pillars have particularly impacted on this institution:

> More than any other actor, the Commission has struggled with the major boundary problem between CFSP/CSDP and non-CFSP/CSDP competences, and thus also between being centre stage, backstage or not on the stage at all. [...] These [...] problems have led to a succession of 'border conflicts' or outright 'wars' or stalemates, not only between the Commission and the Council [...], but also within the Commission's own internal structures.
>
> (Keukeleire and Delreux, 2014: 72–3)

In the pre-Lisbon period, the presence of the EU's pillar structure, the lack of coordination mechanisms between the key institutions involved in the EU's foreign policy decision-making process, as well as within the Commission itself, have thus created significant hurdles for the formulation of a coordinated EU foreign policy, which would necessarily translate into attempts to include provisions pertaining to individual policy areas into the EU's Association Agreements.

The Treaty of Lisbon then formally did away with the distinction between the EU's various pillars and introduced new language as to the coherence of the EU's foreign policy under a specific heading entitled External Action. On the surface, this resolves some of the problems that some member states had wanted to address since the Treaty of Amsterdam. First of all, the treaty's Article 21 sets out a number of objectives for the Union's External Action, such as a reference to certain universal values:

> The Union's action on the international scene shall be guided by the principles which have inspired its own creation, development and enlargement, and which it seeks to advance in the wider world: democracy, the rule of law, the universality and indivisibility of human rights and fundamental freedoms, respect for human dignity, the principles of equality and solidarity, and respect for the principles of the United Nations Charter and international law.
> (Official Journal of the European Union, 2008, Article 21, 1)

More specifically, it tasks specific institutions in the EU with the coordination of its foreign policy by stating that:

> The Union shall ensure consistency between the different areas of its external action and between these and its other policies. The Council and the Commission, assisted by the High Representative of the Union for Foreign Affairs and Security Policy, shall ensure that consistency and shall cooperate to that effect.
> (Official Journal of the European Union, 2008, Article 21, 3)

While the treaty upholds the language that gives both the Council and the Commission a role in policy coordination, the inclusion of the newly created HRVP (making use of the EEAS at its service) attributes the roles somewhat more clearly to the different institutions. It is important to note, however, that the European Parliament is still not mentioned in this context.

Despite this, the treaty did not define a specific framework for the HRVP's and the EEAS' powers, functions, and competencies (Holland and Doidge, 2012: 124). Thus, the "Lisbon Treaty left the *modus operandi* of any more detailed coordination within the EEAS and between the Service and the EU institutions open" (Duke, 2012: 53). This once more created room for conflict between the institutions, only this time with an entirely new actor involved in the process. Furthermore, despite formally abandoning the former three-pillar structure,

> The Lisbon Treaty emphatically does not take one step that integrationists would have wished it to take, namely any significant extension within the area of foreign policy of the traditional 'Community method' of decision-making.
> (Donnelly, 2010: 18)

The presence of different modes of decision-making was thus not abandoned with the new treaty either.

The creation of an entirely new institution at the EU level externalized some of the necessity for intra-institutional coordination that had formerly been addressed within the European Commission and the Council itself, thus disrupting established mechanisms for policy coordination (Schade, 2019). This is mainly related to the fact that the separation of parts of the Commission bureaucracy to be included in the new service created the potential for policy overlap within the structures of the EEAS, as well as between the EEAS and the Commission. Attributing this to the hybrid origin of the different policies contained under the External Action heading, Smith has pointed out that, even after Lisbon, due to

> constant challenges of adjustment and institutional boundary-drawing [...] the institutional context for EU diplomacy has remained uncertain, as has the more material dimension of institutional resources and capacity.
>
> (Smith, 2013: 655–6)

While the EEAS gained a formal role in providing political guidance for the EU's External Action, the Commission retained important competencies throughout and after the set-up of the EEAS (Morgenstern-Pomorski, 2018: 146–52). Crucially, most relevant funding sources and implementation powers remained with the European Commission (Balfour, 2015: 37). As a consequence, new realms of overlapping competences were introduced, while reducing the EEAS' possibility to provide guidance due to its lack of resources (Carta and Duke, 2015: 60). Furthermore, given that the EEAS itself is staffed by personnel of different origins within the Council, the Commission, and member state foreign services, its activity will likely have been shaped by the continued presence of differing administrative cultures internally (Lequesne, 2015: 46–8).

After a few years of operation, the HRVP suggested changes to the functioning of the EEAS to increase its role in ensuring the coherence of the EU's foreign policy. The 2013 EEAS review document that is the result of this process then devoted an entire chapter to the issue of policy coherence (EEAS, 2013: 7–12), stressing that:

> It is not always easy to achieve this [policy coherence] since it requires the establishment of linkages between: related geographic or thematic topics; the work in different institutions, and even the different levels of discussion in the Council bodies (European Council, Ministerial Council formations, PSC, thematic working groups).
>
> (EEAS, 2013: 7)

While the document made some suggestions as to how to change its functioning to increase its coordination role, there is only anecdotal evidence that coordination between the EEAS and Commission DGs has increased ever since. This is despite the fact that the EEAS has formally been included in internal

Commission coordination meetings (Vanhoonacker and Pomorska, 2016: 55), has reshaped its internal structure, and that political guidance for good cooperation between Commission services and the EEAS was given by political leaders (Morgenstern-Pomorski, 2018: 172–4).

Conclusions

This chapter has further detailed the functioning of the EU's foreign policy decision-making that is relevant for analysing the EU's conduct in complex negotiations. In so doing, it has provided an overview over the institutional set-up of the EU's external relations bureaucracy over time and thereby highlighted potential sources of bureaucratic conflict that may arise in such negotiations.

While many attempts have been made to increase the coordination and coherence of the EU's foreign policy, these efforts appear to have had only a limited success up to now. This can be attributed primarily to the fact that the roles of the different actors in the coordination of the EU's foreign policy are not clearly defined, creating the potential for competence overlap, and that existing mechanisms have been disrupted by nearly continuous reforms to the foreign policy decision-making system in itself.

Notes

1 European Parliament official, Brussels (Interview 25).
2 DG DEVCO officials, Brussels (Interview 24).
3 Prior to the 2004 enlargement round large member states appointed two, rather than one Commissioner.
4 Former Barroso cabinet official, London (Interview 3).
5 Former Barroso cabinet official, London (Interview 3).
6 EEAS officials, Brussels (Interview 8).
7 Former DG RELEX official, Brussels (Interview 18).
8 Former EU official, Brussels (Interview 17).
9 Member state diplomat, Brussels (Interview 19); Member state diplomat (Interview 29).
10 Former EU official, Brussels (Interview 17).
11 EU officials, Brussels (Interview 11).

Bibliography

Balfour R (2015) Change and Continuity: A Decade of Evolution of EU Foreign Policy and the Creation of the European External Action Service. In: Balfour R, Carta C, and Raik K (eds) *The European External Action Service and National Foreign Ministries: Convergence or Divergence?* Farnham: Ashgate, pp. 31–44.

Billiet S (2009) Principal-Agent Analysis and the Study of the EU: What About the EC's External Relations? *Comparative European Politics* 7(4): 435–454. DOI: 10.1057/cep.2008.45.

Blom T and Vanhoonacker S (2015) The European External Action Service (EEAS), the New Kid on the Block. In: Bauer MW and Trondal J (eds) *The Palgrave Handbook of the European Administrative System*. Basingstoke: Palgrave, pp. 208–226.

Bretherton C and Vogler J (1999) *The European Union as a Global Actor*. Abingdon: Routledge.

Cameron F (2007) *An Introduction to European Foreign Policy*. London: Routledge.

Cameron F and Spence D (2004) The Commission-Council Tandem in the Foreign Policy Arena. In: Dimitrakopoulos DG (ed.) *The Changing European Commission*. Manchester: Manchester University Press, pp. 121–137.

Carta C and Duke S (2015) Inside the European External Action Service's Institutional Sinews: An Institutional and Organizational Analysis. In: Balfour R, Carta C, and Raik K (eds) *The European External Action Service and National Foreign Ministries: Convergence or Divergence?* Farnham: Ashgate, pp. 55–71.

Christiansen T (2001) Intra-Institutional Politics and Inter-Institutional Relations in the EU: Towards Coherent Governance? *Journal of European Public Policy* 8(5): 747–769. DOI: 10.1080/13501760110083491.

Conceição-Heldt E da (2011) Variation in EU Member States' Preferences and the Commission's Discretion in the Doha Round. *Journal of European Public Policy* 18(3): 403–419. DOI: 10.1080/13501763.2011.551078.

Delreux T (2015) Bureaucratic Politics, New Institutionalism and Principal-Agent Models. In: Jørgensen KE, Aarstad ÅK, Drieskens E, et al. (eds) *The SAGE Handbook of European Foreign Policy*. London: SAGE, pp. 152–165.

Devuyst Y (2012) The European Council and the CFSP After the Lisbon Treaty. *European Foreign Affairs Review* 17(3): 327–349.

DG DEVCO (2019) *International Cooperation and Development—European Commission*. European Commission. Available at: https://ec.europa.eu/europeaid/policies/european-development-policy_en (accessed 12 May 2019).

Diedrichs U and Wessels W (2006) The Commission and the Council. In: Spence D (ed.) *The European Commission*. London: John Harper, pp. 209–234.

Dimitrakopoulos DG (2004) Introduction. In: Dimitrakopoulos DG (ed.) *The Changing European Commission*. Manchester: Manchester University Press, pp. 1–11.

Dominguez R (2008) *The Foreign Policy of the European Union (1995–2004): A Study in Structural Transition*. Lewiston: Edwin Mellen.

Donnelly B (2010) Europe in the World: All Change or No Change in Foreign Policy After Lisbon? *The International Spectator* 45(2): 17–22. DOI: 10.1080/03932729.2010.489311.

Duke S (2012) The European External Action Service: Antidote Against Incoherence? *European Foreign Affairs Review* 17(1): 45–68.

Dür A and Elsig M (2011) Principals, Agents, and the European Union's Foreign Economic Policies. *Journal of European Public Policy* 18(3): 323–338. DOI: 10.1080/13501763.2011.551066.

EEAS (2013) *EEAS Review*. Brussels: European External Action Service. Available at: http://eeas.europa.eu/library/publications/2013/3/2013_eeas_review_en.pdf (accessed 15 January 2016).

Elsig M (2007) The EU's Choice of Regulatory Venues for Trade Negotiations: A Tale of Agency Power? *JCMS: Journal of Common Market Studies* 45(4): 927–948. DOI: 10.1111/j.1468-5965.2007.00754.x.

EU–CELAC Summit (2015) *Brussels Declaration*. Brussels: European Council. Available at: www.consilium.europa.eu/en/meetings/international-summit/2015/06/EU-CEL-AC-Brussels-declaration_pdf/ (accessed 1 August 2015).

European Council (2019) *Sharm El-Sheikh Summit Declaration*. European Council. Available at: www.consilium.europa.eu/en/press/press-releases/2019/02/25/sharm-el-sheikh-summit-declaration/ (accessed 25 May 2019).

European Union (1997) *Treaty of Amsterdam*. Available at: http://europa.eu/eu-law/decision-making/treaties/pdf/treaty_of_amsterdam/treaty_of_amsterdam_en.pdf (accessed 1 December 2016).

Frennhoff Larsén MF (2007) Trade Negotiations Between the EU and South Africa: A Three-Level Game. *JCMS: Journal of Common Market Studies* 45(4): 857–881. DOI: 10.1111/j.1468-5965.2007.00751.x.

García M (2008) *The Path to the 2002 Association Agreement Between the European Union and Chile: A Case Study in Successful Political Negotiation*. Lewiston, NY: Edwin Mellen.

Gauttier P (2004) Horizontal Coherence and the External Competences of the European Union. *European Law Journal* 10(1): 23–41. DOI: 10.1111/j.1468-0386.2004.00201.x.

General Secretariat of the Council (2019) *List of Council Preparatory Bodies*. Available at: http://data.consilium.europa.eu/doc/document/ST-10075-2017-INIT/en/pdf   (accessed 25 May 2019).

Hayes-Renshaw F and Wallace H (2006) *The Council of Ministers*. 2nd ed. Basingstoke: Palgrave.

Hillman J and Kleimann D (2010) *Trading Places: The New Dynamics of EU Trade Policy Under the Treaty of Lisbon*. Economic Policy Paper Series. Washington, DC: The German Marshal Fund of the United States.

Holland M and Doidge M (2012) *Development Policy of the European Union*. Basingstoke: Palgrave Macmillan.

Kassim H and Menon A (2004) EU Member States and the Prodi Commission. In: Dimitrakopoulos DG (ed.) *The Changing European Commission*. Manchester: Manchester University Press, pp. 89–104.

Kassim H, Peterson J, Bauer MW, et al. (2013) *The European Commission of the Twenty-First Century*. Oxford: OUP.

Keukeleire S and Delreux T (eds) (2014) *The Foreign Policy of the European Union*. 2nd ed. Basingstoke: Palgrave Macmillan.

Lequesne C (2000) The European Commission: A Balancing Act Between Autonomy and Dependence. In: Neunreither K and Wiener A (eds) *European Integration After Amsterdam: Institutional Dynamics and Prospects for Democracy*. Oxford: OUP, pp. 36–51.

Lequesne C (2015) At the Centre of Coordination: Staff, Resources and Procedures in the European External Action Service and in the Delegations. In: Balfour R, Carta C, and Raik K (eds) *The European External Action Service and National Foreign Ministries: Convergence or Divergence?* Farnham: Ashgate, pp. 45–54.

Lister M (1997) *The European Union and the South: Relations with Developing Countries*. New York, NY: Routledge.

Meunier S (2007) Managing Globalization? The EU in International Trade Negotiations. *JCMS: Journal of Common Market Studies* 45(4): 905–926. DOI: 10.1111/j.1468-5965.2007.00753.x.

Meunier S and Nicolaïdis K (2011) The European Union as a Trade Power. In: Hill C and Smith M (eds) *International Relations and the European Union*. Oxford: Oxford University Press, pp. 275–298.

Morgenstern-Pomorski J-H (2018) *The Contested Diplomacy of the European External Action Service: Inception, Establishment and Consolidation*. Abingdon: Routledge.

Nugent N (2001) *The European Commission*. Basingstoke: Palgrave.

Nugent N and Saurugger S (2002) Organizational Structuring: The Case of the European Commission and Its External Policy Responsibilities. *Journal of European Public Policy* 9(3): 345–364. DOI: 10.1080/13501760210138787.

Official Journal of the European Communities (1992) *Treaty on European Union*. Available at: www.cvce.eu/content/publication/2002/4/9/2c2f2b85-14bb-4488-9ded-13f3cd04de05/publishable_en.pdf (accessed 12 February 2016).

Official Journal of the European Union (2008) *Consolidated Version of the Treaty on European Union*, 9 May. Brussels: Official Journal of the European Union. Available at: http://eur-lex.europa.eu/LexUriServ/LexUriServ.do?uri=OJ:C:2008:115:0013:0045:EN:PDF (accessed 15 May 2019).

Orbie J (2008) The European Union's Role in World Trade: Harnessing Globalisation? In: Orbie J (ed.) *Europe's Global Role: External Policies of the European Union*. Burlington, VT: Ashgate, pp. 35–66.

Orbie J and Versluys H (2008) The European Union's International Development Policy: Leading and Benevolent? In: Orbie J (ed.) *Europe's Global Role: External Policies of the European Union*. Aldershot: Ashgate, pp. 67–90.

Peterson J (1999) *Decision-Making in the European Union*. New York, NY: St. Martin's Press.

Radtke K (2012) The EU's Common Foreign and Security Policy (CFSP) After the Lisbon Treaty: Supranational Revolution or Adherence to Intergovernmental Pattern? In: Laursen F (ed.) *The EU's Lisbon Treaty: Institutional Choices and Implementation*. Farnham: Ashgate, pp. 41–62.

Schade D (2019) Fuzzy Roles in EU External Relations Governance: The Difficult Construction of Informal Policy Coordination Frameworks. In: van Heumen L and Roos M (eds) *The Informal Construction of Europe*. Routledge, pp. 199–216.

Smith M (2013) Beyond the Comfort Zone: Internal Crisis and External Challenge in the European Union's Response to Rising Powers. *International Affairs* 89(3): 653–671. DOI: 10.1111/1468-2346.12038.

Smith ME (2001) The Quest for Coherence: Institutional Dilemmas of External Action from Maastricht to Amsterdam. In: Stone Sweet A, Sandholtz W, and Fligstein N (eds) *The Institutionalization of Europe*. Oxford: OUP, pp. 171–193.

Smith ME (2004) *Europe's Foreign and Security Policy: The Institutionalization of Cooperation*. Cambridge: CUP.

Spence D (2006a) The Directorates General and the Services: Structures, Functions and Procedures. In: Spence D (ed.) *The European Commission*. London: John Harper, pp. 128–155.

Spence D (2006b) The President, the College and the Cabinets. In: Spence D. (ed.) *The European Commission*. London: John Harper, pp. 25–74.

Stetter S (2007) *EU Foreign and Interior Policies: Cross-Pillar Politics and the Social Construction of Sovereignty*. Routledge Advances in European Politics 43. New York, NY: Routledge.

Tannous I (2013) The Programming of EU's External Assistance and Development Aid and the Fragile Balance of Power Between EEAS and DG DEVCO. *European Foreign Affairs Review* 18(3): 329–354.

Telò M (2013) The EU: A Civilian Power's Diplomatic Action After the Lisbon Treaty. Bridging Internal Complexity and International Convergence. In: Telò M and Ponjaert F (eds) *The EU's Foreign Policy: What Kind of Power and Diplomatic Action?* Farnham: Ashgate, pp. 27–63.

van den Hoven A (2007) Bureaucratic Competition in EU Trade Policy: EBA as a Case of Competing Two-Level Games? In: Faber G and Orbie J (eds) *European Union Trade Politics and Development: 'Everything But Arms' Unravelled.* New York, NY: Routledge, pp. 60–73.

Van der Loo G (2017) The Dutch Referendum on the EU–Ukraine Association Agreement: Legal Implications and Solutions. In: Kuijer M and Werner W (eds) *Netherlands Yearbook of International Law 2016: The Changing Nature of Territoriality in International Law.* Netherlands Yearbook of International Law. The Hague: T.M.C. Asser Press, pp. 337–350. DOI: 10.1007/978-94-6265-207-1_14.

Vanhoonacker S and Pomorska K (2016) EU Diplomacy Post-Lisbon: The Legacy of the Ashton Era. In: Smith M, Keukeleire S, and Vanhoonacker S (eds) *The Diplomatic System of the European Union: Evolution, Change and Challenges.* Abingdon: Routledge, pp. 49–63.

Woolcock S (2010) EU Trade and Investment Policymaking After the Lisbon Treaty. *Intereconomics* 45(1): 22–25.

WZB (2014) *Position Formation in the EU Commission (PEU) Database.* Berlin: Social Science Research Center Berlin (WZB). Available at: www.wzb.eu/de/forschung/internationale-politik-und-recht/positionsbildung-in-der-eu-kommission/publikationen/database (accessed 15 January 2016).

Part II

Complex EU negotiations in the Latin American region

4　Testing the water

Initial attempts for cross-cutting negotiations in the Latin American region

Like all chapters in this second empirical part of the book, its main aim is to explore how relevant factors of bureaucratic politics and reforms to the EU's institutional and decision-making set-up have shaped complex EU Association Agreement negotiations in practice. Both this book section and this chapter are organized roughly chronologically, so as to be able to trace the dynamics of complex EU negotiations over time and in line with changes to the EU's institutional set-up. The main focus of this chapter is then the EU's initial complex negotiations with Mexico, Mercosur, and Chile, in the late 1990s and early 2000s. The later revival of the EU negotiations with Mercosur, however, also means that more recent developments in this particular case are also considered.

Ultimately, the initial negotiations considered here have been a testing ground for future complex negotiations for EU Association Agreements, as the EU–Mexico Global Agreement is the first of its kind and the EU–Chile Association Agreement was unmatched in ambition at the time. The EU's negotiations with Mercosur, in turn, represent the EU's first attempt to conclude an Association Agreement in the region and have turned out to be the EU's longest-running Association Agreement negotiations overall as formal negotiations began in 1999 and an agreement in principle was only found in 2019. Through a side-by-side analysis of the parallel negotiations with both Mercosur and Chile, the chapter is able to point to the effect that the preferences of individual institutional actors within the Commission have had on the outcome of each negotiation, all while distinguishing the differing developments later on in the process.

Establishing the context of the EU's complex negotiations with Latin America

The EU's attempts to conclude Association Agreement negotiations with countries and regional organizations in the Latin American region can ultimately be attributed to an increasing desire of the EU to develop ties to third actors after the Maastricht Treaty (del Arenal, 1997: 112, 122–3), as well as to promote its own model of regional integration (Börzel and Risse, 2015: 56). The initial aim was to achieve this through developing ties to other regional integration mechanisms across the globe (De Lombaerde et al., 2015: 752). While attempts were made in the South East Asian context, efforts to develop ties to Latin American regional organizations predate these (Allison, 2015) given the density of regional integration mechanisms there (Devlin, 2001: 79).

Prior to such attempts, the EU had not focused on Latin America, as the economic and political turmoil in large countries like Brazil rendered them relatively unattractive partners at the time.[1] As an example, the so-called San José Dialogue on peace in the Central American region first established in 1984 (Smith, 1995: 78–80) remained the only dialogue format with the region for a long period of time. This, in turn, was meant to increase the EU's soft power amidst attempts to provide the European Communities with a more active role in foreign affairs.[2] It was only in 1990 that a dialogue format with all of Latin America was set up under the guise of annual ministerial meetings with the Rio Group.[3]

The EU's formal ties to the region then grew only gradually, in particular given its activity in the realm of development cooperation and through the conclusion of a number of bilateral, yet relatively weak dialogue and political agreements. While there were some differences between individual of these so-called third generation agreements concluded (IRELA, 1997), they nonetheless shared a large number of features. By 1993, the EU's ties with the entire Latin American region were then structured by these types of agreements which created only few mutual obligations for cooperation. While these were mainly bilateral in nature, the EU also concluded similar agreements with incipient regional integration mechanisms such as Mercosur at the time (Agence Europe, 1992). These agreements were also flanked by an important increase of the EU's ODA towards the region, which was a policy developed under the leadership of a Spanish Commissioner (Agence Europe, 1990).

A turn in the EU's approach towards Latin America was then, however, developed by Manuel Marín, the EU's Spanish Development Commissioner from 1993 onwards. His advocacy for developing closer ties to the region has even been described as a "Marín Effect" (García, 2008). In particular, he first suggested the signing of Association Agreements with actors in the region (García, 2008: 199) and was responsible for the development of a document outlining an EU–Latin America strategy (European Commission, 1995a). All of these developments were possible as his role within the Commission at the time gave him a large degree of autonomy over his policy realm. The strategy in turn outlined and began a process which has been described as a "one-size-fits-all" (Börzel and Risse, 2009: 10) approach towards Latin America which would see the EU gradually attempt to conclude Association Agreements with actors in the region.

Negotiating the EU–Mexico Global Agreement

The EU's negotiations for the EU–Mexico Global Agreement, which was initially signed in 1997 and supplemented by an FTA in 1999 is the first instance of a successful complex EU negotiation in the Latin American region. The pioneering role of this agreement not just in this specific context, but also for other EU Association Agreements is not the only reason that makes this agreement stand out, however. While in most instances of complex EU negotiations, it is the actual negotiation dynamics at hand which can be explained by an analysis of underlying bureaucratic politics, in this instance the choice to undertake negotiations with the country also needs to be explained by a consideration of bureaucratic dynamics internal to the EU.

While the EU's relations with Mexico initially did not differ from those with other countries in the region, the coming into force of NAFTA in 1994 set it apart economically from the remainder of the region. This provided for an external development which would ultimately be the backdrop for the EU's early negotiations with the country. While it was the NAFTA experience that ultimately made Mexico a case apart, the precise nature of the policy change towards the country and its distinction from the "one-size fits all" approach which initially favoured ties to regional organizations can be explained by different factors of bureaucratic politics.

In line with considerations of policy inertia, the EU's policy change towards the country was facilitated by the fact that, just like for the rest of the region, the EU's relations with the country were limited, and an existing political agreement even set to expire in 1996. This allowed for the EU to develop a novel approach towards the country. While internal EU actors largely agreed on the necessity to react to NAFTA with the conclusion of an FTA with the country, dissent as to the precise nature of the agreement rendered the process time-consuming. This was primarily due to the lack of strong coordination mechanisms within the European Commission at the time.

NAFTA as an important external development emerged in the same context as the EU's increasing interest in Latin America, albeit somewhat earlier. Much like the US became increasingly interested in strengthening its ties with the region as a whole, Mexico's inclusion in the NAFTA project between the US and Canada was only natural given the country's geographic proximity and the strong existing economic ties between the countries involved. With the signature of the agreement in 1992, only two years after the beginning of talks on the issue, and its coming into force in 1994, the process itself was speedy. The process and its progress have been explained by difficulties in liberalizing multilateral trade at the time (García, 2008: 60).

NAFTA left EU officials and member states worried about its terms of trade not only with Mexico itself, but also with all of the three North American countries, thus influencing the thought process that would lead to the EU's negotiations with the country (De Lombaerde et al., 2009; García, 2008: 75; Page, 2001: 127). While an FTA with the US or Canada was regarded as unrealistic at the time, Mexico would be able to provide a back door into NAFTA, all while the country signalled its interest in negotiating an FTA with the EU in an attempt to diversify the structure of its external trade. Furthermore, Mexico could serve a bridging function between North America and Latin America (Grevi and Khandekar, 2011; Hess, 2009), thus justifying a political focus on the country.

Concerns over worsening terms of trade became more and more widespread after NAFTA had entered into force[4] and its negative economic effects for the

EU could be felt in the rapid growth of US trade with the country compared to a limited growth in EU–Mexican trade. All of this would set Mexico apart from the upgrade of relations with the rest of the region (Sanahuja, 2000, 45–6), as FTAs with other Latin American countries were not envisioned at the time.

While EU member states and Commission officials agreed on the ultimate goal of an FTA with Mexico, discord over the details of the kind of agreement to be signed and the negotiation process rendered the process relatively lengthy and contributed to the separation of the EU's Mexico policy from the remainder of its Latin America policy. The key institutional factor in this development was the autonomy of the different portfolios within the European Commission.

The idea to upgrade EU–Mexico relations was initially discussed during the December 1994 European Council meeting in Essen, which urged the Commission to "put ideas on the future form of treaty relations with Mexico [...] into concrete form without delay" (European Council, 1994), recognizing the threat from NAFTA and taking note of the scheduled expiry of the existing agreement with the country in 1996 (Szymanski and Smith, 2005: 180). The shape of the proposed agreement with Mexico, however, was then developed in the Commission itself.

In essence, the document outlining its proposal for the evolution of the EU's treaty-based ties with the country proposed the conclusion of an Association Agreement, including an FTA, in all but its name (European Commission, 1995b). This was in line with Mexico's desire to deepen the relationship, which it voiced as early as September 1993, and which was already well received by the responsible European Commissioners of the time (Agence Europe, 1993). In 1995, and in parallel to the Commission's proposal, Mexico began strong lobbying efforts in Europe in support of such an agreement (Sanahuja, 2000: 46; Szymanski and Smith, 2005: 180), thus creating an additional external factor contributing to the EU's rationale to handle Mexico as a case apart.

While the Commission's 1995 paper specifically framed the proposed negotiations with the country in the context of the EU's Latin America strategy, its focus on economic and trade issues already set it apart in form. This is unsurprising given the division of Commission portfolios in the Santer Commission, with its previously noted negative consequences for the coordination of the EU's external policies (Dominguez, 2008: 132). Under this set-up, relations with Mexico formed part of Leon Brittan's portfolio which included North America, while the Latin America policy was Manuel Marín's responsibility, a state of affairs mirrored in the divisions between DG I and DG IB at the time. Brittan was thus able to initiate the process for an agreement with Mexico without extensive consultation and policy coordination with Marín and his DG, underlining the relevance of the autonomy of individual institutional actors.

In order to render Brittan's proposal and priorities for Mexico compatible with the wider Latin America strategy in more than rhetoric, and so as to overcome the divergence of positions between him and Marín, extensive coordination between these two portfolios and DGs would have been necessary, but was largely absent given the independence of Commissioners at the time. To make things worse, as mentioned previously, there was considerable hostility between Commissioners Brittan and Marín (Lister, 1997: 14).

The complexity of decision-making and the divergence of the positions of different member states further contributed to making the EU's Mexico policy a case apart. While member states agreed to Brittan's idea in principle, differences nonetheless arose between them as to the exact shape of negotiations and which elements to include, contributing to the relatively lengthy negotiation period overall. The main discord arose over whether the agreement to be negotiated with Mexico would contain an FTA component from the outset, as favoured by the Mexican side (Agence Europe, 1996c), or whether the political and dialogue component (for which negotiations would be led by Marín's DG) would come first, followed by a lengthier process of FTA negotiations. Agricultural issues were behind these disagreements despite the fact that trade in agricultural goods would play a considerably lesser role in negotiations with Mexico than in those with Mercosur (Allen and Smith, 1990: 104) discussed later on. Ultimately, the provision of an important safeguard to more sceptical countries, as well as putting the agreement on the agenda of pro-FTA Council presidencies over the negotiation period, helped to overcome these difficulties.

While Spain and the UK were particularly vocal as to the necessity of speedy FTA negotiations, thus advocating for a negotiation in a single undertaking (Agence Europe, 1996a, 1997d) given the negative economic effects of NAFTA, other countries voiced fears over the potential effects on European agricultural markets. In this case, a coalition centred around France, Portugal, and Austria opposed the negotiation of all elements at the same time, fearing that this would set a precedent for negotiations with Mercosur (Page, 2001: 127). Their concerns were shared by the Commissioner for Agriculture Franz Fischler (Peterson, 1999: 105).

These differences were slowly resolved by different Council presidencies— pointing to the importance of their autonomy at the time—which made progress on the agreement a policy priority. Spain's 1995 Council presidency made Latin American relations a focal element and included a goal to reach an agreement on negotiations with Mexico itself. However, a compromise on negotiations for the Global Agreement with Mexico was only reached under the Italian Council presidency in the first half of 1996. This was achieved by making concessions to the more reluctant camp by allowing for a two-tier process. Nonetheless, Spain provided the necessary groundwork for this to occur.[5] In line with its commitments towards the Latin American region, the German Council presidency in the first half of 1999 then allowed for important progress in the FTA negotiations (von Kyaw, 1999: 14), which was effectively concluded during Finland's tenure in the second half of 1999.

While previous research has pointed to important discord between the EU and Mexico in the negotiations concerning the inclusion of the "democracy clause" (Szymanski and Smith, 2005), interviews conducted for this book have provided for a different account of the events. Since 1995, a standard "democracy clause"— allowing for the suspension of the agreement if democratic principles were in danger—was to be included in all EU international agreements[6] and would thus also have to form part of the Global Agreement. Mexico had already attempted to resist the inclusion of a prior version in the 1991 Framework Agreement (del Arenal, 1997: 124) and did show a similar reluctance in the negotiations for the PCA. While the Commission initially agreed to modify the standard text for the agreement (Agence Europe, 1997b), this led to protests by a majority of member states (Agence Europe, 1997a) and finally Mexico agreed to the inclusion of the standard formulation (Agence Europe, 1997c).

Szymanski and Smith (2005) explain Mexico's initial reluctance by referring to the country's concerns that the clause would represent a limitation of its rights as a sovereign nation and that references to democratic governance would alter the technical nature of trade negotiations. Asked about this, however, an interviewee familiar with the negotiations asserted that the discord over the democracy clause had less to do with Mexico's position in itself, but rather with the position of Armen Dariz, Mexico's ambassador to the EU at the time.[7] According to this account, once the ambassador was recalled on the behest of the EU, the difficulties in the negotiations disappeared.

While the role of the European Parliament in the conclusion of international agreements was limited at this period of time, concerns of some of the political groups represented in it nonetheless briefly threatened the conclusion of the Global Agreement as its assent was nonetheless required due to the agreement being one for an Association, rather than a pure FTA. This development supports the analytical lens based on the complexity of the EU's decision-making system. The EP's concerns were due to Mexico's human rights track record, which led to the country's government to lobby the EP (see footnote 162 in Dominguez, 2008: 77), and Mexico's foreign minister was even questioned by it before the Members of the European Parliament (MEPs) agreed to its 1997 version (Szymanski and Smith, 2005: 127).

While NAFTA provided the rationale for the EU to separate Mexico from the remainder of its Latin America policy, the main influence on the shape of the ultimate agreement can be found in factors of bureaucratic politics. It is here that the final decision to negotiate all of the agreement's components in a single, yet two-step undertaking can be attributed directly to discord between the member states. Ultimately, the agreement reached during the Italian Council presidency of 1996 meant that this concession to the more sceptical countries was granted. As such, the version of the Global Agreement concluded in 1997 (European Commission, 1997) did not yet cover trade relations, for which negotiations only concluded in November of 1999, with the agreement entering into force in 2000. The agreement represented the first successful instance of a transatlantic free trade accord that was unprecedented in its depth and the number of cross-policy linkages at the time (Szymanski and Smith, 2005). The communication on its conclusion once more emphasized the important link to NAFTA, as it stated that the FTA component would see the EU receive similar treatment in Mexico as was the case for the US and Canada (European Commission, 2000).

Overall, the specific nature of the agreement and its outlier status from the EU's Latin America policy can be attributed to the fact that the responsibility for relations with the country in the Commission resided with Leon Brittan rather than Manuel Marín and that these could act largely independently, while a majority of member states was concerned over a loss of market share in the country to the US. While the issue of the democracy clause is important in itself, it has only shaped the timeline of the EU's negotiations, rather than the nature of the agreement.

Association Agreement negotiations with Mercosur and Chile

The negotiations with Mercosur were the EU's first attempt to conclude an Association Agreement with a regional organization. While the EU's decision to undertake negotiations was a logical continuation of the EU's Latin America strategy, the process was ultimately marred by many difficulties and a number of lengthy interruptions of the negotiations before these were finally concluded in principle after 20 years in 2019. This contrasts with the case of negotiations with Chile which were successfully concluded in 2002 already.

Both negotiations are discussed in parallel in this chapter, as they had been treated as such by the EU from the moment when negotiations were first envisioned. Consequently, the progress of EU decision-making on both negotiation mandates occurred in parallel until the negotiation phase when both processes were decoupled. The initial rationale for this link was the belief that Chile would ultimately enter into Mercosur itself, given that it didn't fit into any of the other regional integration mechanisms in the region.

> The underlying logic to this rationale was that if the EU created a free trade area with Mercosur and aided Mercosur to improve its own integration, there would be a greater incentive for Chile to fully enter Mercosur.
>
> (García, 2008: 123)

While the initiation of negotiations with Mercosur and Chile can be explained through a number of external factors, their development and the decoupling of negotiations with Chile need to consider bureaucratic politics within the EU.

Envisioning negotiations amidst Latin American integration dynamics

A number of external developments prompted the European Commission to begin the process of implementing its Latin America strategy by focusing on Association Agreement negotiations with Mercosur and Chile. While Manuel Marín was successful in pushing for the signature of a Framework Cooperation Agreement (FCA) with both Mercosur and Chile in 1995 and 1996, respectively, these fell short of the ambitions of Association Agreements. Preparatory work on the Association Agreements began as early as 1996 (Robles, 2008b: 338), but the process that would see the European Commission receive its negotiation mandate from the Council would take almost four years to complete (Faust, 2004: 46).

The main external motivating factor for the Commission's focus on these negotiations was the creation of Mercosur itself as the emergence of this new regional actor allowed the Commission to devise plans for the implementation of its Latin America strategy in absence of existing commitments.[8] As one interviewee put it, "Mercosur was the flavour of the month in the 1990s."[9] While Mercosur's creation was a strong external incentive in itself, once more broader trends in international trade policy need to be considered as well, such as problems arising in the negotiations for the Doha Development Agenda (DDA) at the WTO, and the shift of US trade policy towards the region.

The Commission's emphasis on implementing the EU's Latin America strategy can be seen in the trajectory of EU–Mercosur and Chile negotiations. While the FCAs with Mercosur and Chile had to be emptied of any trade component due to member state divisions, the Commission's negotiators were nonetheless successful in injecting language into these that would foresee the process of Association Agreement negotiations.

For instance, the EU's 1995 FCA with Mercosur states that:

> Parties shall undertake to forge closer relations with the aim of increasing and diversifying trade, preparing for subsequent gradual and reciprocal liberalization of trade and promoting conditions which are conducive to the establishment of the subsequent interregional Association.
>
> (Council of the European Union, 1995: Title 2, Article 4)

A similar provision can be found in the 1996 FCA with Chile (Council of the European Union, 1996: Title 3, Article 4). The parallel negotiations for the EU's Association Agreement with Mercosur provided an additional grounding for the Commission strategy, as the outcome from such negotiations would certainly serve as a blueprint for future agreements of the same type.

Even before the Commission officially envisioned entering into Association Agreement negotiations with these partners, DG IB under Marín's leadership had thus successfully pushed for a rhetorical commitment to such negotiations, aiming to help regional integration processes in the region. While it is advisable to question such publicly voiced rationales, research has pointed to the fact that this motivation was indeed present in the Commission and the wider EU foreign policy community at the time (Doctor, 2007: 291), supported by claims to this end by the EU's later chief negotiator (Falkenberg in Doctor, 2007: 291). Other researchers also agreed with this assessment, albeit also mentioning EU attempts to counterbalance US political influence in the region (Working Group on European Union–Mercosur Negotiations, 2005: 15).

While considerations of support for regionalism have provided for a rhetorical leitmotif for the Association Agreement negotiations with Mercosur and Chile, external developments in the realm of trade policy also coincide with Marín's attempts for these negotiations to get underway. This is a view favoured by Doctor:

Once one stripped away the 'distractions' offered by the many named or explicit objectives, it was patent that the substantive core of any agreement would be measured by the potential economic impacts of a bi-regional association as well as public perceptions thereof.

(Doctor, 2007: 297)

Though somewhat surprising given the rhetorical emphasis on regionalism support for its own sake at the time, the argument makes sense in the wider context of developments in trade policy.

Neither Chile nor Mercosur were major trade partners of the EU at the time, with Mercosur only accounting for 2.4% of the EU's total trade volume in goods in 2000, and Chile accounting for 0.4%. Nonetheless, economic growth on the continent rapidly increased the economic importance of both Mercosur and Chile. While the 1997–1998 financial crisis in emerging markets and the 2001–2002 Argentinian crisis put a brief dent into this positive track record and made Mercosur appear less economically attractive (Doctor, 2007: 290), in the 10 years after the FCA of 1995 the economies of the five countries concerned nevertheless managed to sustain average economic growth levels of 2% annually.

While this is lower than the growth rates in other emerging regions at the time, when the European Commission first proposed the draft negotiation mandates in July of 1998, it seemed as though the much more rapid economic growth of the previous years would continue into the future. Furthermore, over the course of the 1990s, the EU's positive trade balance with Mercosur gradually developed into a deficit, contributing to the EU's desire to pursue FTA negotiations with the organization (Robles, 2008a: 191).

While developments in the region hence provide an important backdrop for the Association Agreement negotiations, the wider context of WTO negotiations is more relevant. After the creation of the WTO in 1995, negotiations were underway under this new framework to liberalize trade in services and agriculture. In this context, Mercosur countries were extremely vocal in the late 1990s that the EU would have to liberalize its market to allow access for Latin American products (Müller-Brandeck-Bocquet, 2000: 573), and particularly agricultural products. This even led to an alliance of Mercosur, Chile, and the US in April 1999 ahead of a WTO negotiation round so as to pressure the EU into reforming its CAP (Agence Europe, 1999m) and thereby allowing the liberalization of trade in agriculture. In contrast, the European Union was particularly keen on the liberalization of services (covered under the ongoing WTO negotiations) and the public procurement sector.

As the areas discussed under WTO negotiations touched on many sensitive issues that would arise in the negotiations with Mercosur and Chile, important parallels are drawn below in the timeline of both negotiations. Overall, it is important to note that one can consider the decision to undertake and continue negotiations with Mercosur as a rational reassurance of the EU for the potential failure of the WTO DDA (Doctor, 2007: 291).

Aside from the factors outlined above, much like in the case of Mexico, the trade strategy of the US loomed over the thinking process within the European Commission. While discussed since 1994, negotiations for a Free Trade Area of the Americas (FTAA)[10] (Nelson, 2015: 79–83) finally started to take shape in the late 1990s (see Nelson, 2015: 63–112). The possibility of such an agreement coming to fruition put the EU under pressure to ensure continued market access in Latin America (Doctor, 2007: 291; Müller-Brandeck-Bocquet, 2000: 578). As Doctor has noted:

> Peaks in EU negotiation seriousness [for the EU-Mercosur Association Agreement] tended to coincide with peaks in perceived US influence in the region.
>
> (Doctor, 2007: 290)

This view of developing EU–Mercosur relations as a counterweight to the rapprochement of the US with Latin America under the FTAA project had at the time been voiced by French President Jacques Chirac, who saw the EU's ties with Mercosur as an important component of a multipolar world order (Barrau, 1999: 43; Santander, 2001: 62). After all, the creation of the FTAA could have jeopardized the EU's position as a more important trade partner for Mercosur than the US and was therefore an important background consideration for EU trade officials.[11]

Such thoughts were even more relevant in the case of the negotiation between the European Union and Chile.[12] It was the aim of both the EU and the US to sign FTAs with the country, with the EU's negotiations on the Association Agreement concluding a few months before the beginning of negotiations between the US and Chile. The EU's agreement with Chile entered provisionally into force in 2003, while negotiations between the US and Chile concluded in December 2002 only. The latter then entered into force in 2004.

The underlying economic factors for negotiations with Mercosur and Chile and the dynamism of regional integration in Mercosur thus provide for important external developments that contributed to the EU's desire to launch negotiations. Anecdotal evidence suggests that these views were indeed shared by different actors in the EU's foreign policy decision-making system and have thus served as the basis for the EU wanting to open negotiations with both. While the Commission desired to begin Association Agreement negotiations with Mercosur earlier on, by the late 1990s, this view had diffused throughout the EU's foreign policy decision-making system.

Commission divisions over proposed mandates

The process leading to the negotiations cannot be understood without a consideration of factors of bureaucratic politics, as divisions within the European Commission shaped the timeline for the granting of a negotiation mandate and the content of the mandate itself. This was primarily due to the fact that Commissioner Marín and Agriculture Commissioner Franz Fischler had diverging interests on the issue ahead of asking the Council to grant a negotiation mandate in July 1998. These divisions led to the rare event of a contested vote in the College of Commissioners before the process continued in the Council. The absence of functioning coordination mechanisms between Commission portfolios in the Santer Commission then shaped the EU's decision-making process once the Council discussed the negotiation mandate.

The autonomy of Commissioner Marín and DG IB in driving the Association Agreement process forward was crucial under the geographical division of competencies until 1999 (García, 2008: 135), as

> Manuel Marín [...] was a vehement advocate and driving force of a close partnership between EU and MERCOSUR.
>
> (Müller-Brandeck-Bocquet, 2000: 570–1)

Aside from the motivation arising out of Marín's own Latin America strategy, the prospect of the FTAA discussed above contributed to similar dynamics in the Commission as had been the case for negotiations with Mexico. Already in February of 1998, in a brief outlining the EU's preparations for the 1999 EU–Latin America summit, Commissioner Marín had promised that the Commission would draft a negotiation mandate by June (Agence Europe, 1998i). It would eventually take until 22 July for the Commission to submit such a proposal to the Council over disagreements with Franz Fischler.

Under normal circumstances, draft negotiation mandates prepared within the Commission's bureaucracy typically see very little opposition in the College of Commissioners due to their general nature. The case of the draft mandate for Mercosur and Chile negotiations thus differed, as the disagreements between Commissioners had more to do with diverging preferences as to the overall orientation of the EU's foreign policy, rather than the specific content of the mandate in itself (García, 2008: 139, 143). Franz Fischler's views on the mandate were influenced by powerful agricultural lobby groups, and particularly the Committee of Professional Agricultural Organisations (COPA). This grouping, as well as national farmer lobbies, started to voice opposition against EU negotiations with Mercosur around the time of the negotiations for the FCAs (Faust, 2004: 51), fearing that the European agricultural sector could be negatively affected by any kind of rapprochement with the region.

For instance, COPA voiced concerns in 1996 when the FCA with Mercosur came into being, arguing that the EU's agricultural products were essentially the same as those of Mercosur (Agence Europe, 1996b) and hence fearing that this would negatively affect the EU's CAP. In the more specific context of the EU–Mercosur FTA, organizations from the agricultural sector believed that ultimately it would be them who would have to pay for the benefits that others—and principally the industrial and services sectors—would gain from any form of agreement with Mercosur (Copa-Cogeca in García, 2008: 142; Working Group on European Union–Mercosur Negotiations, 2006: 27).

These groupings then pointed to the difficulties that any agreement with Mercosur would create in the ongoing process of CAP reform, while arguing that the agricultural issues at stake could only be resolved in the context of WTO negotiations (Doctor, 2007: 295). COPA additionally mentioned that the European Commission had committed itself at the Amsterdam Council meeting in 1998 not to conclude any further FTAs (Turner, 1998a). Fischler and his DG adopted this position, mentioning that agriculture would suffer the most under any Mercosur Association Agreement, while complicating the ongoing CAP reform even further (García, 2008: 141–2). This formed the basis for an important divergence of positions between two influential Commissioners.

The Commissioner responsible for relations with most of the developed world as well as the EU's position in the WTO, Leon Brittan, was initially similarly opposed to Marín's attempts, not only for the previously mentioned personal reasons, but because he favoured a different approach to EU FTA negotiations (Müller-Brandeck-Bocquet, 2000: 571). Instead of pushing for negotiations with emerging economies, Brittan was a strong advocate for developing ties with North America, and particularly the US, submitting a proposal to this end in March of 1998. His opposition weakened considerably when his project for what could have been a previous iteration of proposals for a Transatlantic Trade and Investment Partnership (TTIP) (European Commission, 1998) was dropped due to member state insistence, and particularly that of France (Müller-Brandeck-Bocquet, 2000: 570–1). Despite this, Brittan was already vocal in public about a date for the proposed mandate on a tour of Mercosur countries in April 1998 and even stressed that negotiations could begin at the 1999 EU–Latin America summit (Agence Europe, 1998j).

Despite Fischler's position extensive preparatory works for FTA negotiations were carried out within the Commission due to the autonomy of individual portfolios and their supporting DGs, completing an overview of existing trade relations and barriers between Mercosur and the EU, a so-called photography in April 1998 (Turner, 1998c) and officially by mid-May (Dauster, 1998: 447). While dissimilar from today's scoping exercises ahead of EU trade negotiations,[13] this was nonetheless a necessary precondition included in the previous FCA with Mercosur for putting Marín's proposal for Association Agreement negotiations on the table at a meeting of the College of Commissioners. The photography and an analysis by the European Commission found that there were no significant issues of trade sensitivity that would prevent the negotiation of a beneficial and WTO-compatible agreement with Mercosur (Müller-Brandeck-Bocquet, 2000: 570). Given that most development and political dialogue aspects were already covered by the previous FCA, no apparent difficulties would be present in those areas either, rendering it possible for Marín to table his proposal.

Before the initial vote scheduled on the draft mandate in the College on 8 July, Fischler sought to build a coalition of fellow Commissioners from France and southern Europe to postpone its decision to submit the mandate (Agence Europe, 1998k). He indeed received some support from Commissioners whose nationality was that of important agricultural producers: The two French Commissioners,

Yves-Thibault de Silguy (Economics and Finance) and Edith Cresson (Research, Science & Technology), and the Irish Commissioner Pádraig Flynn (Employment and Social Affairs) were all against Marín's proposal (Santander, 2001: 62–3).

A delay was indeed granted until 22 July (Agence Europe, 1999g) so as to study some of the reservations voiced by Fischler (Agence Europe, 1998h, 1998k). In the end, however, these views did not prevail and the proposal was transmitted to the Council for approval on that date. Most unusually for the consensus-driven decision-making process at this level, this resulted in a contested vote with four Commissioners voting against the proposed mandate after an extensive debate (Agence Europe, 1998e; García, 2008: 142). It appears though that four Commissioners, including Fischler, voted against submitting the proposed mandate to the Council. One account additionally lists de Silguy, Cresson, and Flynn (Agence Europe, 1998e); another mentions President Santer himself (García, 2008: 142).

In the end, the proposed mandate was indeed based on past agreements, and particularly the EU's most advanced agreements (García, 2008: 136–7) such as the Europe Agreements with Eastern Europe and the EU–Mexico Global Agreement. While the proposal remained vague on agriculture, leading to fears that Mercosur would reject the offer (Turner, 1998b), the negotiations were ultimately meant to cover all sectors of the economy (Müller-Brandeck-Bocquet, 2000: 573). Overall, the Commission had hence attempted to balance the sensitivity of agriculture with WTO requirements (Müller-Brandeck-Bocquet, 2000: 571), as well as the EU's trade interests. Marín framed the issue of the negotiations within the context of the FCAs at the press conference (Agence Europe, 1998e), downplaying both his personal role in the process and the divisive nature of the vote.

Ultimately, the Commission's proposal for a negotiation mandate was motivated primarily by the market prospects in Mercosur and Chile, as well as its possibility to support regional integration in the region (García, 2008: 137). However, the autonomy of the different Commission portfolios in the Santer years and the lack of functioning coordination mechanisms once more allowed Commissioner Marín to develop his preferred alternative further. Nonetheless, the presence of opposition within the Commission demonstrates that not all actors in the EU's foreign policy system shared the same views on the issue, leading to the contested vote on the draft negotiation mandate and a slight delay in the process. These differences of opinion, once extended to the realm of the Council, would ultimately prove fatal for the original negotiations with Mercosur while allowing those with Chile to move forward.

Agreeing the mandates in the Council

The period during which the Council deliberated on the negotiation mandates for the proposed Association Agreements with Mercosur and Chile lasted almost a year and was shaped by important disagreements between member states. Replicating the concerns elaborated on above in parts of the Commission, these were mainly related to agricultural questions and the strategy to pursue in the context of WTO negotiations.

The fact that the go-ahead for negotiations was ultimately given to the Commission in June 1999 can be explained by a number of factors. On the one hand, advocates for the agreement, such as the German Council presidency in the first half of 1999 and Commissioner Marín, used their positions to influence more sceptical actors. On the other, the previous commitments included in the FCAs by Marín, as well as the looming June 1999 EU–Latin America summit meant that the EU was already publicly committed to the project. In this case, policy inertia contributed to the EU beginning the negotiations in the first place.

While most member states agreed that it was necessary to support Mercosur integration and the democratization process in the region by negotiating agreements with both Mercosur and Chile (García, 2008: 147), differences in the realm of trade policy and related agricultural questions (García, 2008: 144) threatened to derail the process altogether. This is due to the fact that decisions on opening negotiations for Association Agreements require unanimity voting in the Council, hence giving every single member state a veto over the matter.

The agreements' strongest supporters in the Council were Spain and Germany, largely due to their economic interests in the region (García, 2008: 143). While not opposed to the negotiations per se, another group of member states, and particularly the Netherlands and the UK, favoured multilateral, rather than regional, trade negotiations (Agence Europe, 1999a) in the context of the WTO.

The strongest opponent of the proposed negotiations, however, was France. The country became vocal about it at the same time as these were being decided on in the College of Commissioners (Turner and Neligan, 1998). The French criticism was based on their own analysis of the likely impact of agricultural questions, and the country made the proposal to focus on the elimination of non-tariff barriers rather than to negotiate a full FTA with Mercosur (Agence Europe, 1998d).

At an Agriculture Council meeting on the same day as the College's meeting, the matter was discussed due to French insistence. At that point in time, 12 agricultural ministers noted concerns about the proposed mandate (Agence Europe, 1998a) with ministers from France, Germany, and Belgium seemingly the most concerned. While the Spanish minister showed some concerns as well, he simultaneously pointed to the potential positive aspects. At the same time, the Swedish, Danish, and British ministers appeared on the other side of the fence (Agence Europe, 1998a; European Voice, 1998). It is important to note here that the position of certain agricultural ministers did not match the overall structure of countries favouring and opposing an agreement with Mercosur, with the German minister being the most relevant outlier here.

The French reaction was not limited to the discussions in the Agriculture Council, as the French Foreign Ministry once more voiced its concerns and claimed that the Framework Agreements did not provide for FTA negotiations, hence accusing the Commission of non-compliance with the earlier agreements (Agence Europe, 1998f). In September, French Foreign Minister Hubert Vedrine reiterated the country's position himself and set conditions for a French agreement, namely wanting the prior completion of the ongoing CAP reform and WTO negotiations, as well as further prior integration within Mercosur itself (Agence Europe, 1998g). This was a set of conditions that would be impossible to fulfil, hence equating to a French veto on the opening of negotiations.

COPA and its allies continued their opposition by lobbying France and the different agricultural ministers to be sceptical of the Commission's proposal for both negotiations (García, 2008: 140–3). While other highly competitive sectors would have stood to gain from the negotiations (Faust, 2004: 51), their lobbying efforts were not as organized at the time, and civil society interest[14] was almost absent (García, 2008: 186–9). Initially, agricultural interest groups pointed to an incompatibility between the EU's reform agenda and any EU–Mercosur agreement. This view found some support with the French, Irish, and Dutch agriculture ministers (Santander, 2001: 62). When it became clear that some kind of agreement would be found in the Council, this strategy was altered, and the agricultural lobbies suggested that EU–Mercosur negotiations would have to be linked to the progress of WTO negotiations (Doctor, 2007: 295).

Given the difficulties of the Council in reaching an agreement on the proposed negotiation mandate, the responsible DG under Marín's leadership did not remain idle in attempting to influence the Council's decision-making process. It did so by using a variety of strategies, such as support for lobbying groups, re-emphasizing the necessity of interregional ties with Latin America, and conceding on some of the points raised by the critical member states in the Council. Once more, an available policy space, albeit constrained by the activity in the Council, was utilized by Marín to ensure the survival of his political agenda towards the end of his mandate.

Marín used his autonomy as a Commissioner to shape the rhetoric of the EU's relations with Latin America ahead of the 1999 Rio summit by publishing an updated Latin America strategy document in March of 1999. This coincided with the Commission's collective resignation and Marín taking over as the caretaker Commission president until the arrival of the Prodi Commission later on, further increasing his autonomy to shape the Commission's policy. The document portrays the negotiations with both actors as a natural progression from the FCAs signed earlier:

> Following the successes of the 1995 and 1996 agreements aimed inter alia at paving the way for free trade, the EU is examining new initiatives with a view to establishing interregional association agreements [with Mercosur and Chile] covering three key areas: the strengthening of political dialogue, the progressive establishment of a free-trade area and deeper cooperation.
>
> (European Commission, 1999: 5)

It also emphasizes that developing these ties in a similar manner as those with Mexico was only logical (European Commission, 1999: 5). At the same time, the document ensured that a distinction was made between entities with whom Association Agreement negotiations would be sensible and those with whom they would not, thus excluding a similar possibility for the Andean Community and Central America (Agence Europe, 1999b). As the date of the summit approached,

Commissioner Marín also became increasingly vocal about his antipathy towards the French position and mentioned the potential loss of face for the EU if it were to go to the EU–Latin America summit without a mandate for negotiations (Harding, 1999a).

But DG IB's actions did not remain limited to attempting to influence the Council's decision-making process through mere rhetoric. Facing the opposition of agricultural lobbies and the positions of some Commissioners and member states, Marín's bureaucrats became actively involved in rallying businesses that would benefit from an envisioned FTA with Mercosur. It thus helped to create the Mercosur–Europe Business Forum (MEBF) (Santander, 2005: 295; Torrelli, 2003: 9–10), which was meant to act as a counterpart to COPA and its allies. While it was dominated by German firms at first during the Council's decision-making phase (García, 2008: 146), its membership would rise over the course of the actual negotiations.

The MEBF then launched a campaign to convince the Council to agree to a mandate, all while lobbying respective national governments. The forum had privileged access to decision-makers at the national and EU levels due to the involvement of CEOs from large companies across the continent, but particularly in Germany and Mediterranean EU countries (for a list of the companies involved in the MEBF see Torrelli, 2003: 7). The lobbying attempts appear to have had an influence at the very least in the case of Germany, as officials from that country have admitted to trying to forge a consensus in the Council largely due to German business interests (García, 2008: 146). While the companies represented in the MEBF on the European side all had similar interests in Chile, no specific organization was set up for that purpose, nor did the MEBF specifically address the Chile negotiations (García, 2008: 194).

Given these differences not only between individual member states, but also within the Commission itself, the ultimate go-ahead for negotiations with Mercosur and Chile can be attributed to successful bargaining in the Council as mediated by Germany and Spain (García, 2008: 146–7; Müller-Brandeck-Bocquet, 2000: 571), as well as the looming deadline of the 1999 EU–Latin America summit (García, 2008: 135–6). Germany's position was particularly privileged as it disposed of an important autonomy to shape the process given its Council presidency in the first half of 1999.

While the differences between the EU's member states remained unresolved over the course of 1998, attempts to reconcile the different positions were made by Germany once it had taken over the presidency, with the aim of coming to an agreement during the General Affairs Council (GAC) meeting on 31 May (Agence Europe, 1999h)—just in time for the 1999 EU–Latin America summit. Given the symbolic nature of this first-ever summit of its kind, it needed to be filled with some relevant content, and the announcement of negotiations between the EU and Mercosur and Chile would have been ideal for this purpose.[15]

Within this framing, important efforts got underway to build coalitions in order to reach an agreement ahead of the deadline that the Council had set itself. This also helped to sway the French position, as by February 1999 its strategy had shifted to trying to delay any actual decision on negotiations with Mercosur until after the summit itself (Agence Europe, 1999a), all while symbolically launching them during the summit.

Nonetheless, over time, different proposals were floated to overcome the internal differences. For instance, France, Ireland, and the UK were behind a proposed formula that would see the negotiations only aim for an FTA (rather than necessitating one) (Agence Europe, 1999j), with the Scandinavians and Benelux countries backing similar compromise solutions by the German Council presidency (Agence Europe, 1999j). On the other side of the divide were Spain, Portugal, and Italy as strong supporters of spelling out the goal of an FTA in itself. Similar coalition patterns could be found on whether the mandate should include a proposed timeline for the negotiations.

Nonetheless, no agreement was found by the self-imposed deadline and the topic put on the agenda of the June Cologne European Council meeting (Agence Europe, 1999e). To the surprise of different observers (Agence Europe, 1999i; Riccardi, 1999), the European Council's conclusions then made no mention of the issue. Ultimately, the Council only came to a last-minute agreement during a special session of the GAC on 21 June (Agence Europe, 1999d), just prior to the start of the EU–Latin America summit itself. Nonetheless, it would then take until 15 September for the actual negotiation briefs to be decided on in a GAC meeting (Agence Europe, 1999k), allowing the negotiations to get underway in earnest.

The ultimate compromise reached was a Franco-Spanish one (Agence Europe, 1999d). It aimed for tariff negotiations with Mercosur by July 2001—and hence implicitly linking it to the scheduled conclusion of WTO trade talks, while removing the necessity for the creation of an FTA and thereby potentially easing WTO rules that would have required a large opening in the agricultural realm (Agence Europe, 1999d). This was also possible due to the Commission conceding on the wording with the ultimate formulation to "negotiate a commercial liberalization *aiming* at the creation of an FTA" (García, 2008: 147), allowing everyone to read into it what they chose. Lastly, due to French insistence, the mandate did not contain a date by which negotiations were supposed to be finalized. Unofficially, however, Mercosur's countries, as well as member states like Italy and Spain, wanted to see the conclusion of negotiations by 2005 (Harding, 1999b).

Ultimately, France gave in on many of the issues due to their belief in counterbalancing the FTAA project and providing an insurance policy against the failure of ongoing WTO negotiations (Agence Europe, 1999h). Nonetheless, the country's ultimate change of position has been explained as follows:

> President Chirac himself had launched the idea of an EU-Latin American summit [...] and France would have been threatened by a serious loss of face if it had continued to offer resistance.
>
> (Müller-Brandeck-Bocquet, 2000: 571)

While in the end the Commission (and its negotiation partner Mercosur) appeared to be relatively happy with the Council compromise on the mandate (Agence

Europe, 1999f), it nevertheless severely restricted the room for manoeuvre of the European Commission (Working Group on European Union–Mercosur Negotiations, 2005: 15), rendering it difficult for the institution to conduct negotiations as it saw fit (see below). This came about despite the Commission's expertise in the area and its access to a large pool of information on trade relations with Mercosur due to its preparatory work. It is hence possible that part of the initial failure of the Mercosur negotiations was premeditated due to the negotiation compromise found in the Council.

While the Council ultimately reached a consensus on opening negotiations with Mercosur and Chile, this section has shown that the process was shaped importantly by bureaucratic politics affecting the negotiation strategy of the EU. Once more, the divergence of positions, primarily along the lines of member states supporting free trade with Mercosur and those concerned over the likely impact on the EU's CAP, put the suggested timeline at risk and led to a negotiation mandate that tied the Commission negotiators to the timeline of ongoing WTO talks. Furthermore, the autonomy of individual actors helped the formulation of the compromise proposal, alongside the EU's policy inertia arising out of previous (rhetorical) commitments towards Mercosur and Chile.

Negotiations with Mercosur

After the just-in-time agreement by the Council that the EU would indeed undertake negotiations with Mercosur, the EU–Latin America Rio de Janeiro summit final communiqué included wording that the negotiations would officially begin at an EU–Mercosur Joint Council—an institution set up under the previous FCA—to be held on the fringe of the November 1999 GAC meeting (Agence Europe, 1999l).

While a launch date for the negotiations was hence found, the communique explicitly did not include a timeframe within which negotiations should be concluded. Technical talks on the overall structure and chapters of negotiations were then underway in the second half of 1999, with the Cooperation Council[16] setting the agenda for the actual negotiation rounds that began in April 2000 (Agence Europe, 1999c, 1999l).

By this time, the new Prodi Commission had taken office, fundamentally revamping the portfolios of the Commission, as well as the underlying DGs. This meant that a new team of Commissioners took over with responsibilities for individual EU policies. Consequently, negotiations on the trade components of the proposed agreement were led by the newly created DG Trade under Commissioner Pascal Lamy, while DG RELEX under Chris Patten was responsible for the remainder and coordination of policies under the agreement, creating further potential for diverging interests between both entities in the Commission. The only remaining Commissioner from the previous Commission was Franz Fischler, whose portfolio was enlarged to include fisheries. Despite their nominal supervisory role, all three Commissioners would take an active role in the negotiations.

What is most fascinating though is that the Commission's new set-up was divided by policy areas rather than geographical regions. This shake-up of personnel and the fact that its negotiation mandate was relatively clear appears to have put an end to most divisions internal to the Commission. While Brazilian officials felt that Fischler's former scepticism negatively affected the launch of negotiations, they argued that as these continued the Commission appeared to be united, as opposed to the EU's member states.[17] This is even more surprising as the new RELEX Director-General Guy Legras previously held the same position in DG Agriculture and had voiced strong concerns over the prospects of an EU–Mercosur agreement (Agence Europe, 2000d). Despite this, all three Commissioners appear to have defended the negotiations against criticism from other internal EU actors and acknowledged that the EU would have to make important concessions on agriculture early on (Agence Europe, 2000e).

While negotiations on the political dialogue and cooperation elements supervised by DG RELEX proceeded quickly (Agence Europe, 2000b), given their similarity to the previous FCA, the broader trade agenda and agricultural issues were initially bracketed from the negotiations in line with the Council-mandated WTO link. This meant that early reports over quick progress in the negotiations were necessarily exaggerated by the focus on these issues.

Despite the fact that no progress was made in the Doha Round until July 2001, the trade chapter was nonetheless opened after that date in line with the original mandate from the Council. It is from this critical phase of the negotiations onwards that difficulties between the parties and within the EU itself once more came to the fore. An external factor complicating the talks was the fact that Mercosur's institutions were not as integrated as the EU's, leading to confusion amongst the EU's negotiators as to who was authorized to speak on Mercosur's side.[18] Furthermore, while the trade chapter was opened in 2001, one interviewee cautioned that none of the difficult questions had truly been addressed in talks up to an initial breakdown of negotiations in 2004.[19]

Looking at the constellation of actors on the EU's side, the opening of the trade negotiations meant that lobbying organizations came to be increasingly active once more, with aggressive lobbying by the industrial and services sectors (Doctor, 2007: 294). While the creation of the MEBF had helped to ensure that negotiations would go ahead in the first place, its lobbying efforts were less prominent at this stage. Its members had previously been able to agree on the benefits of launching negotiations with Mercosur; however, its diverse membership now rendered the formulation of a coherent position more and more difficult (Doctor, 2007: 295; Faust, 2004: 52). This was also related to the fact that Spanish firms took a more and more active role in the MEBF as negotiations progressed (Torrelli, 2003: 8–9), counterbalancing the previous domination of German firms in this entity.

The Commission continued to be a strong supporter of the agreement, for instance flanking the negotiations with heavily increased development budgets for regionalism support in 2002 (Agence Europe, 2002g, 2002h). The Commission's activities led Mercosur officials to state publicly that they believed the

Commission was more favourable towards the negotiations than the member states (Agence Europe, 2002f). Its view was further supported by the European Parliament, which repeatedly called on member states to remove the restriction on negotiations for trade issues ahead of the July 2001 deadline, and thus positioning itself against the more sceptical member states (Agence Europe, 2001a).

The most relevant actors on the EU's side at this stage were the member states, given that the Commission's room for manoeuvre in the negotiations had been severely limited beforehand by the negotiation mandate. During the negotiation rounds, they were continually present in the form of a special committee to observe the process and so as to provide constant input for the Commission's negotiators. As this process is entirely secret and unrecorded, very little public information is available on it. García has argued, however, that the member state presence in the form of the committee had a significant impact on the progress of the negotiations (García, 2008: 185), and their differing views determined the progress and dynamics of the entire process.

The coalitions of supporters and more sceptical member states did not change radically, with Germany continuing to be the strongest proponent for the agreement. While Spain and Portugal were keen on supporting Mercosur through this process (Agence Europe, 2002d), the former's position was somewhat mixed. On the one hand, Spain accused the Commission of neglecting Latin America in its development policy, while insisting that agricultural concessions to Mercosur would have been carefully balanced internally (Agence Europe, 2000c). France, on the other hand, retained its scepticism across the board.

Given that the most difficult questions were bracketed from the negotiations at first, the largest risks during this part of the negotiation phase occurred with the Argentinian crisis in April 2002 (Agence Europe, 2002e, 2002i), and the election of Luiz Lula da Silva as president of Brazil in 2003, which weakened the country's attitude towards free trade. Commission officials were furthermore increasingly worried that Mercosur's regional integration hadn't gone far enough to ensure the successful conclusion of negotiations.[20]

While these external developments could have altered the EU's reasoning to abandon the negotiations, a number of other external developments, the EU's policy inertia, and the autonomy of the Commission negotiators meant that these continued for the time being. Negotiations at this stage were helped by a continued lack of progress in the realm of the WTO Doha Round and the continuing talks towards an FTAA. It was the overall absence of a multilateral WTO deal on the trade issues to be considered in the Mercosur negotiations (García, 2008: 150) that enabled the negotiations to get underway in the first place.

The lack of progress on agricultural issues in the WTO then also took pressure off the EU to make important concessions in the talks with Mercosur (Müller-Brandeck-Bocquet, 2000: 577–8). This overall lack of progress in the WTO realm has probably kept the negotiations alive for longer than they would have otherwise as "abandoning talks was not on the cards, partly as a hedge against the (increasingly likely) possible failure of the Doha Round" (Doctor, 2007: 291).

This external factor was aided by the fact that DG Trade had already invested heavily in the negotiations by then and that the Commission's negotiators were sufficiently autonomous to keep making offers despite some reservations in the Council.[21] Commission officials were conscious of the fact nonetheless that they would have to negotiate with the member states internally over which concessions they could offer.[22]

These developments led high-level officials to believe that negotiations could indeed conclude successfully, so that at a November 2003 ministerial meeting a timetable was set to end negotiations in October 2004 (Agence Europe, 2003b, 2003c, 2003d). This goal was reiterated at the May 2004 EU–Latin America summit in Guadalajara (Agence Europe, 2004f). Nonetheless, negotiations would ultimately break down once more difficult aspects were put on the table, and particularly in the realm of agriculture. By 2004, detailed market access offers were discussed between both sides, with the Commission's negotiators making extensive offers including in the agricultural realm so as to enable a successful conclusion of the negotiations (Agence Europe, 2004h).

Internal EU differences were then quick to crop up again as multiple member states voiced their criticism as to the willingness of the Commission to open up the EU's agricultural market for imports from Mercosur (Agence Europe, 2004i), with Commissioner Fischler stepping in to defend the offer made by the Commission, pointing in particular to the Commission's previous impact assessments (Agence Europe, 2004e). Member state criticism was partly fuelled by COPA's renewed lobbying against the agreement at critical junctures during the negotiation process (Agence Europe, 2004a, 2004b).

The concerns over agricultural issues did not only come to the fore once more at this point in time because they were on the table by then, but also because the perceived risk of losing market access with the FTAA had been averted due to the failure of these negotiations in 2004 (Nelson, 2015: 110). Despite these difficulties and the reduced incentives for the EU, the Guadalajara Declaration issued during the EU–LAC summit in May 2004 reiterated the rhetorical link between Association Agreements and the support of regional integration:

> In view of the progress achieved, we reconfirm the positive signal given by the Madrid Declaration in relation to the negotiation of Association Agreements, including Free Trade Agreements. Such Association Agreements are our common strategic objective. The Parties recognise that the prospect of Association Agreements should give a new impetus for strengthening regional economic integration processes.
>
> (Council of the European Union, 2004: 8)

The document also officially welcomed the progress in the negotiations and set a deadline for October 2004 for these to conclude (Council of the European Union, 2004: 8). Nonetheless, negotiations had come to an effective deadlock at the next negotiation round less than a month later in mid-June of 2004 over agricultural and public procurement issues (Agence Europe, 2004c). While the EU's chief negotiator Karl Falkenberg initially remained optimistic, stating that negotiations could still conclude before the end of the term of the Commission at the end of October that year (Agence Europe, 2004h), no progress was made at further negotiation rounds (Agence Europe, 2004k) and a final ministerial meeting on 20 October led to a suspension of negotiations (Agence Europe, 2004j).

The main differences between both sides occurred over the degree to which each other's markets would have to open up. While the initially proposed FTA would ultimately have to liberalize at least roughly 90% of trade within 10 years under WTO rules (García, 2008: 138–9), both sides disagreed on whether this was actually the case. An EU official has put the blame on Mercosur's market access offer stating that it was non-compliant with WTO rules.[23] Brazilian officials, however, have put the blame on the limited agricultural concessions offered by the EU.[24]

There is some truth in both sides of the argument, as the Council's Article 133 Committee on 7 June 2004 made clear to the Commission that the member states would not accept any further concessions to Mercosur (Agence Europe, 2004d), having been critical of the Commission's negotiation strategy for some time (Agence Europe, 2004g). While several attempts were made to relaunch the process throughout 2005 and 2006 (Agence Europe, 2005, 2006), the EU had essentially frozen negotiations as of 2005.[25]

However, negotiations were never officially abandoned but left in limbo for a very long period of time. It took until 2010, and therefore after the institutional changes of the Lisbon Treaty (including a change of most EU-level politicians involved), for the process to be relaunched (DG Trade, 2010). This was mainly down to internal political divisions within Mercosur, but also the considerable differences of both sides' positions.[26] While the pace of negotiations then picked up initially, this then slowed down alongside decreasing public interest in the process. It would then take close to another 10 years for significant progress to be made on the matter.

It was ultimately another attempt to inject new dynamism into the negotiations by exchanging detailed offers in 2016 (DG Trade, 2016) which contributed to a situation whereby the negotiations could be successfully concluded in the following years. What is relevant, however, is that over the course of the entire negotiations the initial negotiation mandate from the period predating the Treaty of Lisbon ultimately survived. In consequence, much like other negotiations taking place in the aftermath of the treaty (as discussed in Chapter 6), negotiations could relaunch under the leadership of DG Trade.[27] DG Trade's activity from 2016 onwards and the exchange of market access offers were then in turn the result of coordination with other relevant Commission DGs, such as DG Agriculture.[28]

Given the age of the original mandate for negotiations with the bloc, the activity of the new EEAS has been somewhat more muted in this regard as the original mandate for political negotiations is rather limited, and the fact that trade negotiations happen with four individual countries, rather than Mercosur's central institutions.[29] This can also explain why the non-trade related parts of the ultimate Association Agreement could already be sealed over the course of 2018, while an agreement in principle on its FTA portion was only found in June of 2019 (DG Trade, 2019).

Nonetheless, these negotiations were not the only activity in the realm of the EU's ties to the region, as the EU decided to intensify its political ties to Brazil during the hiatus in negotiations by declaring the country a strategic partner of the EU in 2007. While this intensified the EU's rhetorical commitment to its relationship with one of only four Mercosur countries, it ultimately remains of a declaratory nature and has strained the EU's relations to other Mercosur members, and Argentina, in particular (Schade, 2019).

The negotiation phase with Mercosur was thus shaped by a number of parallel dynamics. While a number of external developments have indeed altered the EU's rationale at the time when negotiations were first opened, these are not sufficient to explain the dynamics of the negotiation process. This was shaped in part through dynamics in the realm of bureaucratic politics, such as the limitations of the previous negotiation mandate, which made for the most difficult issues being bracketed from the initial negotiations, thus underpinning the complexity of the EU's decision-making underpinning Association Agreements and its ultimate policy inertia. On the other hand, the initial reorganization of the European Commission and the change of personnel led to a disappearance of the divergence of interests internal to the Commission, and the autonomy of its (trade) negotiators meant that the negotiations proceeded despite divisions amongst the member states in the Council.

Yet it is this presence of diverging interests on agricultural issues and the failure of the FTAA project that led to the initial breakdown of negotiations with Mercosur. It was only the relative policy autonomy of DG Trade after the switchover to the EU's post-Lisbon set-up had occurred that then allowed for negotiations to resume and conclude in principle by the middle of 2019.

Negotiations with Chile

Following from the parallel nature of the decision-making process in the Commission and then the Council, the EU–Latin America summit of 1999 also marked the official start of negotiations with Chile, and these were then still tied to the timeframe for the Mercosur negotiations. Nonetheless, these were decoupled later on in the process. In this case, it was the relative absence of agricultural issues in the relationship, the prospect of a US–Chilean FTA, Chilean lobbying, and the EU's policy inertia that meant that once Mercosur negotiations started to become more difficult, the EU decoupled the processes to speed up negotiations with Chile itself. This would lead to a conclusion of negotiations in April 2002, just in time to be announced at the 2002 EU–Latin America summit in Madrid.[30]

While the parallelism of both processes was initially meant to contribute to Chile's rapprochement with Mercosur, the country made it clear that it was interested primarily in bilateral ties with the EU.[31] Chilean officials had been critical of the fact that the EU desired to couple the processes together from the outset (Agence Europe, 1998g), arguing that FTA negotiations with Chile would be much simpler than within the complex setting of Mercosur and given differences over agricultural questions (Agence Europe, 1998b), a view confirmed by inter-viewees who mentioned only some difficulties in the realm of fisheries due to Spanish demands.[32]

Some officials in the European Commission shared this assessment already in 1998, fearing that the difficulties of the Mercosur progress could derail the Chilean negotiations (Agence Europe, 1998c). While the Chile negotiations were technically subject to the same delay due to the ongoing WTO negotiations, the Commission's Chief Negotiator Guy Legras first mentioned its desire to decouple the Chile negotiations from the WTO process in late June 2001 at an EU–Chile Cooperation Council (Agence Europe, 2001b), as it became clear that a multi-lateral consensus at the WTO appeared to be out of sight. Additionally, Com-missioner Patten—who had taken a personal interest in the EU–Latin America summit format (Agence Europe, 2001c)—had already stressed in 2000 that, in his opinion, negotiations could conclude in time for the 2002 EU–Latin America summit (Agence Europe, 2000a).

The main supporter of decoupling at the time was Spain (Agence Europe, 2001b), as it would host the 2002 summit during its Council presidency, and the conclusion of negotiations would be a worthwhile announcement. While by early 2002 some difficulties remained in the negotiations for a few member states, a GAC meeting on 28 January officially affirmed that negotiations would be sped up (Agence Europe, 2002b) and the WTO link removed. Ultimately, negotiations concluded on 26 April, in time for the agreement to be initialled at the II EU–Latin America summit in Madrid (Agence Europe, 2002a). The signature followed in November after legal revisions and translations (Agence Europe, 2002c), with the trade chapter of the agreement coming into effect on 1 February 2003 (Agence Europe, 2003a).

During the actual negotiations, the member states were represented similarly to the Mercosur negotiations in a special committee to give continuous input to the Commission's negotiators. Their influence through this official body appears to have been relatively limited in this instance however (García, 2008: 185), as no significant divergences of opinion existed, and member states and DG Trade under Pascal Lamy were concerned about the progress of FTAA negotiations and the prospect of a separate US–Chile agreement from the outset. Interestingly, and contrasting with the case of negotiations with Mercosur, it was the EU that ultimately concluded an agreement with the country first, with bilateral Chilean–US negotiations only being launched afterwards in August 2002 (Agence Europe, 2002j).

While the process for EU–Chile negotiations was initially coupled with that for EU–Mercosur negotiations, the slow progress in the latter and the looming risk of once more losing market access to the US ultimately contributed to a change of heart amongst both the new Commission and the member states, allowing for a bilateral EU–Chile Association Agreement to be signed. It is striking that there appears to be no evidence for the decoupling of the negotiations being discussed in the context of the EU's wider Latin America strategy, which is likely down to the autonomy of DG Trade during the Prodi years and thus the source of a wider inconsistency of the EU's policy towards the wider region at the time.

Conclusion

This chapter has shown various elements of bureaucratic politics at play that have been identified in the analytical framework beforehand. When considering the process that led to the EU–Mexico Global Agreement, it is clear that the autonomy of individual Commissioners and their DGs within the Commission has helped the project move forward outside of the context of the EU's wider relations with the Latin American region. At the same time, the economic concerns of the member states helped to forge a consensus on the necessity of concluding an FTA with Mexico, thus demonstrating how a specific constellation of bureaucratic factors has helped in the successful conclusion of said agreement.

This was somewhat different in the case of negotiations with Mercosur and Chile. While similar issues of Commissioner autonomy helped lay the groundwork for both negotiations, the differing views between various Commissioners on the prospect of negotiations with Mercosur in the agricultural realm made it more difficult for the Commission to officially launch the process leading to the granting of a negotiation mandate. Something similar could then be observed in the Council. Aside from factors internal to Mercosur, it was then similar issues which contributed to the initial failure of negotiations with this organization.

The negotiations with Chile then demonstrate how both path dependence and an absence of similar issues for internal conflict could lead to a relatively rapid conclusion of an Association Agreement. Lastly, the process leading to the now likely conclusion of an Association Agreement with Mercosur then demonstrated the effect that the long duration of particular EU negotiations can have on the underlying bureaucratic structure and hence the bureaucratic politics in play.

Notes

1 Former DG RELEX official, Brussels (Interview 18).
2 Former EU official, Brussels (Interview 17); Member state diplomat, Brussels (Interview 29).
3 This international organization was founded in 1986. At the time of the signature of the Rome Declaration, its membership included all hispano- and lusophone countries of South America and Mexico. Over time, its membership has grown to include all Latin American and some Caribbean states.
4 Former EU official, Brussels (Interview 17) and Szymanski and Smith (2005: 173).
5 Former EU official, Brussels (Interview 17).
6 For a detailed discussion of the evolution of the democracy clause, see Crawford (1997).
7 Former EU official, Brussels (Interview 17).
8 Former EU official, Brussels (Interview 17).

9 Former Latin American diplomat, Hamburg (Interview 2).
10 This was an attempt to conclude a continent-wide FTA in the Americas.
11 Former EU official, Brussels (Interview 17).
12 Former EU official, Brussels (Interview 17).
13 DG Trade official, Brussels (Interview 12).
14 For an overview over interest group, and particularly civil society involvement in Mercosur and Chile, see Cecilia Alemany (2004).
15 Former EU official, Brussels (Interview 17).
16 A regular meeting at the ministerial level established through the FCA. Similar mechanisms were established with Mexico and Chile.
17 Latin American diplomats, Brussels (Interview 7).
18 European Parliament official (Interview 14).
19 Former EU official, Brussels (Interview 17).
20 European Parliament official (Interview 14).
21 Latin American diplomats, Brussels (Interview 7).
22 EU trade official, Brussels (Interview 12).
23 EU officials, Brussels (Interview 11).
24 Latin American diplomats, Brussels (Interview 7).
25 Member state diplomat, Brussels (Interview 19).
26 Member state diplomat, Brussels (Interview 9).
27 DG Trade official, Brussels (Interview 32).
28 DG Trade official, Brussels (Interview 32).
29 Senior EEAS official, Brussels (Interview 32).
30 For a more detailed overview over the EU–Chile negotiation process, see García (2008, 2011).
31 Former EU official, Brussels (Interview 17).
32 Former EU official, Brussels (Interview 17).

Bibliography

Agence Europe (1990) Development Council—Future Cooperation with Asia and Latin America. *Agence Europe*, 30 November. Brussels. Available at: Factiva Document AGEU000020011129dmbu0039h (accessed 9 April 2018).

Agence Europe (1992) Conclusions of Ministerial Meeting Between the EC and the Rio Group. *Agence Europe*, 30 May. Brussels. Available at: Factiva Document AGEU000020011122do5u00ae2 (accessed 9 April 2018).

Agence Europe (1993) Mexico—Messrs Delors and Salinas Express Intention to Make Existing Accord More Complete. *Agence Europe*, 25 September. Brussels. Available at: Factiva Document AGEU000020011121dp9p007w3 (accessed 9 April 2018).

Agence Europe (1996a) EU15 Disagree on Nature and Contents of Mexican Agreement. *Agence Europe*, 14 February. Brussels. Available at: Factiva Document AGEU000020011016ds2e005tj (accessed 9 April 2018).

Agence Europe (1996b) EU/Mercosur—Cooperation Agreement Enters into Operational Phase. *Agence Europe*, 7 June. Brussels. Available at: Factiva Document AGEU000020011016ds6700811 (accessed 9 April 2018).

Agence Europe (1996c) Mexico Stresses Specific Nature of Agreement Envisaged with EU. *Agence Europe*, 17 February. Brussels. Available at: Factiva Document AGEU000020011016ds2h0060w (accessed 9 April 2018).

Agence Europe (1997a) EU/Mexico—'Adjustments' to Human Rights Clause Raise Difficulties. *Agence Europe*, 20 June. Brussels. Available at: Factiva Document AGEU000020010928dt6k000em (accessed 9 April 2018).

Agence Europe (1997b) EU/Mexico—End of Negotiations for an Interim, Global and Political Agreement. *Agence Europe*, 13 June. Brussels. Available at: Factiva Document AGEU000020010928dt6d007sm (accessed 9 April 2018).

Agence Europe (1997c) EU/Mexico—Negotiations Are Over. *Agence Europe*, 21 June. Brussels. Available at: Factiva Document AGEU000020010928dt6l000hr (accessed 9 April 2019).

Agence Europe (1997d) EU/Mexico—Negotiations for an Interim Agreement Begin Tuesday. *Agence Europe*, 10 June. Brussels. Available at: Factiva Document AGEU000020010928dt6a007om (accessed 9 April 2018).

Agence Europe (1998a) EU/Agriculture Council—Majority of Agriculture Ministers Express Concerns and Reluctance Regarding Plans for a Free Trade Area with Mercosur. *Agence Europe*, 23 July. Brussels. Available at: Factiva Document AGEU000020010921du7n000ze (accessed 9 April 2018).

Agence Europe (1998b) EU/Chile—Chile's Authorities Say Free Trade Project Raises Few Problems That Could Be Settled Easily. *Agence Europe*, 14 October. Brussels. Available at: Factiva Document AGEU000020010921duae002g6 (accessed 9 April 2018).

Agence Europe (1998c) EU/Chile/Mercosur. *Agence Europe*, 15 May. Brussels. Available at: Factiva Document AGEU000020010921du5f0074e (accessed 9 April 2018).

Agence Europe (1998d) EU/Mercosur/Chile. *Agence Europe*, 17 July. Brussels. Available at: Factiva Document AGEU000020010921du7h000vr (accessed 9 April 2018).

Agence Europe (1998e) EU/Mercosur/Chile—Commission Recommendation to Council for Approval to Negotiate Association Comprising Free Trade Area, Enhanced Cooperation, Political and Security Partnership. *Agence Europe*, 23 July. Brussels. Available at: Factiva Document AGEU000020010921du7n000zd (accessed 9 April 2018).

Agence Europe (1998f) EU/Mercosur/Chile—France Affirms That Commission Proposal on Free-Trade Area Does Not Conform to What Was Agreed and Recommend 'Other Ways' of Strengthening Relations. *Agence Europe*, 25 July. Brussels. Available at: Factiva Document AGEU000020010921du7p00120 (accessed 9 April 2018).

Agence Europe (1998g) EU/Mercosur/Chile—France Gives Qualified Confirmation of Its Position on Trade Negotiations. *Agence Europe*, 23 September. Brussels. Available at: Factiva Document AGEU000020010921du9n001x5 (accessed 9 April 2018).

Agence Europe (1998h) EU/Mercosur/Chile—Postponing Future Trade Relations. *Agence Europe*, 9 July. Brussels. Available at: Factiva Document AGEU-000020010921du790044z (accessed 9 April 2018).

Agence Europe (1998i) EU/Rio Group—Preparing for a Summit. *Agence Europe*, 7 February. Brussels. Available at: Factiva Document AGEU000020010921du27004tm (accessed 9 April 2018).

Agence Europe (1998j) EU/Trade—Sir Leon Confirms That a Negotiating Brief for Trade Liberalization with Mercosur Will Be Put Before the Council in June and Argues in Favour of the 'Millennium Round' in the WTO. *Agence Europe*, 17 April. Brussels. Available at: Factiva Document AGEU000020010921du4h006gx (accessed 9 April 2018).

Agence Europe (1998k) Mercosur/Chile. *Agence Europe*, 4 July. Brussels. Available at: Factiva Document AGEU000020010921du7400416 (accessed 9 April 2018).

Agence Europe (1999a) EU/Chile/Mercosur—Framework Agreement with Chile Comes into Force. *Agence Europe*, 20 February. Brussels. Available at: Factiva Document AGEU000020010831dv2k000ib (accessed 9 April 2018).

Agence Europe (1999b) EU/Latin America—Commission Proposes to Focus Assistance on Lesser Developed Latin American Countries and on Limited Number of Priority

Actions, and to Integrate the Civil Society in Political Dialogue. *Agence Europe*, 10 March. Brussels. Available at: Factiva Document AGEU000020010831dv3a004uw (accessed 9 April 2018).

Agence Europe (1999c) EU/Latin America—Discussions on Follow-up to Give Rio Summit—First Meeting with Mercosur on 24 November. *Agence Europe*, 24 September. Brussels. Available at: Factiva Document AGEU000020010831dv9o004fk (accessed 9 April 2018).

Agence Europe (1999d) EU/Latin America—Franco-Spanish Compromise Allows Negotiating Brief with Mercosur and Chile to Be Brought Out of Deadlock. *Agence Europe*, 21 June. Brussels. Available at: Factiva Document AGEU000020010831dv6l006rz (accessed 9 April 2019).

Agence Europe (1999e) EU/Mercosur—Council Calls on Cologne Summit to Take Stance on Projects for Liberalisation of Trade with Mercosur and Chile. *Agence Europe*, 2 June. Brussels. Available at: Factiva Document AGEU000020010831dv62006f8 (accessed 9 April 2018).

Agence Europe (1999f) EU/Mercosur—Council Compromise on Timing of Future Trade Negotiations Satisfies Both the European Commission and Mercosur Countries. *Agence Europe*, 25 June. Brussels. Available at: Factiva Document AGEU000020010831dv6p00708 (accessed 9 April 2018).

Agence Europe (1999g) EU/Mercosur—Council to Examine Compromise on Monday Allowing Tariff Negotiations to Begin in July 2002. *Agence Europe*, 16 June. Brussels. Available at: Factiva Document AGEU000020010831dv6g006l7 (accessed 9 April 2018).

Agence Europe (1999h) EU/Mercosur—EU Stance on Trade Chapter Still Not Decided. *Agence Europe*, 1 June. Brussels. Available at: Factiva Document AGEU000020010831dv61006d4 (accessed 9 April 2018).

Agence Europe (1999i) EU/Mercosur—Final Text of Summit's Conclusions Make No Mention of Negotiating Brief with Mercosur and Chile. *Agence Europe*, 4 June. Brussels. Available at: Factiva Document AGEU000020010831dv64006ne (accessed 9 April 2018).

Agence Europe (1999j) EU/Mercosur—German Presidency Will Attempt to Bring the General Affairs Council on Monday Next to a Compromise on the EU's Position for Liberalising Trade with Mercosur and Chile. *Agence Europe*, 28 May. Brussels. Available at: Factiva Document AGEU000020010831dv5s0068o (accessed 9 April 2018).

Agence Europe (1999k) EU/Mercosur/Chile—Council Adopts Negotiating Briefs. *Agence Europe*, 16 September. Brussels. Available at: Factiva Document AGEU000020010831d-v9g000xp (accessed 9 April 2018).

Agence Europe (1999l) EU/Mercosur/Chile—Negotiations Over the Free-Trade Areas Are Launched. *Agence Europe*, 25 November. Brussels. Available at: Factiva Document AGEU000020010831dvbp00235 (accessed 9 April 2018).

Agence Europe (1999m) EU/Mercosur/United States. *Agence Europe*, 16 April. Brussels. Available at: Factiva Document AGEU000020010831dv4g0058z (accessed 9 April 2018).

Agence Europe (2000a) (EU) EU/CHILE—Third Negotiating Session for Association and Free Trade Agreement Begins Monday in Santiago. *Agence Europe*, 13 November. Brussels. Available at: Factiva Document AGEU000020020702dwbd000me (accessed 9 April 2018).

Agence Europe (2000b) EU/Mercosur—Both Parties Define Structure and Preliminary Timetable of Negotiations. *Agence Europe*, 17 June. Brussels. Available at: Factiva Document AGEU000020010803dw6h001jl (accessed 9 April 2018).

Agence Europe (2000c) EU/MERCOSUR—Negotiators Try to Clarify Objectives and Modalities of Future Association and Free-Trade Agreement, but Many Differences Appear Beyond Conciliatory Words. *Agence Europe*, 9 November. Brussels. Available at: Factiva Document AGEU000020020703dwb90005t (accessed 9 April 2018).

Agence Europe (2000d) EU/Mercosur/Chile. *Agence Europe*, 5 April. Brussels. Available at: Factiva Document AGEU000020010803dw45006xx (accessed 9 April 2018).

Agence Europe (2000e) EU/Mercosur/Chile. *Agence Europe*, 1 November. Brussels. Available at: Factiva Document AGEU000020010803dwb1003zs (accessed 9 April 2018).

Agence Europe (2001a) EP/Mercosur/Chile. *Agence Europe*, 9 February. Brussels. Available at: Factiva Document AGEU000020010709dx29001pp (accessed 9 April 2018).

Agence Europe (2001b) (EU) EU/CHILE—Rate of EU/Chile Trade Talks Could Be Accelerated. *Agence Europe*, 28 June. Brussels. Available at: Factiva Document AGEU000020010911dx6s0007r (accessed 9 April 2018).

Agence Europe (2001c) EU/Latin America—Lindh and Patten Visit American Continent to Prepare Next EU/Latin America Summit. *Agence Europe*, 23 March. Brussels. Available at: Factiva Document AGEU000020010709dx3n002np (accessed 9 April 2018).

Agence Europe (2002a) (EU) EU/CHILE—Association and Free Trade Agreement Initialled. *Agence Europe*, 12 June. Brussels. Available at: Factiva Document AGEU000020020612dy6c000xh (accessed 9 April 2018).

Agence Europe (2002b) (EU) EU/CHILE—EU and Chile to Intensify Rate of Negotiations on Free Trade Agreement. *Agence Europe*, 26 January. Brussels. Available at: Factiva Document AGEU000020020127dy1q00009 (accessed 9 April 2018).

Agence Europe (2002c) (EU) EU/CHILE—'It Will Not Be Easy' to Conclude 'Such an Ambitious' Agreement with Other Latin. *Agence Europe*, 20 November. Brussels. Available at: Factiva Document AGEU000020021120dybk00005 (accessed 9 April 2018).

Agence Europe (2002d) (EU) EU/GENERAL AFFAIRS—EU Confirms Intention to Conclude Negotiations with Chile on EU/Latin American. *Agence Europe*, 28 January. Brussels. Available at: Factiva Document AGEU000020020130dy1s00007 (accessed 9 April 2018).

Agence Europe (2002e) (EU) EU/MERCOSUR—7th Association Agreement Negotiating Meeting Focuses on Facilitating Trade, Failing. *Agence Europe*, 10 April. Brussels. Available at: Factiva Document AGEU000020020410dy4a000mb (accessed 9 April 2018).

Agence Europe (2002f) (EU) EU/MERCOSUR—8th Negotiating Session for Free Trade Agreement to Be Held from 10–14 November In. *Agence Europe*, 8 November. Brussels. Available at: Factiva Document AGEU000020021108dyb8000be (accessed 9 April 2018).

Agence Europe (2002g) (EU) EU/MERCOSUR—Commission Affirms Its 'Confidence' in Mercosur by Presenting Strategies For. *Agence Europe*, 3 August. Brussels. Available at: Factiva Document AGEU000020020803dy830005p (accessed 9 April 2018).

Agence Europe (2002h) (EU) EU/MERCOSUR—Commission Approves Regional Programme of EUR 48 Million. *Agence Europe*, 28 September. Brussels. Available at: Factiva Document AGEU000020020928dy9s000bq (accessed 9 April 2018).

Agence Europe (2002i) (EU) EU/MERCOSUR/CHILE—Mr Lamy Invites Mercosur Countries to Extend Relations with EU—Commission. *Agence Europe*, 8 March. Brussels. Available at: Factiva Document AGEU000020020312dy38000bo (accessed 9 April 2018).

Agence Europe (2002j) (EU) EU/TRADE—Pascal Lamy Welcomes Senate's Approval of 'Fast Track'. *Agence Europe*, 3 August. Brussels. Available at: Factiva Document AGEU000020020803dy8300063 (accessed 9 April 2018).

Agence Europe (2003a) (EU) EU/CHILE—Trade Association Agreement Takes Effect. *Agence Europe*, 4 February. Brussels. Available at: Factiva Document AGEU000020030204dz24000b7 (accessed 9 April 2018).

Agence Europe (2003b) (EU) EU/MERCOSUR—EU and Mercosur Seek Solution to Reconcile Bilateral and Multilateral Negotiations In. *Agence Europe*, 14 November. Brussels. Available at: Factiva Document AGEU000020031114dzbe0000h (accessed 9 April 2018).

Agence Europe (2003c) (EU) EU/MERCOSUR—New Negotiation Agenda for Association and Free Trade Agreement to Be Set At. *Agence Europe*, 11 November. Brussels. Available at: Factiva Document AGEU000020031111dzbb0000i (accessed 9 April 2018).

Agence Europe (2003d) (EU) EU/MERCOSUR—Timetable to End Negotiations in October 2004. *Agence Europe*, 13 November. Brussels. Available at: Factiva Document AGEU000020031113dzbd0000o (accessed 9 April 2018).

Agence Europe (2004a) (EU) EU/AGRICULTURE—EU Farmers Concerned at Concessions That Could Be Offered to Mercosur Countries. *Agence Europe*, 2 April. Brussels. Available at: Factiva Document AGEU000020040402e04200016 (accessed 9 April 2018).

Agence Europe (2004b) (EU) EU/MERCOSUR—COPA Is Critical of Any Further Agricultural Concessions to Brazil and Argentina. *Agence Europe*, 30 April. Brussels. Available at: Factiva Document AGEU000020040430e04u0000o (accessed 9 April 2018).

Agence Europe (2004c) (EU) EU/MERCOSUR—Free Trade Negotiations Continue This Week, Despite Lack of Progress Last Week On. *Agence Europe*, 15 June. Brussels. Available at: Factiva Document AGEU000020040615e06f0000h (accessed 9 April 2018).

Agence Europe (2004d) (EU) EU/MERCOSUR—Member States Call on Commission Not to Give Way on Agriculture During Buenos Aires Talks. *Agence Europe*, 8 June. Brussels. Available at: Factiva Document AGEU000020040608e0680000g (accessed 9 April 2018).

Agence Europe (2004e) (EU) EU/MERCOSUR—Ministerial Meeting in Guadalajara to Launch Last Phase of Free Trade Talks. *Agence Europe*, 28 May. Brussels. Available at: Factiva Document AGEU000020040528e05s0000a (accessed 9 April 2018).

Agence Europe (2004f) (EU) EU/MERCOSUR—Ministers and the Commission Confirm Their Aim to Conclude the Free Trade. *Agence Europe*, 29 May. Brussels. Available at: Factiva Document AGEU000020040529e05t0000i (accessed 9 April 2018).

Agence Europe (2004g) (EU) EU/MERCOSUR—Parties Due to Present Improved Free Trade Offers on Friday. *Agence Europe*, 16 April. Brussels. Available at: Factiva Document AGEU000020040416e04g0000h (accessed 9 April 2018).

Agence Europe (2004h) (EU) EU/MERCOSUR: Commission Prudently Optimistic About Free Trade Negotiations Despite Recent Breakdown. *Agence Europe*, 30 June.

Brussels. Available at: Factiva Document AGEU000020040630e06u0000i (accessed 9 April 2018).

Agence Europe (2004i) (EU) EU/MERCOSUR/AGRICULTURAL—Mr Fischler Repudiates Member States' Criticism of EU's Free-Trade. *Agence Europe*, 26 May. Brussels. Available at: Factiva Document AGEU000020040526e05q0000d (accessed 9 April 2018).

Agence Europe (2004j) (EU) EU/MERCOSUR/TRADE: After Failure of Lisbon, Continuation of Free-Trade Negotiations Postponed Until 2005. *Agence Europe*, 22 October. Brussels. Available at: Factiva Document AGEU000020041022e0am0000a (accessed 9 April 2018).

Agence Europe (2004k) (EU) EU/TRADE: EU and Mercosur Suspend Negotiations on Free-Trade Agreement. *Agence Europe*, 23 July. Brussels. Available at: Factiva Document AGEU000020040723e07n0000c (accessed 9 April 2018).

Agence Europe (2005) (EU) EU/MERCOSUR: Talks Between Europeans and South Americans Resume on Free Trade Agreement. *Agence Europe*, 6 September. Brussels. Available at: Factiva Document AGEU000020050906e1960000f (accessed 9 April 2018).

Agence Europe (2006) (EU) EU/MERCOSUR: South American Offer Could Be Improved, but Their Agriculture Demands Will Be Greater. *Agence Europe*, 13 September. Brussels. Available at: Factiva Document AGEU000020060913e29d0000i (accessed 9 April 2018).

Alemany C (2004) *La sociedad civil del Mercosur y Chile ante la asociación con la Unión Europea*. Montevideo: ALOP.

Allen D and Smith M (1990) Western Europe's Presence in the Contemporary International Arena. *Review of International Studies* 16(1): 19–37.

Allison L (2015) *The EU, ASEAN and Interregionalism: Regionalism Support and Norm Diffusion Between the EU and ASEAN*. Houndmills, Basingstoke: Palgrave Macmillan.

Barrau A (1999) *Rapport d'information sur les relations entre l'Union européenne et le MERCOSUR*. Paris: Assemblée nationale. Available at: www.assemblee-nationale.fr/europe/rap-info/i1721.pdf (accessed 1 May 2018).

Börzel T and Risse T (2009) *The Rise of (Inter-)Regionalism: The EU as a Model of Regional Integration*. APSA 2009 Toronto Meeting Paper, 13 August. SSRN. Available at: http://papers.ssrn.com/abstract=1450391 (accessed 15 January 2018).

Börzel TA and Risse T (2015) The EU and the Diffusion of Regionalism. In: Telò M, Fawcett L, and Ponjaert F (eds) *Interregionalism and the European Union: A Post-Revisionist Approach to Europe's Place in a Changing World*. Farnham: Ashgate, pp. 51–65.

Council of the European Union (1995) *Interregional Framework Cooperation Agreement Between the European Community and Its Member States, of the One Part, and the Southern Common Market and Its Party States, of the Other Part*, 15 December. Madrid: European Union. Available at: http://ec.europa.eu/world/agreements/prepare-CreateTreatiesWorkspace/treatiesGeneralData.do?step=0&redirect=true&treatyId=405 (accessed 16 March 2018).

Council of the European Union (1996) *EU–Chile Framework Cooperation Agreement*, 21 June. Florence: European Union. Available at: www.sice.oas.org/TPD/CHL_EU/CHL_EU_e.ASP (accessed 17 March 2018).

Council of the European Union (2004) *Guadalajara Declaration*. Final Declaration. Guadalajara:CounciloftheEuropeanUnion.Availableat:http://alcuenet.eu/dms-files.php?action=doc&id=363 (accessed 12 June 2018).

Crawford G (1997) Los derechos humanos, la democracia y el desarrollo: Hacia un trato justo e igualitario. *Revista Española de Desarrollo y Cooperación* (1): 63–101.

Dauster J (1998) Guest Editorial: MERCOSUR and the European Union: Prospects for an Inter-Regional Association. *European Foreign Affairs Review* 3(4): 447–449.

De Lombaerde P, Pietrangeli G, and Schulz M (2009) EU Support to Latin American Regionalism. In: Franck C, Defraigne J-C, and de Moriamé V (eds) *L'Union Européenne et la montée du régionalisme: Exemplarité et partenariats*. Louvain-La-Neuve: Academia Bruylant, pp. 247–261.

De Lombaerde P, Söderbaum F, and Wunderlich J-U (2015) Interregionalism. In: Jørgensen KE, Aarstad ÅK, Drieskens E, et al. (eds) *The SAGE Handbook of European Foreign Policy*. London: SAGE, pp. 750–765.

del Arenal C (1997) Los acuerdos de cooperación entre la Unión Europea y América Latina (1971-1997): Evolución, balance y perspectivas. *Revista Española de Desarrollo y Cooperación* (1): 111–138.

Devlin R (2001) Les processus ALCA et Union européenne-Mercosur : quels enseigne-ments réciproques ? In: Giordano P, Vallãdao A, and Durand M-F (eds) *Vers un accord entre l'Europe et le Mercosur*. Paris: Presses de Sciences Po, pp. 75–103.

DG Trade (2010) *European Commission Proposes Relaunch of Trade Negotiations with Mercosur Countries*, 4 May. Brussels: European Commission. Available at: www.sice. oas.org/TPD/MER_EU/negotiations/EU_relaunch_052010_e.pdf (accessed 15 June 2019).

DG Trade (2016) *EU–Mercosur Joint Communiqué on Exchange of Negotiating Offers*. Available at: www.sice.oas.org/TPD/MER_EU/negotiations/EU-Mercosur_exch_neg_offers_e.pdf (accessed 10 June 2016).

DG Trade (2019) *EU and Mercosur Reach Agreement on Trade*, 28 June. Brussels: European Commission. Available at: http://trade.ec.europa.eu/doclib/press/index.cfm?id=2039.

Doctor M (2007) Why Bother with Inter-Regionalism? Negotiations for a European Union–Mercosur Agreement. *JCMS: Journal of Common Market Studies* 45(2): 281–314. DOI: 10.1111/j.1468-5965.2007.00712.x.

Dominguez R (2008) *The Foreign Policy of the European Union (1995–2004): A Study in Structural Transition*. Lewiston: Edwin Mellen.

European Commission (1995a) *The European Union and Latin America: The Present Situation and Prospects for Closer Partnership 1996–2000*. Communication from the Commission to the Council and the European Parliament COM(95) 495 Final, 23 October. Brussels: European Commission. Available at: http://eur-lex.europa.eu/LexUriServ/LexUriServ.do?uri=COM:1995:0495:FIN:EN:PDF (accessed 17 March 2018).

European Commission (1995b) *Towards Closer Relations Between the European Union and Mexico*. Communication from the Commission to the Council and the European Parliament COM(95) 03 Final, 8 February. Brussels: European Commission. Available at: http://eur-lex.europa.eu/LexUriServ/LexUriServ.do?uri=COM:1995:0495:FIN:EN:PDF (accessed 17 March 2018).

European Commission (1997) *Proposal for a Council Decision Concerning the Conclu-sion of the Economic Partnership, Political Co-ordination and Cooperation Agreement Between the European Community and Its Member States, on the One Part, and the United Mexican States, on the Other Part*. COM(97) 527 Final. Brussels: Office for Official Publications of the European Communities.

European Commission (1998) *The New Transatlantic Marketplace*. Communication from the Commission to the Council, the European Parliament and the Economic and Social

Committee COM(1998) 125 Final. Brussels: European Commission. Available at: http://aei.pitt.edu/6799/1/6799.pdf (accessed 6 January 2018).

European Commission (1999) *A New European Union–Latin America Partnership on the Eve of the 21st Century*. Communication from the Commission to the Council and the European Parliament COM(99) 105 Final, 9 March. Brussels: European Commission. Available at: http://aei.pitt.edu/38376/1/A4438.pdf (accessed 6 April 2018).

European Commission (2000) *Commission Gives Green Light to EU–Mexico Free Trade Agreement*. European Commission Press Release IP/00/54, 18 January. Brussels: European Commission. Available at: http://europa.eu/rapid/press-release_IP-00-54_en.htm (accessed 15 April 2018).

European Council (1994) *Conclusions of the Presidency*. European Council in Essen 9–10 December 1994. Essen: European Council. Available at: www.consilium.europa.eu/ueDocs/cms_Data/docs/pressData/en/ec/00300-1.EN4.htm (accessed 12 June 2018).

European Voice (1998) 20 July Agriculture Council. *European Voice*, 23 July. Brussels. Available at: Factiva Document evoice0020010923du7n000ph (accessed 9 April 2018).

Faust J (2004) Blueprint for an Interregional Future? The European Union and the Southern Cone. In: Aggarwal VK and Fogarty EA (eds) *EU Trade Strategies: Between Regionalism and Globalization*. Houndmills, Basingstoke, Hampshire: Palgrave Macmillan, pp. 41–63.

García M (2008) *The Path to the 2002 Association Agreement Between the European Union and Chile: A Case Study in Successful Political Negotiation*. Lewiston, NY: Edwin Mellen.

García M (2011) Incidents Along the Path: Understanding the Rationale Behind the EU–Chile Association Agreement. *JCMS: Journal of Common Market Studies* 49(3): 501–524. DOI: 10.1111/j.1468-5965.2010.02149.x.

Grevi G and Khandekar G (eds) (2011) *Mapping EU Strategic Partnerships*. Madrid: FRIDE.

Harding G (1999a) Mercosur Failure Looms Over Rio Summit. *European Voice*, 3 June. Brussels. Available at: Factiva Document evoice0020010905dv63000dc (accessed 9 April 2018).

Harding G (1999b) Mercosur Welcomes Trade Talks Mandate. *European Voice*, 24 June. Brussels. Available at: Factiva Document evoice0020010905dv6o000z4 (accessed 9 April 2018).

Hess NM (2009) *Brasilien, Mexiko und LAC-Staaten—Inflation der strategischen Partner der EU in Lateinamerika?* GIGA Focus Lateinamerika 6/2009. Hambug: German Institute of Global and Area Studies.

IRELA (1997) *Los Acuerdos de Tercera Generación entre la UE y América Latina: ¿Plataforma para un nuevo tipo de cooperación?* Informe IRELA. Madrid: IRELA.

Lister M (1997) *The European Union and the South: Relations with Developing Countries*. New York, NY: Routledge.

Müller-Brandeck-Bocquet G (2000) Perspectives for a New Regionalism: Relations Between the EU and the MERCOSUR. *European Foreign Affairs Review* 5(4): 561–579.

Nelson M (2015) *A History of the FTAA: From Hegemony to Fragmentation in the Americas*. New York, NY: Palgrave Macmillan.

Page S (2001) Les autres accords de libre-échange de l'Union européenne. In: Giordano P, Vallãdao A, and Durand M-F (eds) *Vers un accord entre l'Europe et le Mercosur*. Paris: Presses de Sciences Po, pp. 117–134.

Peterson J (1999) *Decision-Making in the European Union*. New York, NY: St. Martin's Press.

Riccardi F (1999) A Look Behind the News. *Agence Europe*, 7 June. Brussels. Available at: Factiva Document AGEU000020010831dv67006ps (accessed 9 April 2018).

Robles AC (2008a) EU FTA Negotiations with SADC and Mercosur: Integration into the World Economy or Market Access for EU Firms? *Third World Quarterly* 29(1): 181–197. DOI: 10.1080/01436590701726608.

Robles AC (2008b) The EU and ASEAN: Learning from the Failed EU–Mercosur FTA Negotiations. *ASEAN Economic Bulletin* 25(3): 334–344.

Sanahuja JA (2000) Trade, Politics, and Democratization: The 1997 Global Agreement Between the European Union and Mexico. *Journal of Interamerican Studies and World Affairs* 42(2): 35–62. DOI: 10.1111/j.1548-2456.2000.tb00136.x.

Santander S (2001) La légitimation de l'Union européenne par l'exportation de son modèle d'intégration et de gouvernance régionale. Le cas du Marché commun du sud (Note). *Études internationales* 32(1): 51–67.

Santander S (2005) The European Partnership with Mercosur: A Relationship Based on Strategic and Neo-Liberal Principles. *Journal of European Integration* 27(3): 285–306. DOI: 10.1080/07036330500190156.

Schade D (2019) Of Insiders and Outsiders: Assessing EU Strategic Partnerships in Their Regional Context. *International Politics* 56(3): 375–394. DOI: 10.1057/s41311-017-0132-y.

Smith H (1995) *European Union Foreign Policy and Central America*. Houndmills, Basingstoke: Macmillan.

Szymanski M and Smith ME (2005) Coherence and Conditionality in European Foreign Policy: Negotiating the EU–Mexico Global Agreement. *JCMS: Journal of Common Market Studies* 43(1): 171–192. DOI: 10.1111/j.0021-9886.2005.00551.x.

Torrelli C (2003) *Mercosur for Sale? The EU's FTAA and the Need to Oppose It*. CEO & TNI Info Brief. Amsterdam: Transnational Institute.

Turner M (1998a) Farm Lobby Urges Second Thoughts on Latin America Pact. *European Voice*, 9 July. Brussels. Available at: Factiva Document evoice0020010923du79000ki (accessed 9 April 2018).

Turner M (1998b) Marin Side-Steps Bid to Block Mercosur Talks. *European Voice*, 23 July. Brussels. Available at: Factiva Document evoice0020010923du7n000o7 (accessed 9 April 2018).

Turner M (1998c) Union Takes 'Snapshot' of Mercosur Trade. *European Voice*, 30 April. Brussels. Available at: Factiva Document evoice0020010923du4u001lt (accessed 9 April 2018).

Turner M and Neligan M (1998) France Steps Up Campaign Against Free-Trade Accords. *European Voice*, 16 July. Brussels. Available at: Factiva Document evoice-0020010923du7g000m3 (accessed 9 April 2018).

von Kyaw D (1999) *Prioritäten der deutschen EU-Präsidentschaft unter Berücksichtigung des Europäischen Rates in Wien*. Discussion Paper C33. Bonn: Center for European Integration Studies, Rheinische Friedrich-Wilhelms-Universität Bonn. Available at: http://aei.pitt.edu/312/1/dp_c33_kyaw.pdf (accessed 6 April 2018).

Working Group on European Union–Mercosur Negotiations (2005) *EU–Mercosur Negotiations and the Doha Round: What Next?* Annual Report 2004–2005. Paris: Chaire Mercosur de Sciences Po.

Working Group on European Union–Mercosur Negotiations (2006) *No Doha Round, No EU–Mercosur Negotiations?* Annual Report 2005–2006. Paris: Chaire Mercosur de Sciences Po.

5   Institutional complexity and the Lisbon transition

Negotiating with Central America and the Andean region

The negotiations for Association Agreements with the Andean Community of Nations[1] and the Central American Common Market[2] are perfect illustrations of the role of the EU's institutional complexity in the period prior to the implementation of the changes of the Treaty of Lisbon. Both can also illustrate how the long duration of EU Association Agreement negotiation processes shapes the outcome of the negotiations, as the ratification of the agreements which ultimately resulted from these negotiations occurred only after the implementation of the Lisbon changes. While the negotiations for both agreements were initially envisioned and conducted in parallel within the EU's institutions, the processes increasingly diverged and an Association Agreement was only concluded in the case of negotiations with Central America, all while an FTA was signed with only two of the Andean Community's members, namely Colombia and Peru.

As this chapter shows, a number of external developments can partially explain the divergent negotiation outcomes. However, when considering factors of bureaucratic politics, the dynamics of the negotiations can be explored in much more detail in both cases. First of all, the EU's policy inertia can explain why negotiations were opened with both regional organizations in the first place, and why the EU's rhetoric of regionalism support in the Andean region wasn't abandoned even after the interregional Association Agreement negotiations had failed.

Secondly, the importance of diverging interests between different institutional actors on the EU's policy outputs can also be seen at play. While the interests of DG RELEX and DG Trade largely aligned for the Central America negotiations, this was not the case for negotiations with CAN. Furthermore, the autonomy of individual Commission DGs can help us understand why the EU's development cooperation funding towards the Andean region did not cohere with the developments in the EU's negotiations with the region. Lastly, the slow pace of ratification of the relevant agreements demonstrates the influence of the complexity of EU foreign policy decision-making over time.

The remainder of this chapter is organized as follows: After outlining the factors contributing to the opening of negotiations for Association Agreements with both regional organizations, it then elaborates on a number of different developments in the negotiations with both regions, which can best be understood through the lens of bureaucratic politics. While these will be elaborated on broadly in sequence, the analysis is divided into three parts: The first is the process of internal deliberations that led to the granting of negotiation mandates in the first place. This is followed by an analysis of the factors that led the EU to abandon the Association Agreement framework in one case, while successfully concluding negotiations in the other. Lastly, the ratification process in the aftermath of the Treaty of Lisbon and the difficulties that arose in this context are further elaborated on.

An unlikely case for negotiations

The negotiations for Association Agreements with the two regions mentioned above may not appear to be relevant developments in the EU's foreign policy in and of itself. If one considers the existence of a previous EU–Latin America strategy that has aimed to create deeper links between both regions with a focus on regional integration organizations, it would appear hardly surprising that the EU chose to open negotiations in both cases. Yet, the consideration of a number of political and economic factors prior to the process shows that only a consideration of bureaucratic factors can explain the underlying dynamics.

First and foremost, the economic case for negotiations between the EU and both regions was very weak. In the early 2000s, the focus of the EU's trade policy was clearly limited to the multilateral realm, with the hope of reaping the economic benefits of a successful conclusion of the WTO's DDA. This preference was expressed during the Prodi Commission under then Trade Commissioner Pascal Lamy by imposing a *de facto* moratorium on the launch of new EU FTA negotiations (Woolcock, 2007: 5) which was supported by many EU member states.

After all, Doha's liberalization measures would have had to be known before being able to realistically assess the potential and possible depth of any further bilateral trade negotiations.[3] Furthermore, Spain, the EU's most prominent advocate for strengthening EU–Latin American ties, had desired to undertake negotiations for an FTA with the entirety of Latin America in the late 1990s,[4] mirroring the approach of the US under the FTAA project. This would have rendered Association Agreement negotiations with subregional negotiations in Latin America unnecessary.

The EU's trade with the region was also much more limited than that with Mercosur discussed before. After all, imports and exports between the EU and CAN's four member states after Venezuela's withdrawal accounted for less than 1% of the EU totals in each case (see Table 5.1). Furthermore, most imports from these regions were already liberalized under the EU's GSP and GSP+[5] schemes for the foreseeable future, and neither region was a particularly relevant recipient of European exports.

The European Commission, and DG Trade more specifically, also faced important human resource constraints on the number of trade negotiations that could be undertaken at that point in time.[6] This is mainly due to the complexity of such negotiations, creating a number of barriers before any EU negotiation would receive the go-ahead. Internally, the EU was undergoing important changes with the 2004 enlargement round, leading to an overall inward focus

Table 5.1 EU–CAN and EU–SIECA trade in goods

	2005		2010		2015	
	Imports	Exports	Imports	Exports	Imports	Exports
Bolivia	140 (0.0)	171 (0.0)	335 (0.0)	307 (0.0)	645 (0.0)	738 (0.0)
Colombia	3,277 (0.3)	2,475 (0.2)	4,783 (0.3)	3,945 (0.3)	6,589 (0.4)	6,533 (0.4)
Ecuador	1,580 (0.1)	883 (0.1)	2,035 (0.1)	1,403 (0.1)	2,585 (0.2)	2,009 (0.1)
Peru	2,444 (0.2)	1,087 (0.1)	5,190 (0.3)	2,312 (0.2)	4,949 (0.3)	3,730 (0.2)
Venezuela	3,778 (0.3)	2,848 (0.3)	3,808 (0.2)	4,133 (0.3)	2,161 (0.1)	3,003 (0.2)
CAN	7,441 (0.6)	4,616 (0.4)	12,343 (0.7)	7,967 (0.6)	14,768 (0.9)	13,010 (0.7)
SIECA	4,835 (0.4)	3,715 (0.4)	5,654 (0.4)	4,597 (0.3)	5,169 (0.3)	5,723 (0.3)

In million € (% of total EU trade in goods). CAN excludes Venezuela.

Source: Eurostat (2014).

that further strained the EU's capacity to undertake significant foreign policy initiatives, especially in a region that did not play an important role for any of its 10 new member states.[7]

Lastly, the EU's political focus was not on either of these regions, unlike when the EU first started official dialogues with them in the 1980s. While Mercosur had evolved rapidly, the same could not be said of the Andean Community (though it has been in existence for much longer than Mercosur). While its institutions were relatively developed, it still lacked integrated policies. In the case of SICA and SIECA, neither the institutions nor the associated political and economic integration projects functioned very well.[8] With SIECA reuniting countries as distinct as Nicaragua, with the second-lowest GDP in all of Latin America, and Costa Rica, an upper-middle-income economy, the region's countries furthermore diverge significantly. While this is not quite as extreme in the case of CAN, there are nevertheless important differences between its different member states.

For these reasons, the EU was initially wary of replacing the existing political ties to the Central American and Andean region by new and untested mechanisms. This can be seen by the fact that already the establishment of formal political relations with both regional groupings through the 1996 Declaration of Rome, as well as the EU–Central America FCA of 1993, was accompanied by fears on the European side that these could break up the then successful Rio Group and San José dialogue formats.[9] The latter were regarded at the time as having contributed to the peace processes and democratization wave in the region in important ways. Despite this, the EU nevertheless eventually signed Political Dialogue and Cooperation Agreements with both regions in 2003.[10] This ultimately made renewed negotiations within a few years unlikely.

The EU's reluctance to enter into negotiations for any kind of agreement that would include trade provisions with both regions at the time is demonstrated by its reaction to various Latin American calls to do so. As early as 1997, Peru openly approached the EU Council presidency troika about a potential EU–Andean Community FTA.[11] Similarly, with the Doha negotiations dragging on, Colombia started to join in such calls, while Costa Rica began to advocate for a similar agreement for itself.[12]

This originally engendered disbelief and negative reactions from the EU's side,[13] as it was believed that none of the Latin American countries would stand to benefit economically from this. After all, most of these countries' significant exports to the EU were already unilaterally liberalized under GSP and GSP+. Furthermore, EU representatives were doubtful as to whether any of the countries concerned had the necessary experience and capacity to negotiate what would necessarily be complex FTAs.

Bilateral negotiations with individual countries would likely strain the EU's human resources too much for only a small economic benefit (in contrast to the potential of an FTA with Mercosur discussed previously), with EU officials further doubting the institutional capacity of both regional organizations to enter into talks.[14] Lastly, by the early 2000s, the successful negotiation of a FTAA had largely dissipated.

The Guadalajara Declaration that came out of the 2004 EU–Latin America summit perhaps best illustrates the important barriers facing the potential of negotiations with both regions, stating that any

> future Free Trade Agreement shall be built upon the outcome of the Doha Development Agenda and the realization of a sufficient level of regional economic integration.
>
> (Council of the European Union, 2004: 8)

The EU's general commitment to interregionalism aside, there are very few factors that could rationally explain the EU's opening of Association Agreement negotiations with both regions given their lack of economic importance, the EU's moratorium on new FTAs, the absence of competing FTA negotiations by the US, and the fear that both regional integration mechanisms weren't sufficiently advanced to negotiate successfully with the EU. It is thus only a consideration of elements of bureaucratic politics that can explain the opening of negotiations in both instances.

A lengthy pre-negotiation phase: Overcoming diverging internal views

Bureaucratic developments within the EU's institutions can explain the ultimate opening of negotiations with CAN and Central America despite the manifold reasons against. This section outlines the developments from a first consideration of negotiations within the institutions and up the approval of the negotiation mandates by the Council. While this is only a small part of the overall negotiation experience, the timeframe covered here spans two and a half years between November 2004 and the adoption of the negotiation mandates in April 2007. Ultimately, this section once more demonstrates the role that the autonomy of individual Commissioners and Commission DGs can play in the EU's foreign policy, all while the divergence of views on specific issues increases the duration of EU foreign policy decision-making processes.

Envisioning negotiations

Given the political context outlined above, the opening of negotiations with both organizations appeared nowhere on the horizon in the early to mid-2000s. The initial factor that provided for the first consideration of the negotiations within the Commission's DG RELEX was the inauguration of the Barroso Commission in November 2004. Here, it was a combination of a change of the responsible Commissioner combined with the renewed autonomy of Commission DGs that provided the initial impetus for a consideration of the negotiations.

The inauguration of the Barroso Commission meant an important change for the composition of the Commission as a whole, with the most important posts being staffed with new Commissioners. While, as Portugal's former prime minister, Commission President José Manuel Barroso had an obvious interest in Latin America, it was ultimately two other Commissioners who played a crucial role in the process to begin negotiations with both regions: RELEX Commissioner Benita Ferrero-Waldner and Trade Commissioner Peter Mandelson.

Having served as Austria's foreign minister under the conservative government of Prime Minister Wolfgang Schüssel until her nomination to the post of Foreign Relations Commissioner in the autumn of 2004, Ferrero-Waldner was instrumental for the EU's renewed focus on Latin America, and the relevant subregions in particular.[15] While it is unclear what exactly motivated her to take a prominent role in shaping the EU's relations with the region, she already showed a keen interest in it as Austria's foreign minister and is married to an expert on Latin American literature.[16]

The important role that Ferrero-Waldner played for the launch of negotiations can also be attributed to an important change in management style within the Commission. While Barroso did not return to the old organizational system of attributing portfolios by region, he did decide to preside over a special group of Commissioners with external relations portfolios himself (Dominguez, 2008: 121). This could have given him the possibility to weigh significantly into the Commissioners' separate portfolios. However, as a former member of Mr. Barroso's cabinet pointed out, the Commission president "picked his fights" and did not want to micromanage the work of any of the important external relations Commission portfolios, thus allowing individual Commissioners significant leeway in their specific policy area.[17]

It is in this changed institutional context that the reflection process on the future of EU–Latin American relations began. Given the failure of the Mercosur negotiations at the end of the previous Commission's tenure, these negotiations would no longer be an option to turn the EU's Latin America strategy into practice. The new Commission was then once more approached by both CAN and Central America in short succession with both voicing their desire to negotiate FTAs with the EU amidst the slow progress of the DDA.[18] For a country like Peru, the initial aim was to diversify its external markets in the context of the then ongoing FTAA negotiations and to overcome the limitations of the EU's unilateral GSP scheme[19]—even if this meant concessions that could have adverse economic effects in the short term. This is illustrative of some Latin American governments' belief in the merits of the so-called Washington Consensus, which aimed for a large-scale liberalization of national economies.

What helped Colombia and Peru argue their case were the vague previous commitments for the EU to consider deeper trade ties with the Andean region. These references could be found in the existing agreements with the EU, as well as EU–Latin America summit declarations. The Madrid Declaration of the 2002 summit mentions both the successful conclusion of the Doha Round and the necessity of reaching Political Dialogue and Cooperation Agreements as precursors to trade and association negotiations (Council of the European Union, 2002: 3).

Once the PDCAs were signed in 2003, the formulations on eventual Association Agreement negotiations contained in these could then be used by the Latin American parties (Council of the European Communities, 2003: 2). The Guadalajara Declaration of 2004 was more precise as to eventual Association Agreement negotiations with Central America and the Andean Community, however adding a condition for their "sufficient level of regional economic integration" (Council of the European Union, 2004: 8). Nevertheless, the document included provisions on "a joint assessment phase of the respective integration processes of the Central American and Andean Community's [sic]" that would lead in "due course" to the beginning of negotiations (Council of the European Union, 2004: 8). Given the overall timing of the latter declaration immediately after the EU's big bang enlargement round, and a continued reference to Doha (US Embassy Italy Rome, 2004), this was merely meant as a symbolic gesture by the Europeans at the time.

Therefore, other bureaucratic factors also need to be considered to explain the process leading to the beginning of negotiations with both regional organizations. It is here that the influence of the incoming RELEX Commissioner Ferrero-Waldner needs to be considered. While it is unclear what exactly motivated her to take the initiative on the EU's Latin America policy, she nonetheless asked DG RELEX to study the options for Association Agreement negotiations with CAN and Central America within three months of her taking office.[20] While the DGs' bureaucrats were initially reserved about the idea by making reference to their resource constraints,[21] work to this end got underway due to the new Commissioner's insistence.

It has been noted by multiple interviewees that such a policy shift initiated by an incoming Commissioner is highly unusual. They stated that Commissioners typically need some time to adjust to their new role at the beginning of the mandate and will often find it difficult to overrule or out-manoeuvre the key personnel in the DGs who will typically remain in place. Despite this, the central role of Ferrero-Waldner has been confirmed by most interviewees, while one used the case as an example to underline that the EU's bureaucracy can occasionally rapidly change tracks if the political situation permits, and key bureaucrats are convinced of the merits of such a change in the first place.[22]

In any case, preparatory working groups between the Commission and Central America, as well as with the Andean Community, were set up already in January 2005 (Agence Europe, 2005a, 2005c). At a San José dialogue meeting in May 2005, mention was furthermore made by Ferrero-Waldner that negotiations could officially be launched in 2006—in time for the next EU–Latin America summit—while cautioning that this still depended on the progress of the Doha Round (Agence Europe, 2005b).

This did not mean that there was no resistance to the negotiations on the European side, or to the proposed format on the Latin American end. Alongside the preparatory work, a case needed to be made for the merits of the negotiations to convince the Commission as a whole and the different member states to approve the launch of negotiations.

The upcoming 2006 EU–Latin America summit provided the incentive for Ferrero-Waldner to make her case in a 2005 Commission communication prepared by DG RELEX on *A stronger partnership between the European Union and*

Latin America,[23] which would serve as the basis of discussions for the future of EU–Latin American relations in the preparations for the summit. The document calls specifically for the establishment of

> an enhanced strategic partnership through a network of association agreements (including free trade agreements) involving all the countries of the region and liable to contribute to the integration of the region as a whole.
>
> (European Commission, 2005: 6)

It furthermore makes rhetorical reference to the EU's previous commitments to the region and underlines its responsibility of proving its continued interest in the region even after the Eastern enlargement round (European Commission, 2005: 5).

Overcoming internal bureaucratic reservations

With DG RELEX and the responsible Commissioner convinced of the merits of negotiating with CAN and Central America, a number of other internal EU actors needed to be brought on board for the process to go forward. This ultimately succeeded due to an alignment of preferences of other internal EU actors over a lack of progress in the Doha Round and further DG RELEX activity.

Due to the tripartite structure of Association Agreements, DG RELEX—albeit the lead actor for such negotiations—was not the only entity within the Commission that needed to give its go-ahead before the demand for a negotiation brief could be put to the Council. Given that the political dialogue and cooperation elements had already been dealt with to a large extent in the negotiations leading to the PDCAs of 2003, the trade component would be the most significant—if not the only—substantial addition in the negotiations for the Association Agreements. Aside from securing member state support, gaining that of DG Trade (alongside a number of other relevant DGs, such as AGRI) was the most important element before negotiations could be envisioned.

While DG RELEX's initial internal concerns about the project were limited to timing and workload issues over the DG's small staff footprint,[24] DG Trade's concerns were of a more fundamental nature. For EU trade officials—as was the case for many member states—a number of different elements still stood in the way of the negotiation of Association Agreements with either region. At the time of DG RELEX's Latin America strategy document, the Doha Round was still ongoing and the EU was strongly committed to its successful conclusion, with the moratorium on new FTA negotiations still in place in late 2005. At the same time, DG Trade was busy updating the EU's existing agreements with the rest of the world so as to take into account the effects of the EU's enlargement rounds.

Trade officials also argued that the economic case for agreements with CAN and Central America was relatively weak. While negotiations would occupy an important number of the EU's trade negotiators, the markets of neither region were deemed important or integrated enough economically for the EU to warrant such costly processes.[25] The difficulty for further economic integration at least in

CAN was illustrated by the fact that Venezuela had increasingly begun to embrace principles of socialist economic planning under President Hugo Chavez.[26]

When four of the five CAN members called for the EU to negotiate an FTA with the region in 2003, Venezuela was notably absent (Agence Europe, 2003) and abstained from negotiations with the US. Similar tendencies could be observed in the Central American region, with Honduras, Guatemala, and Nicaragua showing sympathy for the ALBA regional integration project launched by Venezuela and the Petrocaribe project funded by it (Erisman, 2011: 125). The latter would allow these countries to receive Venezuelan oil at significantly reduced rates.

Lastly, the EU was involved in an ongoing dispute at the WTO over its banana quotas and tariffs which involved some Central American and Andean states under the leadership of Ecuador (US Embassy Ecuador Quito, 2005). Given that disagreements over the EU's position on one of these countries' key exports were proving difficult to resolve, the prospect of amicable and successful negotiations for Association Agreements between both sides appeared relatively slim.

Some of these difficulties were addressed by purely coincidental developments, such as the timetable of the Council's rotating presidency or a scheduled biannual EU–Latin America summit which provides a prominent forum for relations between the two regions. With Austria due to take over the presidency in the first half of 2006, and as the host of that year's EU–LAC summit, the country's support for progress in the relationship was virtually assured. On the one hand, this was due to the country still being governed by the very same government from which Ferrero-Waldner emerged. On the other, tangible progress in the EU–Latin America relationship would be a sign of prestige for the country holding the presidency and hosting the summit. The country then used its influence when holding the presidency to ensure that some progress would be made on the Latin American dossier.

The importance that Austria attributed to progress in the EU–Latin America relationship can be seen in the document outlining its presidency priorities. It specifically mentions the EU–LAC summit as "the largest event during the Austrian presidency in 2006" (Federal Ministry of Foreign Affairs, 2005: 28) and acknowledges the presidency's desire for the beginning of negotiations with both regions. This political priority for negotiations did not eliminate the prevalent concern over developments in the DDA, however, as the document states:

> It is hoped that the Sixth Ministerial Conference of the World Trade Organisation WTO in Hong Kong in December 2005 will come up with decisions that will make it possible to conclude the round by the end of 2006, or at the latest by mid-2007. The outcome of this conference will determine the trade policy agenda during the Austrian Presidency.
>
> (Federal Ministry of Foreign Affairs, 2005: 35)

These Austrian concerns were shared by DG Trade. The failure of the December 2005 WTO negotiations in Hong Kong then paved the way for a changed approach in the EU's trade policy in general, in turn softening DG Trade's position towards the Association Agreements with Latin America.

When the Barroso Commission's new Trade Commissioner Peter Mandelson took up his position at the same time as Ferrero-Waldner in 2004, the EU's preferences for the Doha Round and the consequential moratorium on FTAs were still manifest (Agence Europe, 2004). This was based on Mandelson's adamant support for economic liberalization in the multilateral realm. In consequence, this was the primary reason why Mandelson was initially opposed to DG RELEX's proposals for negotiations with both regional organizations.[27] It was only after Doha's failure became apparent in Hong Kong that a significant shift of thinking on the EU's trade strategy started to emerge within the EU's trade policy apparatus. This, combined with Austria's presidency, Ferrero-Waldner's persuasion, as well as the promise of certain safeguards related to progress in the integration process of the regions concerned, ultimately helped to sway DG Trade's position in favour of the proposed negotiations.[28]

While only published after DG Trade had informally agreed to the negotiations with both regions, its *Global Europe* (DG Trade, 2006) communication of October 2006 best illustrates the change of thinking that occurred after Hong Kong's failure. The document outlined an entirely new vision for the EU's trade policy based on bilateral treaties where necessary and thereby proposed to end the moratorium on new FTAs. On the one hand, the document states that "Europe remains committed to the WTO and is working hard to resume negotiations as soon as circumstances in other countries allow" (DG Trade, 2006: 10). On the other, as a departure from previous policy, it mentions that:

> Free Trade Agreements (FTAs), if approached with care, can build on WTO and other international rules by going further and faster in promoting openness and integration, by tackling issues which are not ready for multilateral discussion and by preparing the ground for the next level of multilateral liberalisation.
>
> (DG Trade, 2006: 10)

The document furthermore makes specific reference to the negotiations with both regions, stating that a European focus on FTAs with them was by no means entirely novel (DG Trade, 2006: 10–11). The emergence of this changed approach made negotiations with both regions much more logical from the perspective of the EU's stated trade policy preferences, thus reducing the divergence of views between DG Trade and DG RELEX.

Nonetheless, the language of the document itself reveals that the change of thinking cannot be explained by *Global Europe* alone. Furthermore, given the lack of overall importance of both regions' economies for the EU, DG Trade's actions do not readily square with the priorities of the document. It is instead the free trade policy of the US that served as a further factor in the change of DG Trade's approach. The failure of the FTAA project initially meant that the EU would not have to fear immediate market access issues in the Latin American region.

However, the abandonment of this grand project did not mean that the US ended its advances towards the region. This time around, the focus was on bilateral negotiations with willing Latin American countries, once more creating fears for the EU's market access.[29] US negotiations with a number of countries in both Central America and the Andean region had begun in May 2004, ultimately leading to the conclusion of agreements with Central America in 2005, and with Panama, Colombia, and Peru in 2006.[30]

The agreements had two effects on the EU's trade preferences: On the one hand, a senior EU trade official pointed out that the EU and the US are economic competitors in both regions, and that any move by the US would mean that the EU would naturally have to follow suit[31] despite the region's relative economic insignificance. Furthermore, the capacity of these countries to successfully conclude agreements with the US alleviated some of DG Trade's concerns over their capacity to negotiate such complex agreements bilaterally (US Embassy Peru Lima, 2006), potentially rendering negotiations less costly for DG Trade and increasing their chance of success. While not addressing all of DG Trade's concerns, its position had nevertheless become more favourable with the effective failure of Doha and the conclusion of the US FTAs, thus decreasing the divergence of views within the Commission.

It is here that the issue of the upcoming EU–Latin America summit became relevant again, and meant that the Council could ultimately provide an additional impetus to DG RELEX's project. Given that such summits, as well as the summit declaration, are technically a matter between governments rather than the supranational institutions, the Council (aided by preparatory work within COLAC) had to agree on an approach ahead of the May 2006 Vienna summit that would signal a deepening of the ties between the EU and Latin America despite the failure of the negotiations with Mercosur. The announcement of negotiations with Central America and the Andean Community would hence be an ideal signal.

It is in this context that the GAC conclusions from 27 February 2006 on the Commission's 2005 Latin America strategy document need to be seen. In it, the Council specifically gave its general support for DG RELEX's plans, stating that:

> The Council [...] welcomes the comprehensive Commission Communication on 'A stronger partnership between the European Union and Latin America' which comes at an appropriate juncture in the relationship between the two regions.
>
> (Council of the European Union, 2006b: 12)

With regard to the proposed negotiations specifically, the document affirms the Council's willingness to support these:

> While reiterating its attachment to ongoing multilateral negotiations in the WTO under the DDA, the Council recalls the EU's strategic objective of enhancing the EU-Latin American bi-regional partnership through a network of association agreements, involving all the countries of the region and aimed

at promoting the integration of the region as a whole. [...] It also expects that appropriate decisions can be taken regarding the opening of negotiations on association agreements, including free trade agreements, with the Andean Community and Central America.

(Council of the European Union, 2006b: 14)

While a commitment to Doha remained at this time, more than seven months ahead of the publication of *Global Europe*, it nevertheless signalled the Council's willingness to entertain the negotiations with both regions in principle, including in the realm of trade.

It is necessary to consider that the Council's approval for the process at this stage should not be taken for granted. Rather, it is once more a number of parallel developments that contributed to its positive attitude towards DG RELEX's approach. First and foremost, it is surprising that some of the member states would, at least in principle, welcome negotiations with a regional organization in which Venezuela wielded considerable influence. While Venezuela's increasingly belligerent rhetoric was largely seen as an internal problem of CAN, some of the EU's member states such as Spain and the Czech Republic nevertheless voiced important criticisms as to the democratic credentials of Venezuela's government. In 2002, Spain's conservative government under José María Aznar, which held the rotating Council presidency at the time, even went so far as to welcome the failed coup against Hugo Chavez (BBC News, 2004). Such views were shared in some Eastern European countries like the Czech Republic (US Embassy Czech Republic Prague, 2006), which was also sensitive to the country's close alignment with Cuba.[32] Given the necessary inclusion of democracy and human rights provisions in any EU agreement, this issue had the potential to be a significant hurdle for any negotiations.

By early 2006, however, this Spanish obstacle to negotiations had disappeared. When José Luis Rodríguez Zapatero became prime minister of Spain in 2004 after the electoral victory of the PSO, Spain's social democratic party, the country slowly moved away from its radical opposition to Latin America's socialist governments. Instead, Zapatero opted for a policy of engagement. While the changed political climate dictated from above took some time to permeate inside Spain's bureaucracy,[33] the government even proposed relaxing the EU's so-called Common Position on Cuba (see the following chapter), which had limited European interactions with the island (US Embassy Czech Republic Prague, 2005). The fact that it was the previous Aznar government which had initiated the Common Position makes the reversal of Spain's policy even clearer.

Similarly, agricultural concerns such as those that had contributed to the failure of negotiations with Mercosur were less prevalent in the case of these regions, if one leaves the sensitive issue of bananas aside. This allowed countries like France to take a more positive attitude towards the negotiations than was the case for Mercosur.[34] This was accompanied by what has been described as member states' "permissive consensus"[35] on the Commission's proposed Latin America strategy that developed in parallel with the support for *Global Europe*.

Furthermore, as explained by an Eastern European Trade Policy Committee delegate, the new member states largely lacked clear preferences as to the opening of trade negotiations, with political concerns over some of the left-wing governments not being allowed to interfere with a general liberalization agenda. In any case, it was feared that a refusal of such talks would play into the hands of Venezuela and its anti-liberalization agenda for the region,[36] thereby creating a perceived urgency for negotiations. As someone who is familiar with the discussions in the Council's Latin America working group has explained, while the issue of competition with the US never comes up in formal discussions, "the EU always needs to be on par with the United States when it comes to market access in the region."[37] Lack of member state support for the negotiations was therefore not an inhibiting factor at this stage, as their positions aligned themselves largely with that of DG RELEX and the now convinced DG Trade.

Against this backdrop of shared assessments between the relevant actors, the preparatory work for negotiations with Central America under the joint assessment exercise continued successfully. This eventually contributed to the identification of a number of economic integration steps that the region would have to undertake in parallel to negotiations with the EU. By the May 2006 EU–LAC summit in Vienna, both sides were sufficiently satisfied that the EU–Central American side-summit could announce the decision that formal negotiations would be launched. Nonetheless, the agreement still included safeguards on regional integration, as follows:

> Central America confirmed its commitment to implement as planned the decisions taken by CA Heads of States on 9 March 2006 in Panama, as well as to seek ratification of the CA Treaty on investment and services and to develop a jurisdictional mechanism that could secure enforcement of regional economic legislation throughout the region.
>
> (Council of the European Union, 2006c: 2)

While this did not mean that negotiations could begin straight away—given the absence of a mandate from the Council—the commitment to the opening of negotiations in this public biregional forum nevertheless sent a strong signal and represented rhetorical entrapment on the EU's side. The remaining internal EU policy process could thus be seen as more of a formality than it would have been otherwise.

Similar progress could not be achieved in the context of negotiations with the Andean Community due to a number of developments that destabilized this regional actor ahead of the summit. This was mainly due to a more radical shift in Venezuelan foreign policy, as well as the election of Evo Morales in Bolivia. Much like the conditions imposed on Central America, the EU had already insisted in its preparatory work for the joint assessment in 2005 that CAN would have to establish an internal common tariff before negotiations could begin (US Embassy Peru Lima, 2005). This meant that the Andean Community would have to undertake further integration steps before any future negotiations. With

Venezuela unwilling to deepen regional integration as demanded, a fulfilment of these conditions appeared increasingly unlikely.

In a somewhat surprising move, Hugo Chavez then decided in April 2006 that Venezuela would withdraw from the organization altogether[38] and join Mercosur instead. This radically changed the dynamics of possible negotiations with the EU: On the one hand, it eliminated an internal CAN hurdle to negotiations, with the four remaining members of the organization committed at least in theory to negotiations with the EU. On the other, it temporarily put the organization into administrative disarray, as Venezuela's departure meant a loss of almost one-third of total funding for CAN's institutions.[39] While Chavez's decision was not communicated as a move against free trade in public, it nevertheless appears to have aimed at punishing Colombia and Peru for their free trade agenda that led them to sign the agreements with the US and pursue negotiations with the EU in the first place (US Embassy Venezuela Caracas, 2006).

Aside from a potential blow to the organization's administrative capacity to negotiate with the EU, one additional problem became apparent: The political landscape of Bolivia had been radically changed with its presidential elections of 2005. Evo Morales had been elected president of the country with a landslide victory for his political party supported by the country's indigenous movements. With his inauguration in early 2006, the political view of the country's government on free trade was about to change. While Morales' positions did not appear to be as radical as that of Venezuela's president, the country nevertheless slowly began to alter its domestic economic policies, while also developing ties with Hugo Chavez and ultimately joining ALBA (see Girvan, 2011).

Once more, Spanish and Czech officials, this time joined by the EU's High Representative for the Common Foreign and Security Policy, Javier Solana, voiced fears over these political developments in conversations with US counterparts. The main concerns at the time were the potential of an ever-closer alliance between Bolivia and Venezuela (US Embassy Belgium Brussels, 2006; US Embassy Czech Republic Prague, 2006; US Embassy Spain Madrid, 2006a), which was perceived as a threat to the spread of Western values in the region. Lastly, there were concerns about Bolivia's programme to re-nationalize its oil and gas resources by expropriating foreign companies (Agence Europe, 2006c).

Ultimately, none of these factors altered the EU's willingness to launch negotiations with the Andean Community. The Spanish Foreign Ministry's director for foreign policy discussed the EU's attitude to the negotiations with American diplomats, saying that "the EU was clear at the Summit that the door is open to begin negotiations on a trade agreement right away, whether with three countries or four" (US Embassy Spain Madrid, 2006b). This meant that multiple dynamics were at play on the European side ahead of the summit. On the one hand, the EU was ready to entertain FTA negotiations for economic reasons, while attempting to continue supporting the Andean Community's regional integration. Balancing these goals was rendered particularly difficult by the fact that the Andean Community's four members had not been able to agree to a common position ahead of the summit, which put the declaration for the entire summit at risk.

Ultimately, the European side suggested a compromise proposal that, while not offering a concrete timeframe for negotiations, still made reference to the ultimate scope and a future start of negotiations.[40] In the summit's final declaration, this compromise reads as follows:

> Recalling the common strategic objective established in the Declaration of Guadalajara, we welcome the decision adopted by the EU and the Andean Community to initiate during 2006, a process leading to the negotiation of an Association Agreement which will include political dialogue, cooperation programmes and a trade agreement.
>
> (Council of the European Union, 2006a: 12)

Through this compromise and by its continued insistence on a regional approach, the EU upheld its political pressure on the organization to integrate before any negotiations could begin.[41] In this context, the EU demanded that CAN find a common position for the negotiations ahead of any further meetings (US Embassy Bolivia La Paz, 2006a). Nonetheless, Ferrero-Waldner cautioned in a meeting of the European Parliament's Foreign Affairs Committee that the process would most likely be difficult, and that convincing Bolivia would prove to be challenging (Agence Europe, 2006a).

At CAN's June 2006 meeting, the remaining members of the organization indeed agreed to strengthen its institutions and policies, and indicated their desire to negotiate an Association Agreement with the EU (US Embassy Ecuador Quito, 2006), thereby facilitating the opening of negotiations. What remained, however, were differing positions as to the trade component of the negotiations, with Bolivia arguing that the economies of the region were too disparate for a regional approach (US Embassy Bolivia La Paz, 2006a).

In an attempt to force Bolivia to give up its reservations in the trade realm, the EU gave the country a deadline to join the process (US Embassy Colombia Bogotá, 2006) or be excluded from any trade negotiations with the EU altogether. While Bolivia would eventually leave the negotiations, the country's lack of a clear political position on the negotiations and the political pressure was nevertheless sufficient for it to join the process at the time (US Embassy Bolivia La Paz, 2006b). Both sides then came together at a meeting in July, after having finalized the joint assessment exercise. While the meeting gave the green light for preparations for the negotiations to go ahead, it still demonstrates the EU's insistence that further Andean integration would have to occur before negotiations could get underway properly (EU–CAN High Level Meeting, 2006).

Approving the negotiation briefs

The last step before negotiations could begin was the granting of negotiation briefs to the Commission. Securing an agreement in the Council on these for a number of proposed trade agreements was ultimately one of the priorities of the German presidency in the first half of 2007. By late April 2007, when the GAC gave the go-ahead for the trade element of the Association Agreements, these had become only two of five new mandates for FTAs granted to the European Commission (Agence Europe, 2007) under the new approach announced with Global Europe. Free trade negotiations were also to get under way with ASEAN, South Korea, and India.

This approach of granting negotiating briefs in parallel formally aligned the two negotiations with the EU's overhauled trade strategy and eliminated some of the difficulties of prioritization of trade negotiations that DG Trade was concerned about. At the same time, the agreed negotiation briefs addressed some of the remaining concerns within this DG by including important elements of conditionality on the remaining issues (European Commission, 2007b). The Council thereby demonstrated the existence of what was earlier described as a "permissive consensus" on the negotiations. On the one hand, it showed its awareness of some of the remaining issues, while on the other it entrusted the Commission with a large degree of independence to resolve these.

The negotiation briefs for talks with Central America are not in the public domain. Nonetheless, the conditionality of negotiations can be derived from the discussions surrounding the Commission's mandate to negotiate with CAN. Already the draft mandate prepared by DG RELEX that was approved by the College of Commissioners took note of DG Trade's concerns and those likely to be voiced by the TPC by tasking the Commission's negotiators with ensuring that the agreement contains

> A clause referring to the effective start of the negotiations and the conclusion of the Agreement [...]. This clause should refer to the assessment of the concrete achievements on the commitments undertaken by the Andean Community at the High Level Meeting of July 2006 as regards the strengthening of its regional economic integration.
>
> (European Commission, 2007b: 6)

COREPER, the highest-level Council preparatory body also made sure to further emphasize the importance of this element prior to the Council's go-ahead. The notes of a meeting at which the proposed mandates were discussed contain a declaration that states that

> The Commission will, as appropriate, take into account the possible impact that the evolution of the Andean Community Integration could have on the development of the negotiations, having in mind the importance of developing a strong framework of relations with the Andean Community.
>
> (COREPER, 2007: 13)

A similar declaration was made concerning the ongoing WTO dispute settlement over the EU's banana import regime that Ecuador had filed in November of 2006 and that was then supported by Colombia. After the countries took this step, Commissioner Mandelson had threatened in December that negotiations with CAN could only begin once the complaint had been lifted, as "it is not possible to litigate and negotiate at the same time" (as cited in Agence Europe, 2006b). This was addressed as follows in the context of the upcoming negotiations by COREPER:

> With regard to the CAN negotiating directives, the Commission will take into account the possible impact that the evolution of WTO dispute settlement on bananas could have on the development of the negotiations, having in mind that the Commission is fully aware of the clear limitations and risks to engage in meaningful discussions aimed at improving preferential market access pending the active pursuit of a WTO panel on that key product.
>
> (COREPER, 2007: 13)

The declaration meant that it would be at the Commission's discretion to adequately take the issue into account in its negotiation strategy and thereby added an important political component to the negotiations.

While the two Association Agreements stand out from the "pure" FTA negotiations with Asian countries agreed at the very same meeting, a further COREPER document that is not fully in the public domain demonstrates how the EU aimed to reconcile the difference between the two distinct types of agreements:

> Negotiations on Free-Trade Agreements [...] shall lead to agreements with a clear legal and institutional linkage to the existing or future Partnership and Cooperation Agreements or updated Framework Agreements. Such legal and institutional linkage would entail, inter alia, the [sic] Free-Trade Agreement could be totally or partially suspended if the conditions for such suspension under the Partnership and Cooperation Agreement or updated Framework Agreement apply, and that there would be a coherent institutional framework for the administration of the agreements.
>
> (COREPER document 8598/07 as cited in Okano-Heijmans, 2014: 16)

In essence, this meant that while the other proposed free trade agreements would not be fully fledged Association Agreements, similar political elements would necessarily have to accompany the "pure" free trade agreements either within it or in additional treaties with such countries, thereby rhetorically limiting the differences between the two kinds of agreements that the EU would negotiate in the future.

While DG RELEX as the initial driver for the negotiations with both regional organizations initially faced important internal hurdles to gaining negotiation briefs, these could ultimately be overcome. This was related to the EU's rhetorical entrapment and an alignment of the interests of internal EU actors which led to the relative coherence of their positions over time. While DG Trade ultimately still had some concerns as to the feasibility of the negotiations with both regions, these could be addressed by the inclusion of conditionality in the negotiation briefs. Policy coordination between different institutional actors on the EU's side was thus ultimately successful as the carefully balanced negotiation mandates for the negotiations show.

The negotiation experience: Handling difficulties differently

Negotiation rounds with both regions began shortly after the approval of the mandates in the Council. While these have encountered a number of difficulties—and a radical change of approach has occurred in the case of CAN—it is nevertheless important to note that the parallelism of both processes was upheld during the entire negotiations phase.

Given the important difference that arose during both negotiation processes, these are outlined separately within this section, with a focus first on the Andean Community, which is then contrasted with the negotiation experience with Central America. While a number of external factors have contributed to both negotiations' disparate outcomes, this section argues that bureaucratic politics once more help us gain a fuller picture of the developments underlying the different developments. Here, the lack of diverging positions in the Central American case can explain why the EU insisted on an interregional approach despite a number of external challenges to it. In contrast, an emerging divergence of views with DG Trade combined with its autonomy in the negotiation process can help our understanding as to why the EU ultimately negotiated a free trade agreement with Colombia and Peru only, while abandoning the inclusion of political and cooperation chapters.

Negotiating with the Andean Community

With the go-ahead for negotiations given by the Council, the Commission could shift its focus to a negotiation strategy that would help overcome some of the difficulties internal to CAN that these were facing. While such attempts would ultimately fail, the initial phase of the negotiations nevertheless demonstrated the unity of the EU's position, making use of the different policy tools at its disposal across policy areas to drive forward the negotiation process. This phase hence demonstrates a scenario under which the negotiation mandates have united the European Commission, much as could be observed in the case of the negotiations with Mercosur. The commitment by the member states in this case furthermore allowed the Commission a relative degree of autonomy and served to overcome any possible internal bureaucratic divisions.

The factors that had rendered the announcement of a start to negotiations at the 2006 Lima summit impossible still remained when negotiations were scheduled to go ahead in early 2007. While the EU was originally concerned about the problems for Andean integration that arose due to Venezuela's decision to leave the process, it became increasingly clear that the position of Bolivia would render the negotiations difficult. This was due to ideological as well as economic factors. While the country's membership in ALBA ensured that it was rhetorically opposed to the concept of free trade, the nature of the country's export structure also meant that the negotiation of an FTA with the EU would have provided few benefits for the country.[42]

The difficulty of reconciling the aim for a true biregional agreement with its trade aspect had already become apparent in the July 2006 EU–CAN meeting which gave the green light for the preparation of formal negotiations. In the document, Bolivia had requested "flexibility in the future negotiations considering the different levels of development between the CAN countries" (EU–CAN High Level Meeting, 2006: 2). By early 2007, the issue of dissenting voices within CAN had come to be even more prevalent with the inauguration of President Rafael Correa in Ecuador. Given his political views, the country then began to develop closer ties with Venezuela and Bolivia, ultimately introducing a two-way split within CAN.

While both countries' detailed trade policy preferences were not necessarily clear from the outset of the negotiations, their position was more and more at odds with those of Colombia and Peru, the main proponents of a FTA with the EU. Ahead of the official opening of negotiations in June 2007, EU diplomats voiced their concerns as to these developments to US counterparts (US Embassy Peru Lima, 2007).

Nonetheless, negotiations began somewhat successfully. This can be attributed in large part to the way in which the EU approached the negotiations, emphasizing that trade would only be one of its three constituent pillars. This initially led Ecuador to believe that the EU's aims were different from pure free trade negotiations, which stand in contrast to the country's refusal to pursue FTA negotiations with the US (US Embassy Ecuador Quito, 2007b).

From the outset, the EU had introduced important elements of conditionality, as well as incentives that would accompany the negotiations to boost their success. Much as can be seen in the parallel negotiations with Central America (see below), it was the EU's position that negotiations would only occur in a region-to-region context that was meant to further incentivize regional integration. When communicating with the Andean partners ahead of the first round of negotiations in April 2007, the EU made its conditions clear by stating that:

> it is expected that the CAN will continue making further progress in the definition of a common tariff reduction point, as well as in the process of taking the necessary decisions on the harmonization of the Andean Customs Regimes.
> (EU–Andean Community Ministerial Meeting, 2007)

This condition was accompanied by a clear positive incentive through the EU's development funding. Given DG RELEX's leadership role on the allocation of the EU's multiannual development cooperation frameworks, it was able to alter the funding to the region in support of the negotiations. The 2007–2013 regional strategy document thus voices one of the EU's main development goals for the region as follows:

> to support regional trade and economic integration in the Andean Community, notably by encouraging intensification of this process before and during negotiations on an Association Agreement, including a free trade area.
> (European Commission, 2007a: 15)

This was meant to be achieved by earmarking more than 40% of the EU's total aid to the region for the regional economic integration envelope (European Commission, 2007a: 30). The EU hence provided significant monetary incentives to help the region integrate further economically and therefore to achieve the EU's negotiation conditions.

This mix of conditionality and incentives helped initial progress in the negotiations. Any of the frequent Colombian and Peruvian attempts to convince the EU of the merits of bilateral negotiations, such as by Peruvian President Alan García in November 2007 (Noriega, 2007), were countered by restating the EU's insistence for region-to-region negotiations, while mentioning the potential for side payments to keep Bolivia at the negotiation table (US Embassy Bolivia La Paz, 2007).

EU and member state officials were keen to point out the advantages of the biregional approach for the ultimate passage of an agreement to the Colombians. While there were important concerns about the human rights situation in Colombia amongst European politicians, the issue would likely not be scrutinized as closely in European parliaments if the agreement were to be regional, rather than bilateral (US Embassy Colombia Bogotá, 2008b).

These attempts, alongside the relatively positive attitude of Ecuador during this initial phase, made for a successful start of negotiations. The country's commitment at this point went so far that when Bolivia threatened to leave before the official start, Ecuadorean diplomats successfully intervened and thereby pre-empted a potential Colombian and Peruvian exit from the regional organization (US Embassy Ecuador Quito, 2007b).

While initial negotiation rounds, which were mainly concerned with issues of a general nature, did not make for significant differences of position, difficulties nevertheless began to arise in the spring of 2008 (European Commission, 2009). Nonetheless, there were increasing European political concerns over the situation in Bolivia and Ecuador: The former had undertaken a controversial nationalization project in its natural gas industry, hurting European business interests (US Embassy Bolivia La Paz, 2008b). In the latter case, it became apparent that Ecuador's foreign policy apparatus was suffering from internal divisions, thereby threatening the unity of the country's foreign policy positions (US Embassy Ecuador Quito, 2007a, 2008b).

Looking at the negotiations themselves, these had reached a gridlock ahead of the EU–LAC summit of May 2008, mainly over Bolivia's refusal to negotiate anything but the trade of goods, with Ecuador gradually moving to a similar position (US Embassy Colombia Bogotá, 2008b; US Embassy Ecuador Quito, 2008c). Furthermore, Ecuadorean negotiators voiced their opposition to the agreement's proposed sustainability chapter, as they believed that political conditionality should not form part of the considerations for a trade agreement (US Embassy Ecuador Quito, 2008c). These difficulties also meant that EU officials started to become more and more impatient over a general lack of progress in the process (Haubrich Seco, 2011: 13). For the European side, this was reminiscent of the original negotiation rounds with Mercosur.

Ultimately, it was a further issue that demonstrated the determining influence of external political, rather than economic, factors on the negotiations. Bolivia and Ecuador used the EU's discussion of the Returns Directive to threaten a unilateral withdrawal from negotiations. This piece of legislation in the realm of the EU's immigration and asylum policy was meant to facilitate the expulsion of illegal immigrants from the EU's territory and had no direct link to the negotiations, nor did officials on the EU's side believe that Latin American countries should be concerned about this.[43] Nevertheless, both countries voiced their fear that it would discriminate against their nationals in the EU (Phillips, 2008a, 2008c). Whether these were actual political concerns or mere posturing is unclear. However, a former Latin American diplomat mentioned that Bolivia's main aim was to delay the negotiation process so as to be able to define its own strategy.[44]

When these difficulties became apparent, an attempt to save the regional approach was made at the May 2008 EU–Andean Community summit held on the fringe of the overall EU–Latin America summit in Lima. The difficulties at this stage were summed up succinctly in an internal EU note for the Council presidency ahead of the meeting:

> Bolivia wants a maximum of exceptions, long-term calendars etc,[sic] for its 'asymmetries' which may become the breaking point in negotiations. Ecuador is oscillating, and changed part of its approach during the third round, as well as part of its team. Colombia and Peru are visibly frustrated with these difficulties and have publicly called on the EU to consider giving up its bi-regional approach.[45]

This further shows that the Returns Directive played no role in the actual negotiations at this point in time. In order to defuse the problems outlined in the internal note, both sides agreed on a format that would allow for more flexibility in the negotiations (Phillips, 2008b). The joint communique of the EU–CAN meeting described this as follows:

> They [The heads of state and government] agreed that particular attention would be paid to the specific development needs of member countries of the Andean Community, taking into account the asymmetries between and within the regions and the need for flexibility, in the appropriate manner, granting a special and differentiated treatment for the member countries of the Andean Community, in particular Bolivia and Ecuador, on the part of the EU.
> (CAN–EU Troika Summit, 2008)

The new approach would have enabled the establishment of different levels of liberalization in the trade realm, thereby effectively turning the trade component of the agreement into a series of bilateral accords, all while upholding the overall goal of an Association Agreement. Ultimately, however, this did not help to overcome the difficulties in the process. While this careful and coordinated use of policy tools on the EU's side helped to keep the negotiation alive, this would ultimately not be enough.

Changing the EU's approach in CAN negotiations

It is at this point in the negotiations, during the spring of 2008, that a significant shift in the EU's approach occurred. After previous difficulties, the Commission unilaterally cancelled the next negotiation round scheduled for April. This initial move could be interpreted at the time as a further attempt to demonstrate the EU's desire to proceed only in a region-to-region format. However, the developments over the ensuing month would lead the EU to revert to bilateral trade negotiations with only some of the Andean countries, and thereby a radical change of its negotiation position. While the FTA ultimately reached with Colombia and Peru is a single agreement, the tariff schedules with both parties nonetheless diverge.

This change of policy can be explained by increasing economic concerns in DG Trade that would see the broader political goal of support for regional integration become secondary to trade concerns, as well as to fears of alienating the governments of those countries which were more willing to improve ties with the EU. This meant a decoupling of the political parts of the negotiations from the trade aspect, with the EU thereby abandoning the complex Association Agreement negotiations for more standardized practice in the trade realm. At the same time, the EU all but abandoned the attempts to modernize the political ties to CAN.

Interviewees have offered different accounts of the ultimate motivation for the EU's change of approach, with a member state representative calling it a "pragmatic response"[46] to changing circumstances, while others insisted that the means of achievement for the ultimate goal of a biregional Association Agreement had simply been altered, but not the goal in itself.[47]

Initially, the EU's aim still appears to have been to return to the biregional format by providing the concerned countries with additional incentives to do so. In July, Ferrero-Waldner announced a further development cooperation project that would once more help the economic integration of the region (Agence Europe, 2008c). Ultimately, this last-ditch effort was not successful, however, and other dynamics began to dominate.

When the EU initially decided to suspend negotiations, this was seen by Columbia and Peru as another opportunity to call for bilateral rather than interregional negotiations. The presidents of both countries, Álvaro Uribe and Alan García, sent identical letters to Commission President Barroso to that end in September. This was accompanied by significant lobbying from the diplomatic representations of both countries, arguing that their pursuit of improving ties with the EU should not be held hostage by unwilling third parties.[48]

While the insistence of these countries appears to ultimately have led DG RELEX to accept the concerns of DG Trade (see below), concerns remained over the possible impact on Andean regional integration. It was in this context that the letters, as well as diplomatic representatives from both countries, pointed to the Andean Community's precedent of allowing bilateral free trade—albeit not political—negotiations in the context of their agreements with the US (US Embassy Colombia Bogotá, 2008c).

Reference was made to decision 598 of the Andean Community Commission in 2004, which allowed the organization's member states the following: "If it is not possible to conduct community negotiations for whatever reasons, the Member Countries can negotiate bilaterally with third countries" (Andean Community Commission, 2004, article 2). Making use of this precedent would hence—at least in theory—help to overcome the problem of a bilateral approach's legal impact on the regional integration process. If we are to believe one of the interviewees, the existence of decision 598 was one of the main factors that ultimately convinced Ferrero-Waldner and DG RELEX that a change of approach would not mean a loss of face given its previous policy preferences.[49] This suggests that while its previous promises played a role in DG RELEX's deliberations, ultimately the necessity to uphold these was overcome by the existence of decision 598.

At the same time, DG Trade officials were anxious to allow for continued trade negotiations given their concerns over market access in the Andean Community's two most important economies.[50] Nonetheless, a fear was also present that taking a bilateral approach would reduce pressure on Ecuador to continue negotiating with the EU.

The main concern, however, was once more the potential loss of competitiveness compared to the US. Both Colombia and Peru pursued an aggressive FTA agenda that also included negotiations with Canada (US Embassy Colombia Bogotá, 2007; US Embassy Peru Lima, 2008), and a Colombian FTA with the European Free Trade Association (EFTA) (US Embassy Colombia Bogotá, 2008a). Furthermore, the US Congress had ratified the agreement with Peru in 2007, and it was due to enter into force by 2009. This was not the case for the US–Colombia agreement, as ratification only occurred in 2011,[51] but the continued link between the different negotiations can nevertheless be seen in a US diplomatic cable (US Embassy Colombia Bogotá, 2010).

Comments by EU chief negotiator Rupert Schlegelmilch to US counterparts offer further evidence for the fear of losing market access to the US, stating that the terms of trade agreed in the existing US FTAs would be the EU's lowest aim in those negotiations (US Embassy Colombia Bogotá, 2009b). Additionally, CAN had failed to proceed with the small integration steps towards a customs union that were part of the EU's conditions, and that would have allowed for actual region-to-region negotiations. With the envisioned efficiency gains from an integrated CAN market less likely, the EU's trade interests in Colombia and Peru hence played out in favour of a bilateral approach.

This would come at a further price for a possible negotiation success with Ecuador, however. Given the structure of the country's exports to the EU, which are largely based on agricultural products such as bananas, and the EU's sensitivities, any kind of WTO-compatible bilateral FTA with the country would prove difficult to reach. Given the relatively more diverse economies of both Colombia and Peru, the fulfilment of this legal requirement that any FTA liberalizes a very significant share of trade between both partners would not be a significant issue. A bilateral approach would hence ultimately render an agreement with the already reticent Ecuador even less likely.

Lastly, Commission officials from all camps were worried that any significant change of approach would lead to a reopening of the time-consuming and possibly conflictual process of reaching a new negotiation mandate with the Council, thereby further reducing the EU's credibility in the face of the more willing negotiation partners (US Embassy Colombia Bogotá, 2008c). Additionally, if negotiations had failed at this point, then this would have meant a repeat of the initial Mercosur debacle of having used precious human resources without achieving tangible results.

Ultimately, amidst these complex preference patterns, the views of DG Trade were key given its autonomy in negotiations of the trade aspects of any agreement, and due to the fact that DG RELEX was divided over whether to reward Colombia and Peru's desire to negotiate with the EU despite the prospect of weakening Andean integration. This emergent change of position within the EU was first unofficially communicated to the Andean countries in August (US Embassy Ecuador Quito, 2008b), but it would take longer to reconcile the different EU priorities with a new negotiation format.

DG Trade was nonetheless nominally weakened given that Trade Commissioner Mandelson surprisingly resigned from his position on 3 October 2008 (Agence Europe, 2008d). He was replaced by Catherine Ashton, an official who was entirely new to the European Commission at the time, and hence unlikely to be able to influence important policy decisions at the beginning of her tenure. Nonetheless, the Council in the form of its TPC (still called Article 133 Committee at the time) had demonstrated confidence in DG Trade's assessment as to the options for the Andean region. When discussing the letters that had been sent to President Barroso, the meeting concluded by stating that "the Committee encouraged the Commission to do its utmost to overcome the impasse whilst keeping in mind issues of regional integration" (Article 133 Committee, 2008b). This offered DG Trade large room for manoeuvre. Facing these opposing views, Ferrero-Waldner and DG RELEX ultimately fell in line with DG Trade's preferences by arguing that they favoured a position which would not see Colombia and Peru punished for their membership in CAN.[52] Once this internal change of thinking towards a bilateral approach had occurred, it had to be rendered at least rhetorically compatible with the EU's stated policy aims for the region, based on the promotion of regionalism and the improvement of human rights.

The Commission's preferred strategy to unite these different elements began to emerge in Barroso's response to both presidents on 6 October, which is described in detail in a US diplomatic cable (US Embassy Colombia Bogotá, 2008c). In essence, the EU signalled to its Andean partners that it was willing to negotiate a separate free trade agreement with willing Andean countries. Simultaneously, the other two pillars could be negotiated with all of CAN, with the FTA simply making reference the biregional PDCA of 2003, or a new political agreement to be reached. In the words of the US diplomat who authored the cable, this would have the following advantage:

> This linkage allows the EC to avoid the time-consuming process of having EU member-states change the negotiating instructions and gives the Commission

the political cover it believes it needs against accusations of fracturing the CAN.

(US Embassy Colombia Bogotá, 2008c)

Nonetheless, in a further attempt to demonstrate the EU's commitment to Andean regional integration, the decision as to how to proceed was essentially left to the Andean countries who were due to hold a summit later in October (Agence Europe, 2008b). While one former official involved in the process described this as a decision aimed at respecting the sovereignty of the Andean countries,[53] the weight of the evidence points to a face-saving measure by DG RELEX to try and ensure coherence between the EU's rhetoric and its policy position towards CAN. Nonetheless, the initial idea for a split of the trade from the cooperation and political aspects had already been floated once at the time of the 2006 EU–Latin America summit over Bolivia's negative attitude towards the negotiations (US Embassy Ecuador Quito, 2008c).

While CAN's Guayaquil summit attempted to demonstrate unity in the face of the EU, with CAN's member states agreeing that the political and cooperation pillars would be approached as a group, the summit nevertheless allowed for bilateral negotiations in the trade pillar (Agence Europe, 2008a). Importantly, Ecuadorian President Correa had taken the decision beforehand that he would not attempt to block bilateral negotiations of any of his partners, while leaving the door open for the country to join into the trade portion later on (US Embassy Ecuador Quito, 2008b). This paved the way for the interested parties to move forward with a bilateral approach, with Ecuador remaining part of the group, while Bolivia then left the process for good (US Embassy Bolivia La Paz, 2008a).

Ultimately, the Commission proposed to the Council that the negotiation briefs should be modified in such a way as to split the political and cooperation pillars from the trade aspects, thereby asking that the Council

> authorise the Commission to negotiate a multiparty trade agreement between the European Community and its Member States, of the one part, and the member countries of the Andean Community which share the aim of reaching an ambitious, comprehensive, balanced trade agreement, consistent with the WTO, of the other part, and to designate the Article 133 Committee [Trade Policy Committee] to assist the Commission in that task.
> (Working Party on Latin America, 2008: 2)

In parallel, the Commission asked for the Council to

> authorise the Commission to negotiate a political dialogue and cooperation agreement between the European Community and its Member States and the Andean Community and its member countries, with a view to strengthening and updating the commitments set out in the Political Dialogue and Cooperation Agreement between the European Community and its Member States, of the one part, and the Andean Community and its member

countries, of the other part, signed in 2003 and to designate the Working Party on Latin America to assist the Commission in that task.

(Working Party on Latin America, 2008: 2)

This meant that the negotiation briefs would only have to be modified minimally, since the overall goal of a region-to-region approach was nominally upheld, albeit in the context of two separate negotiations. The formulation on the parties to the free trade agreement would further allow the EU to keep the door open for all of CAN's members, while enabling negotiations with those most willing to do so.

The most important change on the EU's end, however, was that the decision-making processes for both were meant to be decoupled internally, with the negotiations for the multiparty trade agreement being the responsibility of DG Trade and hence of a different Council structure (the TPC) than the negotiations for an updated PDCA which would remain the responsibility of DG RELEX (and COLAC in the Council).

While the member states appear to have received this proposal favourably over-all, in line with their previous trust in DG Trade's judgement, there nevertheless were concerns by some member states as to what this approach would mean for the value of political clauses in the trade agreement if the political pillar were to be excluded from the FTA (Article 133 Committee, 2008a). Ultimately, however, a mandate change along those lines was agreed and trade negotiations with the willing Andean countries could continue.

Despite the above concerns for the political aspects of the negotiations, the attempts to upgrade the political and cooperation pillars in the region-to-region context were abandoned relatively quickly, with progress only occurring in the trade realm.[54] The EU's shift to bilateral negotiations is hence illustrative of the primacy of DG Trade's, rather than DG RELEX's concerns in this context.

When looking at the remaining trade negotiations, initially only Bolivia had decided not to join the process, while Ecuador remained a part of the group of the willing after further internal divisions were overcome (US Embassy Ecuador Quito, 2008a). Bolivia then accused the EU of attempting to break the Andean integration project. Nevertheless, the country was repeatedly invited to join the negotiations under the new format by various EU representatives (US Embassy Bolivia La Paz, 2008a; Willis, 2009). Its government nonetheless upheld its opposition to the agreement, even attempting to block the others' negotiations by claiming that they had violated CAN's ministerial decision 667, which stipulated that negotiations with the EU would be on a region-to-region basis (Fritz, 2010).

These concerns were not addressed by CAN's other members, however, and an initial round of negotiations with the three countries took place in early 2009. The outcome from this round appeared to demonstrate that splitting the negotiations despite the overall common framework allowed for some progress to be made (US Embassy Colombia Bogotá, 2009b). Nonetheless, limitations related to the position of Ecuador became apparent already in the second negotiation round that took place in this format. While Colombia and Peru were getting closer to reaching an agreement with the EU, the continued discord within Ecuador's government, its poor preparation, as well as the outstanding issue of banana prices and quotas, meant that the latter increasingly fell behind (US Embassy Colombia Bogotá, 2009a).

Ecuador then withdrew from the process entirely in July 2009, citing the unresolved WTO banana dispute (Fritz, 2010) and the EU's difficulties to concede sufficiently in the agricultural realm. While this was the official answer, its withdrawal nevertheless mainly related to its growing unease about FTAs and the country's rapprochement with Venezuela and ALBA. As the negotiations with the two remaining partners went on, Bolivia and Ecuador came to be ever more vocal about their opposition to the EU's supposed imposition of a neoliberal model on the region (Agence Europe, 2009b).

Ultimately, this clear-cut divide allowed the negotiations with Colombia and Peru to be sped up, eying a closure in time for the EU–Latin America summit in May 2010. This schedule was then driven as much by a desire to demonstrate progress in the EU's relations with Latin America in time for the summit, Spain's upcoming Council presidency, as well as Ferrero-Waldner's brief move to the trade portfolio with the Commission's Treaty of Lisbon reshuffle. Much like the decision to open negotiations with Central America and the Andean Community in 2006 was driven by the schedule of the EU–Latin America summit, the 2010 Madrid summit would be another moment to demonstrate that progress in the EU's relations with the region had been made despite the apparent diverging views within the EU.

Ecuador's withdrawal from the process created further difficulties for the EU's rhetoric of continued support for regional integration, an issue which was addressed in a Commission document outlining its strategy for Latin America ahead of the entry into force of the Treaty of Lisbon. The document entitled *The European Union and Latin America: Global Players in Partnership* (European Commission, 2009) would be Ferrero-Waldner's final input into the relationship as External Relations Commissioner ahead of the 2010 summit. The document aimed to take stock of the progress in the relationship between the two regions, while also demonstrating that the EU's policy remained compatible with the broader policy goals of regional integration. Lastly, the document offered the possibility of leaving a legacy upon which the new EEAS strategy for the region could be built. In terms of the relations with the Andean region, the document provided the following narrative:

> When negotiations came up against difficulties, the EU presented alternative approaches to support the countries and regions concerned. In the case of the Andean Community (CAN), an attempt to conclude a region-to-region Association Agreement was not successful. However, at the request of a number of Andean countries, the EU offered them the opportunity to conclude a trade agreement with a regional perspective, together with the option of expanding the 2003 Political and Cooperation Agreement.
>
> (European Commission, 2009: 4)

The desire to conclude the agreement was also driven by Spain's impending Council presidency in the first half of 2010, which made the strengthening of the EU's ties with the region a priority (US Embassy Spain Madrid, 2009). This once more demonstrates the importance of the autonomy of the Council presidency ahead of the changes introduced with the Treaty of Lisbon. Given Spain's particular interest in the region, and the prestige of hosting the 2010 summit, Spanish diplomats made significant efforts that ultimately allowed for the timely conclusion of negotiations (Trueb, 2012: 277–8).

This was further aided by the fact that the introduction of the foreign affairs provisions from the Treaty of Lisbon was only gradual, meaning that the Spanish Council presidency was still able to generate policy initiatives in the EU's foreign policy. While it did foresee a reduction of the role of the rotating presidency in the realm of foreign affairs by changing external relations working groups to a permanent chairmanship by EEAS officials, this only occurred in late 2010 in the case of the working group dealing with Latin America (Trueb, 2012: 279). The chairmanship of the relevant Article 133/Trade Policy Committee would furthermore remain the responsibility of the rotating presidency.

This Spanish activism was helped by Ferrero-Waldner's short-term position as the EU's Trade Commissioner until early February 2010, replacing Catherine Ashton who had been selected as the EU's first HRVP. This meant that only the very last phase of the negotiations was overseen by her successor Karel De Gucht. While the agreement could be initialled at the Madrid summit in May,[55] the breakthrough and de facto finish had already occurred in early March (Agence Europe, 2010a). Given that such a summit declaration has to be drafted unanimously between all remaining partners, the announcement was at least somewhat clouded by the inclusion of a footnote which refers to a Bolivian legal challenge to the agreement, filed in the Andean Community's Court of Justice (Council of the European Union, 2010: 7).

The EU's change of track in the negotiations, while initiated by external divisions within the Andean region, can ultimately be explained by the autonomy of DG Trade due to the great importance of trade aspects in the Association Agreement negotiations. Ultimately, DG RELEX's concerns for regional integration were thereby relegated to a secondary role behind DG Trade's view that an FTA with Colombia and Peru was necessary. While the roles of both were initially bound by the negotiation mandate from the Council, the problems that occurred after few negotiation rounds meant that their preferences had started to diverge beforehand. While regional integration remained important for DG RELEX, DG Trade was ultimately happy about the exclusion of more reluctant countries from the free trade negotiations as this increased the likelihood of success.

Negotiations with Central America

While the negotiations with SIECA ultimately succeeded in the same format as originally intended, a number of external developments risked putting this outcome in peril. Despite these, the EU insisted on continuing the negotiations in the interregional framework in this instance. This ultimately kept the negotiations alive and helped to overcome internal divisions amongst the Central American countries.

This difference in the EU's negotiation position when compared to the Andean case can be attributed primarily to the fact that, this time around, the preferences of DG Trade and DG RELEX remained aligned throughout the negotiations. While Commission policy alignment due to the negotiation mandate played a central role for the progress of the negotiations, this was also helped by the member states' position on the matter.

Three external developments had the potential to derail the entire negotiation: Firstly, Costa Rica's continued attempts to diverge into a bilateral approach whenever difficulties arose in the negotiation process; secondly, Nicaragua's ideological proximity to ALBA; and thirdly, the Honduran *coup d'état* of 2009. While it was the EU's threat of ending negotiations in the former two cases that helped overcome SIECA's internal difficulties, it was the return to relative stability in Honduras and the EU member states' pragmatic acceptance of positive developments in the country that allowed for negotiations to conclude successfully.

Much like in Ecuador and Bolivia, it was the election of a left-wing president in Nicaragua that created a first significant risk for the region-to-region negotiations. Daniel Ortega, a member of the former *junta* that ruled the country during the Sandinista Revolution from 1979 to 1990 won the presidential elections of 2006. Initially, as confided to American diplomats, his election was not seen as a problem by the EU (US Mission to the European Union, 2007), and negotiations in the interregional format went ahead as planned. Nevertheless, over time, the country aligned itself ever more closely with ALBA, coinciding with increasing criticism of the free trade chapter of the proposed Association Agreement.

Before any effect could be felt on the negotiations, however, relations between the country and the EU began to worsen ahead of the country's municipal elections of 9 November 2008, when Nicaragua decided to align itself more closely with Russia. This manifested itself in the country's recognition of the independence of South Ossetia and Abkhazia. Thereby, the country directly took sides in the Georgian conflict, triggering anger in the EU institutions and member states alike. Furthermore, a number of opposition parties were barred from participating in the elections, leading to highly critical comments from European officials. As a result, the country upped its rhetoric, accusing European ambassadors of a campaign to "destabilise and topple the legitimately constituted government led by the comrade commander Daniel Ortega" (Nicaraguan diplomat cited in Caroit, 2008, translation mine). The EU took a strong and coherent stance in reaction to these developments, with member states and the EU's institutions freezing development aid to the country (US Mission to the European Union, 2009). For Nicaragua, the consequences of such a decision were important, since European Union aid accounts for 40% of the development aid received, the total of which makes up around 10% of the country's GDP (Caroit, 2008).

While these developments initially did not impact significantly on the negotiation process for the Association Agreement, ultimately the country's political demands did lead to a suspension of negotiations ahead of a round scheduled for April 2009. In an attempt to block further progress, the country asked for the set-up of a compensation fund for economic asymmetries, demanding an astronomical sum of 60 billion euros—more than six times the country's annual GDP. When this elicited a negative response from Brussels, the country unilaterally withdrew from the negotiation process. While the measure was seemingly pointed against the EU, European officials nevertheless believed that it was targeted more at the country's Central American neighbours, who were also increasingly worried about the political development within its government (US Embassy Nicaragua Managua, 2009).

Despite these difficulties, the EU maintained its position that negotiations would only go ahead with the entirety of the Central American region (Gutiérrez Wa-chong, 2009), in line with fears that this would have the potential to weaken the region's integration and further worsen the economic case for an agreement.[56] In this instance, the interests of DG RELEX, pushing for a region-wide negotiation agenda, and those of DG Trade aligned, allowing the EU to maintain its initial stance. After all, given the size of the region's economy, the negotiation of bilateral FTAs would not be warranted, nor would the prospect of a US FTA with some of the countries in the region have any discernible impact on the EU's trade patterns.[57]

Negotiations were able to resume later in the month, after other Central American countries put pressure on Nicaragua.[58] The EU at the same time made a promise that it would study the set-up of an additional funding mechanism for Latin America to tackle some of the existing disparity in the region (Agence Europe, 2009d; *Guatemala Times*, 2009) and thereby addressing the issue of Nicaragua's development funding demands—albeit at a low level. In the words of Guatemala's deputy foreign minister, this meant that:

> Central American and the European Union have [...] decided to install a bi-regional working group to study the establishment of a financial mechanism for the development of Latin America.
>
> (*Guatemala Times*, 2009)

From this proposal would emerge the Latin America Investment Facility (LAIF), once more demonstrating the EU's ability to use development funding as part of its negotiation strategy when the views of actors internal to the Commission cohere.

Ultimately, it was the political conditionality of linking the EU's development policy to the negotiation process and the insistence on the regional format that helped overcome this particular blockade. At the same time, one should not overestimate the sometimes hostile rhetoric of the Nicaraguan government. Guisell Morales-Echeverry, Nicaragua's ambassador to the UK, has mentioned in public[59] that for Nicaragua ALBA and the negotiations with the EU were always seen as complementary, helping to balance out any possible negative side-effects.

Another important setback for the negotiations occurred only a few months later, when the July 2009 negotiation round was suspended in the wake of the

Honduran *coup d'état* (Agence Europe, 2009c). The country's President Manuel Zelaya was deposed by the country's military on 28 June 2009, nominally over a row between his office and the constitutional court. The action was quickly dismissed by external actors including the EU as a de facto military *coup d'état*. This led the EU to suspend political contacts with the country, and all member states withdrew their ambassadors and suspended development funding to the country (Agence Europe, 2009a; US Embassy Tegucigualpa, 2009), once more demonstrating that the views of the Commission and of the member states aligned on this matter.

While the EU was quick to react to this crisis situation, the urge to return to negotiations once the situation had stabilized was also evident. Trueb (2012: 277–8) has pointed out that over the last year of the negotiations Spanish diplomacy played an important role to close the deal in time for the EU–Latin America summit to be held in Madrid. The impact of Spain's activity can once more be attributed to the autonomy of the country's rotating presidency in the first half of 2010.

When Spain's Deputy Prime Minister María Teresa Fernández de la Vega visited Costa Rica in early August, shortly after the coup, she made it clear that the country wished for negotiations to continue, with Honduras returning to the negotiation table once the crisis resolved (Murillo, 2009). An EP delegation visiting Costa Rica in October 2009 was more sceptical as to the possibility for renewed negotiation, mentioning that a solution in Honduras would have to be found first (Long, 2009).

In any case, when a political settlement based on the upcoming elections in November 2009 was found, Ferrero-Waldner was quick to embrace the agreement (Agence Europe, 2009e). Despite some ongoing concerns, the EU slowly returned to *realpolitik* and officially resumed negotiations in early 2010, with an aim to conclude these in time for the upcoming summit.

A further stumbling block was the factor of Costa Rica, the country in the region that has been the most vocal supporter of an agreement with the EU. Being more politically stable and with a more sophisticated economy, the country continually saw itself as a case apart. Whenever negotiations were facing difficulties, it was the EU's categorical opposition to bilateral negotiations that forced the country back into line (Gutiérrez Wa-chong, 2008, 2009).

Nevertheless, the agreement does take stock of some of the disparities in the region and thereby addresses some of Costa Rica's concerns. While the Association Agreement in itself was negotiated between all the partners at hand, the trade chapters are specific to every Central American country. This is not just a means to allow for different tariff schedules, but also a safeguard to allow for a gradual entry of force of the agreement, even when the ratification is blocked in some of the Central American countries.[60]

Ultimately, an alignment of interests on the EU's side, be it amongst different parts of the Commission, or amongst large member states (Trueb, 2012), helped the EU to maintain its initial position throughout the negotiation process. Despite a number of external developments in this instance, it was the primacy of political concerns over the situation in some of the Central American countries, as well as the absence of an economic incentive for bilateral negotiations that could have swayed DG Trade, which helped the EU maintain its position and not change its policy approach. With the positions of all relevant actors internal to the EU aligning, the complexity of the negotiation process never put the EU's approach at risk in this case. This allowed for the conclusion of a full Association Agreement with SIECA and Panama at the 2010 EU–Latin America summit, which contributed to the latter country's ultimate accession to the grouping.

The ratification experience

The conclusion of the Association Agreement with SIECA and of the FTA with Colombia and Peru at the EU–LAC summit in 2010 marked the end of the Commission-driven process of the negotiations. This started another stage leading to their ratification and application. While the latter phase was marked by the Commission leading an external negotiation process, this section is concerned with the ratification stage that would see a return to internal EU bargaining, principally over the EP's new powers gained with the Treaty of Lisbon. This section once more demonstrates the difficulty for EU foreign policy-making in the absence of agreement amongst all the institutional actors involved in the process and amidst the complexity of the EU's decision-making system.

The Treaty of Lisbon's entry into force in 2009 has to be considered as a factor that risked putting the agreements' ratification at stake. Whereas the dynamics of negotiations for international agreements were largely limited to the coordination between different DGs of the Commission, as well as the Council, the Treaty of Lisbon renders this set-up somewhat more complex. The most important bureaucratic change for the EU's foreign policy overall was the creation of the EEAS, and its formal role in the negotiations for international agreements (Woolcock, 2010: 25) (see Chapter 3). This did not prove to be of any importance for the agreements in question, however, given that the remaining negotiations were largely limited to the trade realm, which remained under the auspices of the Commission's DG Trade. The focus of this section is hence on the European Parliament and on individual member states given that the agreements in question were deemed to be of a mixed nature, requiring ratification by all of the EU's member states.

Dealing with the European Parliament

The changes introduced with the Treaty of Lisbon led to an increase of the powers of the EP that would radically alter its attitude towards FTA and Association Agreements. While not gaining a formal input into the formulation of negotiation briefs, the Treaty of Lisbon nevertheless provided it with information rights on the progress of negotiations not dissimilar to those of the Council, and even pure FTAs without political and cooperation provisions now require the European Parliament's consent (Woolcock, 2010: 23). This has the potential to influence the dynamics of the EU's future Association and trade negotiations in important ways, but ultimately did not directly create new hurdles for the negotiations at hand. This can be attributed to the fact that the existing briefs for both negotiations did not lose validity with the entry into force of the treaty, and that both negotiations were very advanced at the time.

The most important internal EU disruption for the cases here can ultimately be attributed to changes in the ratification process for the EU's Association and free trade agreements. Prior to the Treaty of Lisbon, the European Parliament was only consulted for pure FTAs, and thus without decision-making power. Furthermore, the EP had no input into either the negotiation mandate or the actual negotiations. Even when its assent was required for specific international agreements, it was only the very last actor to be involved, after ratification by the EU's member state parliaments had occurred (Hillman and Kleimann, 2010: 5; Woolcock, 2010: 23).

With the Treaty of Lisbon, the Ordinary Legislative Procedure (OLP) now applies to the EU's CCP, increasing the power of the EP on most trade matters. This is particularly relevant as the EU has to adopt bilateral safeguards legislation before any agreement can even enter into force provisionally. This legislation sets out to define technical conditions under which the application of (trade) agreements can be temporarily suspended in case of a disruptive surge of imports. With Lisbon, the passage of such legislation gives the EP equal decision-making powers to those of the Council.

When it comes to the ratification process for international agreements that Parliament already had to assent to previously, the only technical change to the EP's powers is that it can now consent to these with a simple rather than absolute majority (Woolcock, 2010: 23). However, the increase in its powers on trade matters has meant that the EP's role became more important even for agreements such as the EU–Central America Association Agreement. In any case, it decided to test its increased role with regard to the ratification of the EU–Colombia–Peru FTA, hoping to set a precedent for the future. This put the Parliament at odds with the Commission, which was keen to see its successfully negotiated agreement approved.

Given the ultimately different nature of the agreements, one being for an Association and the other for free trade, Parliamentary approval procedures differed. Whereas the EP's AFET holds primary responsibility for Association Agreements, it is INTA that is responsible for trade agreements, as well as giving an opinion on the trade parts of the Central America deal. This differentiated treatment has been pointed out as somewhat inconsequential, given that trade was the primary concern for both of the agreements at hand.[61] Ultimately, it contributed to the fact that only the approval of the Colombia and Peru FTA agreements was put in peril by dynamics within the EP.

Awareness of the potential difficulties that an agreement with CAN or any of its members could have in the EP was apparent even while the negotiations were ongoing. In 2008, a French trade official posted to Colombia mentioned that the regional approach would most likely aid the agreement's ultimate ratification, as the European Parliament would not be able to single out Colombia from the other countries over human rights concerns (US Embassy Colombia Bogotá, 2008b).

Parliamentary opposition became clearer, however, at the point in time when DG Trade had announced that negotiations had concluded in March 2010, with a number of political groups issuing press statements that were very critical of the deal (Agence Europe, 2010b).

The main division lines over this agreement can best be seen in a written question that was put to the Commission by INTA. In it, the latter entity shows its concern about the human rights situation in Colombia and Peru (Moreira et al., 2012) and INTA ultimately puts the agreement's contribution to an improvement of the situation into question. The question acknowledges the existence of a chapter in the FTA on trade and sustainable development which was meant to address these and similar issues. The main issue taken, however, is that these provisions do not fall under the dispute settlement process that applies to its trade aspect, which would ultimately allow for the suspension of the preferences granted under the agreement.

Parliament's interpretation of its new role became clear when the question was debated in a session on 22 May 2012. Bernd Lange, a German Socialist & Democrats (S&D) MEP and head of INTA since 2014, voiced his position on parliament's duties as to the agreements as follows:

> I believe that it is clear that trade is not an end in itself, but a means of improving people's living conditions. [...] Parliament is, of course, investigating very carefully, on the basis of the rights granted to it under the Treaty of Lisbon, whether this trade agreement with Colombia and Peru meets these requirements.
>
> (European Parliament, 2012)

Ultimately, the Parliamentary question and his statement call for an "action plan," in the absence of which Parliament's consent to the agreement would be at risk. In a separate statement on the question, INTA's rapporteur on the agreement, Portuguese European Peoples' Party MEP Mário David, voiced best what was meant by this, namely "a transparent and binding road map, possibly with the support of the Commission, regarding human labour rights [sic] and sustainable development" (European Parliament, 2012).

In his answer, Karel De Gucht, the EU's then Commissioner for Trade, was at pains to point out to what degree the agreement already included human rights safeguards, arguing that binding elements like a road map would only prove to be counterproductive. This is not to say that such concerns did not exist within the Commission (US Mission to the European Union, 2007), but the role that a trade agreement should play was simply interpreted differently. Despite De Gucht's aim to demonstrate that Parliament's demands were already satisfied through the text of the agreement, the issue of the "road map" did continue to play an important role before Parliamentary approval was reached.

The issue came about due to heavy lobbying by human rights groups and church activists who leaned on MEPs, particularly from the S&D Group, to address the issue of the respect for the rights of trade unionists in Colombia, mentioning a number of disappearances and killings (Fritz, 2010: 7). Given a long-standing network of activists which observes Colombia's human rights track record in the context of the ongoing conflict, the focus was soon on this country alone. No similar and strong advocacy groups exist in the case of Peru or the Central American region. Therefore, despite similar problems in some Central American countries, the same hurdles did not occur in the context of the ratification of the Central America agreement.[62]

There is some evidence that the issue of the road map caused concern in the Commission over the agreement's successful and speedy ratification. One NGO employee claimed that DG Trade officials were so unnerved that they told them that they had gone too far with their demands.[63] While the Commission treated the issue as having to be resolved largely by Colombia itself, it did nevertheless intervene when the European Parliament threatened to inject non-technical measures into the safeguards legislation, fearing that this could create a dangerous precedent of politicizing technical aspects of trade policy.[64]

Ultimately, it was the left-wing GUE/NGL group which called for the implementation of the road map, with the S&D Group finding a face-saving compromise that would allow them to back the agreement while Colombia put in place a non-binding road map.[65] An interview with an EEAS official has confirmed that since the passage of the agreement in Parliament the issue of the road map has furthermore not been followed up systematically,[66] which would confirm that the institutions themselves were not interested in this issue.

While the issue in question was ultimately resolved and Parliament's consent given with 72% of the votes in favour, the path to reach approval for it was still rocky and introduced delays in the ratification process. The introduction of the road map furthermore created a distinction between different countries in the region, despite a problematic human rights track record in most of them.

Ultimately, the case in question once more demonstrates the difficulty for EU foreign policy-making amidst diverging views between its key internal actors and the complexity of the EU decision-making process. With the EP only becoming officially involved in the last stage of the process for the EU's international agreements, its actions can threaten the success of EU Association Agreements even when the views of all other relevant internal EU actors cohere. While the Lisbon Treaty changes should provide for more regular talks between MEPs and the EU's negotiators, the EP's consent requirement adds another stumbling block for complex EU negotiations to be successful given the dynamics of the EU's decision-making process over a long period of time.

A difficult ratification process

The European Parliament's approval of both the EU–Colombia–Peru FTA and the Central America Association Agreement allowed the national ratification process to get underway, thereby launching another time-intensive phase before either agreement can fully enter into force. Most importantly, however, it also permitted the provisional application of parts of both agreements. Nevertheless, neither agreement has been ratified or fully implemented at present, once more demonstrating the complexity associated with this element of the EU's foreign policy.

While pure EU trade agreements do not require ratification domestically in every member state of the EU, this is not the case for Association Agreements as these are mixed agreements given their political parts or FTAs which contain some political provisions or trade provisions not in the exclusive competence of the EU (as outlined in Chapter 3). While the Commission argued that the EU–Colombia–Peru FTA is an exclusive EU agreement, the Council disagreed with this assessment and domestic ratification came to be necessary (Brown, 2013: 173).

Once the ratification process at the EU level is finished, however, the parts exclusive to the EU's competence can provisionally enter into force beforehand. That was the case for the FTA with Colombia and Peru, and most of the trade components of the Association Agreement with SIECA, all of which entered provisionally into force in 2013. The promise of provisional application even ahead of the ultimate ratification and full implementation of an agreement can be used as an EU means of pressure on its partners. Typically, this is only granted when ratification is completed in the partner countries concerned, hence putting pressure on both the Central American states and Colombia and Peru to speedily ratify the agreement. At the same time, provisional application gives the EU's member states more time to finish their domestic ratification processes.

Securing provisional application was crucial for some of the partner countries in question, given that the reform of the EU's GSP scheme put the previous unilateral EU preferences under its GSP+ scheme in peril. While initially all of the countries concerned would still have benefitted from the EU's reformed GSP scheme as of 2014 (DG Trade, 2012: 20), its new eligibility criteria based on World Bank development indicators were to remove Colombia and Peru from the list altogether within years. EU and member state representatives in the region then made a concerted diplomatic effort to push for fast domestic ratification. This was the case for instance in Colombia where the EU's ambassador, accompanied by those of Germany, France, and Spain, held a public press conference urging the country to speed up its ratification process (Buckley, 2012).

While for the EU's trade policy an agreement's actual ratification and full implementation are not crucial for most of its trade benefits to accrue, the same cannot be said for some of the other provisions. Without all the EU member states' ratification of the Association Agreement, the political and cooperation pillars remain formally inactive. It is at this point of the process that the EU's institutions are weakest, having no influence over the ratification process within the member states.

Looking at the two agreements in question, all member states with the exception of Belgium had ratified the agreement with Colombia and Peru by mid-2019, while ratification is still pending for Belgium and Greece in the case of the Central America Association Agreement (Council of the European Union, 2019). Typically, ratification is a technical if lengthy process, given the Council's previous formal approval of an agreement. Nonetheless, the outcome of the Dutch referendum on the EU's Association Agreement with Ukraine on 6 April 2016 demonstrates that political concerns can at times hinder this process (see Chapter 7).

It would be impossible to provide an overview here of the domestic ratification processes for both agreements in all member states. Some anecdotal evidence can, however, portray additional difficulties for the EU's foreign policy. A relevant example is the case of Germany, in which the ratification of the EU–Central America Association Agreement and the FTA with Colombia and Peru was risked over domestic political concerns. While the country's representatives in the Council appear to have been somewhat interested in the follow-up of the road map in the latter case,[67] this has not led to a delay in the start of the domestic ratification process of the agreement. In fact, Germany's parliament was the first in the EU to give its approval to the deal with Colombia and Peru.

Throughout the domestic ratification processes for both agreements, a large number of NGOs have nonetheless lobbied politicians to oppose these over a long list of concerns. A majority in Germany's *Bundestag*, the country's chamber of elected representatives, for both agreements could only be reached between the governing Christian Democratic and Free Democratic parties in the spring of 2013 and they were opposed by the three opposition parties represented, thereby leading to its approval by only a relatively small margin. Most relevantly, the social democratic SPD, part of the S&D Group which had approved both agreements in the European Parliament, voted against the agreements within Germany, citing human rights and procedural concerns (Bode, 2013; Neuber, 2012).

Had voting patterns remained the same for both agreements in the *Bundesrat*, the representation of Germany's federated states, the country would have failed to ratify both agreements. The Peru and Colombia FTA was ultimately passed in May 2013 by a majority that involved SPD-governed states, leading to a headline that effectively stated that the "SPD has outvoted the SPD on free trade" (Neuber, 2013, translation mine). The successful approval of the Central America agreement was even more difficult and came down to a change of mind of two SPD-governed states at the last minute (Maier, 2013), revealing a rift in the party over the agreement.

While the concerns in the German case appear to have been of a general nature, individual political aspects also have the potential to delay the ratification process. For instance, the provisional application of the trade chapter of the Central America agreement with Costa Rica and El Salvador was delayed by Italian reservations over its capacity to sell specific protected cheese products in those countries (KAS, 2015).

The ratification of the agreement has also been held up over a political issue in the case of Lithuania, which made its ratification of the agreement dependent on political demands towards Nicaragua. Lithuania informed all of the Central American representations to the EU of its intent to delay ratification of the agreement domestically until Nicaragua ceases to recognize the sovereignty of two disputed and Russian-held territories in Georgia, namely South Ossetia and Abkhazia.[68] While the document dates back to July 2012, just after the Association Agreement was signed in Tegucigalpa, the country indeed took until 2017 to ratify the agreement domestically (Council of the European Union, 2019).[69]

While the seriousness of this threat remains unclear amidst the ultimate ratification in the country, diplomats from both Central America and the Andean countries have nevertheless voiced their impatience with the EU's slow ratification progress over time.[70] Lastly, while overall ratification is pending, it is important to point out that the political processes behind Association and trade agreements do not end with their application. Ultimately, their success also relies on their implementation which necessitates collective decisions in specific joint bodies meant to help administer such agreements.[71]

Conclusions

This chapter has detailed two developments in the EU's foreign policy towards Latin America, one being the negotiation of an Association Agreement with SIECA and the other the conclusion of an FTA with Colombia and Peru. The developments leading to the opening of negotiations and those with SIECA illustrate instances under which the EU was capable of maintaining its stance in complex negotiations over a long period of time due to the absence of a divergence of interests between the relevant actors and the underlying coordination efforts. This was not the case for negotiations with the Andean Community, as DG RELEX and DG Trade held diverging views on the matter.

Preparations for the Association Agreement negotiations were ultimately rendered possible by a reorganization of the European Commission with the arrival of the Barroso cabinet at the end of 2004. The autonomy of DG RELEX and that of the RELEX Commissioner Benita Ferrero-Waldner allowed for the thought process that would lead to the negotiations in the end. While this was initially blocked by internal Commission divergences of view and the requirement for adoption by the College of Commissioners, a gradual alignment of DG Trade's position with that of DG RELEX meant that the Council could be asked for its approval, which was ensured through a "permissive consensus" amongst the EU's member states.

The negotiation briefs then ensured that initially DG RELEX and DG Trade remained united in negotiations with CAN until Bolivia's and Ecuador's threat to leave the negotiations led to a split in their assessment as to the future of negotiations. Ultimately, DG Trade, supported by the TPC, prevailed and negotiations continued for an FTA with only some of CAN's members. The same did not happen in the case of negotiations with SIECA, as the absence of strong economic incentives meant that the preferences of both DGs continued to align on the matter, thus leading to the successful conclusion of an Association Agreement with the organization.

The ratification phase once more demonstrates difficulties that can arise in the EU's foreign policy out of the mere complexity and duration of decision-making in the EU's foreign policy system. While the Treaty of Lisbon allowed the EP to threaten the ratification of the EU–Colombia–Peru FTA at the EU level, the examples of Germany, Italy, and Lithuania furthermore illustrate the risks to EU Association Agreement negotiations due to the necessity for domestic ratification of mixed agreements.

While ultimately both agreements were signed and are provisionally applied at present, the complexity of the EU's foreign policy decision-making process on international agreements is further illustrated by the timeline of the negotiation. With preparatory work in the Commission having begun in 2005, both agreements' ratification is still not completed in the middle of 2019.

Notes

1 This organization's Spanish name is Comunidad Andina (CAN). When negotiations got underway, its membership consisted of Bolivia, Colombia, Ecuador, Peru, and Venezuela. Venezuela later withdrew from the organization.

2 This organization is known as the Sistema de Integración Centroamericana (SICA) with a seat in San Salvador. Its economic branch Secretaría de Integración Económica Centroamericana (SIECA) is based in Guatemala City. The membership of the latter organization is smaller and consists of Costa Rica, El Salvador, Guatemala, Honduras, Nicaragua, and Panama only. However, the latter country initially did not partake directly in the others' attempts to set up a customs union.

3 DG Trade official, Brussels (Interview 6).

4 Former EU official, Brussels (Interview 17).

5 A system granting unilateral tariff-free access to the EU's market for developing economies.

6 Former member of the Barroso cabinet (Interview 3). The problematic nature of these resource constraints in general has been acknowledged by a large number of interviewees.

7 Member state diplomat, Brussels (Interview 9); Former EU official, Brussels (Interview 17).

8 Former Latin American diplomat, Hamburg (Interview 2); Latin American diplomat, Brussels (Interview 27).

9 Former EU official, Brussels (Interview 17).

10 Neither of these has come into force.

11 Former Latin American diplomat, Hamburg (Interview 2).

12 Former EU official, Brussels (Interview 17).

13 Former EU official, Brussels (Interview 17).

14 Former EU official, Brussels (Interview 17), and Latin American diplomat, Brussels (Interview 27). The latter has stressed that the institutions of SICA and SIECA are suffering from a lack of expertise of its bureaucrats, which the interviewee accounted to nepotism in the appointment process, the geographical location of the institution's seat, as well as its lack of funding.

15 Her continuing interest in the region is evidenced by her having served as the president of the European Union–Latin America and the Caribbean Foundation (EU–LAC Foundation) after stepping down as European Commissioner. This is a joint EU–Latin American institution which was created during her tenure as RELEX Commissioner.

16 Former Latin American diplomat, Hamburg (Interview 2).

17 Former member of the Barroso cabinet, London (Interview 3).

18 EU Trade official, Brussels (Interview 6); Former EU official, Brussels (Interview 17).

19 Former Latin American diplomat, Hamburg (Interview 2).

20 Former Latin American diplomat, Hamburg (Interview 2); EU officials, Brussels (Interview 11).

21 Former Commission official, Hamburg (Interview 1).
22 Former EU official, Brussels (Interview 17).
23 This was the first of two Latin America strategy documents prepared during Ferrero-Waldner's tenure as Commissioner.
24 Former EU official, Brussels (Interview 17).
25 Former Latin American diplomat, Hamburg (Interview 2); Latin American diplomat, Brussels (Interview 27); EU officials, Brussels (Interview 8).
26 This is perhaps best illustrated by Venezuela's project for an Alianza Bolivariana para los Pueblos de Nuestra América (ALBA), an alternative regional integration scheme between socialist-leaning countries in the region (Flemes, 2009).
27 EU Trade official, Brussels (Interview 6).
28 EU Trade official, Brussels (Interview 6); Former Latin American diplomat, Hamburg (Interview 2).
29 Former EU official, Brussels (Interview 17).
30 The so-called Dominican Republic Central America Free Trade Agreement (CAFTA-DR) is an agreement with the 5 SIECA states, as well as the Dominican Republic. While negotiations had also begun with Ecuador, these never led to the conclusion of an actual agreement.
31 EU Trade official, Brussels (Interview 6).
32 This can be seen in a number of American diplomatic cables (US Embassy Czech Republic Prague, 2006, 2007) and was confirmed in interviews with a former EU official (Interview 17) and a member state official (Interview 31) in Brussels.
33 MFA officials appear to have been particularly critical of the premier's position towards Venezuela (US Embassy Spain Madrid, 2005).
34 EU trade official, Brussels (Interview 12); Member state official, Brussels (Interview 19).
35 European Parliament Official, Brussels (Interview 25).
36 Member state diplomat, Brussels (Interview 9).
37 EU officials, Brussels (Interview 11)
38 Chavez had made reference to CAN's apparent pro-FTA stance when leaving the organization (Maihold, 2008: 23). Instead, Venezuela's government has since promoted the Bolivarian Alliance for the Peoples of Our America (ALBA), essentially a redistribution scheme towards poorer Latin American countries which chose to align with Venezuela's left-wing policies.
39 Former EU official, Brussels (Interview 17).
40 Former EU official (Brussels, 19.6.2015, Interview 17).
41 Former EU official (Brussels, 19.6.2015, Interview 17).
42 Senior DG Trade official, Brussels (Interview 6).
43 Former EU official, Brussels (Interview 17).
44 Former Latin American diplomat, Hamburg (Interview 2). The interviewee cautions that this was merely an excuse for the Bolivian side to slow down negotiations as the government under Evo Morales was still unsure as to its own preferences in these negotiations.
45 One interviewee showed this document to me.
46 Member state diplomat, Brussels (Interview 29).
47 EU officials, Brussels (Interview 11).
48 Former Latin American diplomat, Hamburg (Interview 2).
49 Former Latin American diplomat, Hamburg (Interview 2).
50 DG Trade official, Brussels (Interview 6).
51 The agreement was originally held up in Congress over human rights concerns, much as would be the case in the European Parliament later on (see below). In the end, the end of negotiations between Colombia and the EU contributed to the ratification in Congress.

52 Former Latin American diplomat, Hamburg (Interview 2).
53 Former EU official, Brussels (Interview 17).
54 Former EU official, Brussels (Interview 17).
55 Earlier drafts of the summit's Madrid declaration seen by the author show that this appears to have occurred on a very tight schedule, given that the announcement of the agreement remained bracketed until the very end.
56 Former EU official, Brussels (Interview 17).
57 Former EU official, Brussels (Interview 17).
58 Latin American diplomat, Brussels (Interview 27).
59 At the 2013 Latin America Adelante conference in London.
60 Former EU official, Brussels (Interview 17).
61 European Parliament official, Brussels (Interview 14).
62 European Parliament official, Brussels (Interview 20).
63 NGO official, Brussels (Interview 23).
64 Latin American diplomat, Brussels (Interview 28).
65 European Parliament official, Brussels (Interview 20); European Parliament official, Brussels (Interview 21).
66 Latin American diplomat, Brussels (Interview 28).
67 European Parliament official, Brussels (Interview 20).
68 A document to this effect and dated July 2012 was seen by the author, and the country's continued position has been confirmed in talks with a Latin American diplomat in Brussels (Interview 28). Given its past relationship with Russia and its geographical position, the country takes issue with a change in the status quo of territories in the post-Soviet space.
69 Representatives from large EU member states who were asked about this in Brussels (Interviews 29, 30) were unaware of this issue.
70 Senior EEAS official, Brussels (Interview 8); Latin American diplomat, Brussels (Interview 27); Latin American diplomat, Brussels (Interview 28).
71 Latin American diplomat, Brussels (Interview 27); Latin American diplomat, Brussels (Interview 28).

Bibliography

Agence Europe (2003) (EU) EU/ANDEAN COUNTRIES—Andean Countries (Except Venezuela) Demand Free-Trade Pact with EU. *Agence Europe*, 31 January. Brussels. Available at: Factiva Document AGEU000020030131dz1v00009 (accessed 9 April 2019).

Agence Europe (2004) (EU) EU/BARROSO COMMISSION/TRADE: Peter Mandelson Recommends Opening Market to Benefit Economic Growth, Social Justice, Sustainable Development and Reduction of Poverty in World—'I Am a Committed European', Independent of Blair Government. *Agence Europe*, 5 October. Brussels. Available at: Factiva Document AGEU000020041005e0a500007 (accessed 9 April 2019).

Agence Europe (2005a) (EU) EU/CENTRAL AMERICA: Launch of Work Group to Open Negotiations for EU/Central American Association Agreement. *Agence Europe*, 21 January. Brussels. Available at: Factiva Document AGEU000020050121e1l0000e (accessed 9 April 2019).

Agence Europe (2005b) (EU) EU/RIO GROUP/SAN JOSE DIALOGUE: Ferrero Waldner Says 2006 Launch of Negotiations for Association Agreement Will Depend on Doha Round Table Results and Progress in Regional Integration in Central America. *Agence Europe*, 27 May. Brussels. Available at: Factiva Document AGEU000020050527e15r0000f (accessed 9 April 2019).

Agence Europe (2005c) EU/ANDEAN COMMUNITY: Working Group Set Up for Opening Talks with View to Association Agreement. *Agence Europe*, 25 January. Brussels. Available at: Factiva Document AGEU000020050125e11p0000p (accessed 9 April 2019).

Agence Europe (2006a) (EU) EU/ANDEAN COMMUNITY: Benita Ferrero-Waldner Says Association Agreement Talks Would Not Be Easy. *Agence Europe*, 24 June. Brussels. Available at: Factiva Document AGEU000020060624e26o0000f (accessed 9 April 2019).

Agence Europe (2006b) (EU) EU/ANDEAN COMMUNITY: Equador's Complaint to WTO in Banana Case Will Make Negotiations on FTA More Difficult. *Agence Europe*, 8 December. Brussels. Available at: Factiva Document AGEU000020061208e2c80000g (accessed 9 April 2019).

Agence Europe (2006c) (EU) EU/LATIN AMERICA AND CARIBBEAN: Europeans and Latin Americans Want to Strengthen Strategic Partnership—Energy at Heart of Discussions—Inability of Latin America to Unite into Regional Units Holding Back Development of Bilateral Relations. *Agence Europe*, 13 May. Brussels. Available at: Factiva Document AGEU000020060513e25d0000d (accessed 9 April 2019).

Agence Europe (2007) (EU) EU/TRADE: Council Green Light to Launch of Negotiations for Bilateral Free Trade Agreements with ASEAN, South Korea and India. *Agence Europe*, 24 April. Brussels. Available at: Factiva Document AGEU000020070424e34o0000g (accessed 9 April 2019).

Agence Europe (2008a) Andean Countries Stick to Target of Negotiating as a Bloc with Margin of Flexibility on Trade Chapter. *Agence Europe*, 21 October. Brussels. Available at: Factiva Document AGEU000020081021e4al00003 (accessed 23 August 2019).

Agence Europe (2008b) Barroso Willing to Consider Bilateral Negotiation of Trade Chapter of Association Agreement. *Agence Europe*, 14 October. Brussels. Available at: Factiva Document AGEU000020081014e4ae00009 (accessed 23 August 2019).

Agence Europe (2008c) (EU) EU/LATIN AMERICA: €10 Mio for Regional Projects of Andean Community for Improving Regional Economic Integration and Strengthening Fight Against Illicit Drugs. *Agence Europe*, 29 July. Brussels. Available at: Factiva Document AGEU000020080729e47t0000j (accessed 9 April 2019).

Agence Europe (2008d) (EU) EU/TRADE: Departure of Peter Mandelson, Fervent Free Trader, Brings Regret and Criticism. *Agence Europe*, 7 October. Brussels. Available at: Factiva Document AGEU000020081007e4a70000g (accessed 9 April 2019).

Agence Europe (2009a) (EU) EU/CENTRAL AMERICA: EU Keeps Up Pressure on De Facto Honduran Government. *Agence Europe*, 23 July. Brussels. Available at: Factiva Document AGEU000020090723e57n00006 (accessed 9 April 2019).

Agence Europe (2009b) (EU) EU/LATIN AMERICA: Bolivia and Ecuador Question Tree-Trade Model on Which EU/Andean Community Talks Are Based. *Agence Europe*, 26 September. Brussels. Available at: Factiva Document AGEU000020090926e59q00005 (accessed 9 April 2019).

Agence Europe (2009c) EU Suspends Negotiations with Central America and Refuses Contact with New Powers in Honduras. *Agence Europe*, 2 July. Brussels. Available at: Factiva Document AGEU000020090702e57200007 (accessed 23 August 2019).

Agence Europe (2009d) EU/Central America. *Agence Europe*, 15 May. Brussels. Available at: Factiva Document AGEU000020090515e55f00008 (accessed 9 April 2019).

Agence Europe (2009e) EU/LATIN AMERICA: EU Support for Agreement Reached in Honduras. *Agence Europe*, 31 October. Brussels. Available at: Factiva Document AGEU000020091031e5av0000g (accessed 9 April 2019).

Agence Europe (2010a) (EU) EU/LATIN AMERICA: EU Concludes Free-Trade Agreement with Peru and Colombia. *Agence Europe*, 2 March. Brussels. Available at: Factiva Document AGEU000020100302e6320000b (accessed 9 April 2019).

Agence Europe (2010b) (EU) EU/TRADE: Bilateral Free Trade Agreements with Peru and Colombia Come Under Fire. *Agence Europe*, 3 March. Brussels. Available at: Factiva Document AGEU000020100303e6330000q (accessed 9 April 2019).

Andean Community Commission (2004) Decision 598: Trade Relations with Third Countries. Available at: www.sice.oas.org/trade/junac/Decisiones/dec598e.asp (accessed 15 December 2018).

Article 133 Committee (2008a) *Outcome of Proceedings Article 133 Committee 23 December 2008.* Outcome of Proceedings 17584/08, 23 December. Brussels: Council of the European Union.

Article 133 Committee (2008b) *Outcome of Proceedings Article 133 Committee 26 September 2008.* Outcome of Proceedings 13197/08, 30 September. Brussels: Council of the European Union.

BBC News (2004) Moratinos Defends Coup Comments. *BBC News*. Available at: http://news.bbc.co.uk/1/hi/world/europe/4059555.stm (accessed 10 January 2019).

Bode B (2013) Abkommen mit Zentralamerika. *Das Parlament.* 18th–20th ed. Berlin. Available at: www.das-parlament.de/2013/18_20/EuropaWelt/44544874/323248.

Brown CM (2013) Changes in the Common Commercial Policy of the European Union After the Entry into Force of the Treaty of Lisbon: A Practicioner's Perspective. In: Bungenberg M and Herrmann C (eds) *Common Commercial Policy After Lisbon.* European Yearbook of International Economic Law. Berlin: Springer, pp. 163–183.

Buckley N (2012) Europe Urges Colombia to Speed Up FTA. *Colombia Reports*, 13 December. Medellin. Available at: http://colombiareports.com/european-union-urges-colombia-to-speed-up-fta/ (accessed 12 December 2018).

CAN–EU Troika Summit (2008) *Andean Community—EU Troika Summit Joint Communiqué*, 17 May. Lima. Available at: www.sice.oas.org/TPD/AND_EU/negotiations/flexible_frame_e.pdf (accessed 10 October 2018).

Caroit J-M (2008) Les Relations entre l'Europe et le Nicaragua s'enveniment. *Le Monde*, 7 November. Paris.

COREPER (2007) *2180th Meeting of the Permanent Representatives Committee Held in Brussels on 17, 18 and 20 April 2007.* COREPER Meeting Summary 8565/07, 4 May. Brussels: Council of the European Union.

Council of the European Communities (2003) *Political Dialogue and Cooperation Agreement Between the European Community and the Andean Community.* Quito: Council of the European Economic Communities.

Council of the European Union (2002) *Madrid Declaration.* Final Declaration. Madrid: Council of the European Union. Available at: http://eulacfoundation.org/sites/eulacfoundation.org/files/2002_EN_Madrid_Decl.pdf (accessed 12 June 2016).

Council of the European Union (2004) *Guadalajara Declaration.* Final Declaration. Guadalajara: Council of the European Union. Available at: http://alcuenet.eu/dms-files.php?action=doc&id=363 (accessed 12 June 2018).

Council of the European Union (2006a) *Declaration of Vienna.* IV EU–LAC Summit Declaration 9335/06 (Presse 137), 12 May. Available at: http://register.consilium.europa.eu/doc/srv?l=EN&f=ST%209335%202006%20INIT (accessed 12 October 2018).

Council of the European Union (2006b) *General Affairs Council Brussels 27 February 2006.* Press Release 6343/06 (Presse 45), 27 February. Brussels: Council of the

European Union. Available at: http://data.consilium.europa.eu/doc/document/ST-6343-2006-INIT/en/pdf (accessed 25 June 2018).

Council of the European Union (2006c) *II. EU–Central American Summit Vienna*. Joint Communiqué 9337/06 (Presse 139), 13 May. Available at: http://eeas.europa.eu/la/previous_summits/vienna_summit/docs/2006_eu-central_america_summit_en.pdf (accessed 12 October 2018).

Council of the European Union (2010) *Madrid Declaration*. Madrid: Council of the European Union. Available at: www.consilium.europa.eu/uedocs/cms_Data/docs/pressdata/en/er/114535.pdf (accessed 12 June 2018).

Council of the European Union (2019) *Agreements Database*. Brussels: Council of the European Union. Available at: www.consilium.europa.eu/policies/agreements/search-the-agreements-database?lang=en (accessed 1 June 2019).

DG Trade (2006) *Global Europe: Competing in the World*. Brussels: European Commission. Available at: http://trade.ec.europa.eu/doclib/docs/2006/october/tradoc_130376.pdf (accessed 3 December 2016).

DG Trade (2012) *The EU's New Generalised Scheme of Preferences (GSP)*, December. Available at: http://trade.ec.europa.eu/doclib/docs/2012/december/tradoc_150164.pdf (accessed 4 December 2018).

Dominguez R (2008) *The Foreign Policy of the European Union (1995–2004): A Study in Structural Transition*. Lewiston, ME: Edwin Mellen.

Erisman HM (2011) Cuba, Venezuela, and ALBA: The Neo-Bolívarian Challenge. In: Prevost G and Campos CO (eds) *Cuban-Latin American Relations in the Context of a Changing Hemisphere*. Amherst, NY: Cambria Press, pp. 101–147.

EU–Andean Community Ministerial Meeting (2007) *EU–Andean Community Ministerial Meeting Santo Domingo 19 April 2007*. Joint Communiqué, 19 April. Santo Domingo. Available at: www.sice.oas.org/TPD/AND_EU/negotiations/Ministerial04_07_e.pdf (accessed 10 October 2018).

EU–CAN High Level Meeting (2006) *EU–CAN High Level Meeting 12/13 July 2006*. Joint Minutes, 13 July. Available at: www.sice.oas.org/TPD/AND_EU/negotiations/highlevel2006_e.pdf.

European Commission (2005) *A Stronger Partnership Between the European Union and Latin America*. Communication from the Commission to the European Parliament and the Council COM(2005) 636 Final. Brussels: European Commission. Available at: http://eeas.europa.eu/la/docs/com05_636_en.pdf (accessed 17 January 2019).

European Commission (2007a) *Andean Community Regional Strategy Paper 2007–2013*. E/2007/678. Brussels. Available at: http://eeas.europa.eu/andean/rsp/07_13_en.pdf (accessed 21 January 2019).

European Commission (2007b) *EU–CAN Association Agreement Draft Negotiation Mandate*. Available at: www.bilaterals.org/?draft-eu-can-negotiating-directive (accessed 15 June 2016).

European Commission (2009) *The European Union and Latin America: Global Players in Partnership*. Communication from the Commission to the European Parliament and the Council COM(2009) 495/3. Brussels: European Commission. Available at: http://eeas.eu/la/docs/com09_495_en.pdf (accessed 17 January 2016).

European Parliament (2012) *Debate on the Question for Oral Answer to the Commission on the Trade Agreement Between the EU on the One Part and Colombia and Peru on the Other Part*, 22 May. Strasbourg: European Parliament. Available at: www.europarl.europa.eu/sides/getDoc.do?pubRef=-//EP//TEXT+CRE+20120522+ITEM-014+DOC+XML+V0//EN (accessed 25 May 2019).

Eurostat (2014) *European Union International Trade Statistics*. Brussels: European Commission.

Federal Ministry of Foreign Affairs (2005) *The Austrian EU Presidency 2006*, 23 November. Vienna: Federal Ministry of Foreign Affairs. Available at: www.eurosfaire.prd.fr/7pc/doc/1134635746_presidence_autrichienne_2006.pdf (accessed 23 June 2018).

Flemes D (2009) *Konkurrierender Regionalismus: Fünf Jahre UNASUR und ALBA*. GIGA Focus Lateinamerika 12/2009. Hamburg: German Institute of Global and Area Studies. Available at: www.giga-hamburg.de/dl/download.php?d=/content/publikationen/pdf/gf_lateinamerika_0912.pdf (accessed 27 November 2018).

Fritz T (2010) *The Second Conquest: The EU Free Trade Agreement with Colombia and Peru*. October. Berlin: Forschungs- und Dokumentationszentrum Chile-Lateinamerika–FDCL e.V.

Girvan N (2011) ALBA, Petrocaribe, and Caricom: Issues in a New Dynamic. In: Clem RS and Eguizábal C (eds) *Venezuela's Petro-Diplomacy: Hugo Chávez's Foreign Policy*. Gainesville, FL: University Press of Florida, pp. 116–134.

Guatemala Times (2009) Central America and the European Union Resume Negotiations for an Association Agreement. *Guatemala Times*, 26 April. Guatemala City.

Gutiérrez Wa-chong T (2008) Europa reitera que no permitirá acuerdos comerciales bilaterales con Centroamérica. *La Prensa Libre*, 30 May. San José, Costa Rica.

Gutiérrez Wa-chong T (2009) Centroamérica: Europeos reiteran que Acuerdo es de 'región a región' o se suspende. *La Prensa Libre*, 3 April. San José, Costa Rica.

Haubrich Seco M (2011) *Decoupling Trade from Politics: The EU and Region-Building in the Andes*. IAI Working Paper 11/20, July. Rome: Istituto Affari Internazionali.

Hillman J and Kleimann D (2010) *Trading Places: The New Dynamics of EU Trade Policy Under the Treaty of Lisbon*. Economic Policy Paper Series. Washington, DC: The German Marshal Fund of the United States.

KAS (2015) *Das Assoziierungsabkommen zwischen den Zentralamerikanischen Staaten und der EU*. San José, Costa Rica: Konrad Adenauer Stiftung. Available at: www.kas.de/costa-rica/de/pages/6207/ (accessed 12 December 2018).

Long C (2009) EU Agreement on Hold Pending Honduras Crisis. *Tico Times*, 28 October. San José, Costa Rica.

Maier J (2013) SPD für EU-Abkommen mit Zentralamerika. *amerika21*, 12 June. Available at: https://amerika21.de/2013/06/83235/abkommen-eu-zantralamerika.

Maihold G (2008) *Außenpolitik als Provokation: Rhetorik und Realität in der Außenpolitik Venezuelas unter Präsident Hugo Chávez*. SWP-Studie 22/2008. Berlin: Stiftung Wissenschaft und Politik. Available at: www.swp-berlin.org/fileadmin/contents/products/studien/2008_S22_ilm_ks.pdf.

Moreira V, David M, and Lange B (2012) *Question for Oral Answer to the Commission on the Trade Agreement Between the EU on the One Part and Colombia and Peru on the Other Part*. O-000107/2012, 27 April. Strasbourg: European Parliament. Available at: www.europarl.europa.eu/sides/getDoc.do?type=OQ&reference=O-2012-000107&language=EN.

Murillo Á (2009) Europa reaviva proceso para TLC, a pesar de Honduras. *La Nación*, 4 August. San José, Costa Rica. Available at: www.nacion.com/nacional/servicios- publicos/Europa-reaviva-proceso-TLC-Honduras_0_1065693519.html.

Neuber H (2012) Regierungsparteien stimmen für Freihandel mit Kolumbien und Peru. *amerika21*, 23 March. Available at: https://amerika21.de/2013/03/81823/bundestag-tlc-kolumbien-peru.

Neuber H (2013) SPD überstimmt SPD im Freihandelsstreit. *amerika21*, 4 May. Available at: https://amerika21.de/2013/05/82737/freihandel-eu-peru-kolumbien.

Noriega C (2007) Alan García se corta solo con la UE. *Página 12*, 1 November. Buenos Aires. Available at: www.pagina12.com.ar/diario/elmundo/4-93878-2007-11-01.html (accessed 14 January 2019).

Okano-Heijmans M (2014) *Trade Diplomacy in EU–Asia Relations: Time for a Rethink.* Clingendael Report, September. The Hague: Clingendael Institute.

Phillips L (2008a) Bolivia Threatens EU–Andes Trade Agreement Over Return Directive (Ticker). *EUobserver*, 6 October. Brussels. Available at: http://euobserver.com/tickers/107340 (accessed 3 November 2018).

Phillips L (2008b) EU–Latin America Summit Achieves Little. *EUobserver*, 19 May. Brussels. Available at: http://euobserver.com/news/26174 (accessed 3 November 2018).

Phillips L (2008c) Latin America Could Halt EU Trade Talks Over Return Directive. *EUobserver*, 23 June. Brussels. Available at: http://euobserver.com/foreign/26374 (accessed 3 November 2018).

Trueb B (2012) Boost or Backlash? EU Member States and the EU's Latin America Policy in the Post-Lisbon Era. In: Cardwell PJ (ed.) *EU External Relations Law and Policy in the Post-Lisbon Era.* The Hague: T.M.C. Asser, pp. 265–286.

US Embassy Belgium Brussels (2006) Message on Latin America Resonates with EU. Available at: https://search.wikileaks.org/plusd/cables/06BRUSSELS472_a.html (accessed 20 March 2019).

US Embassy Bolivia La Paz (2006a) EU Awaits Andean Community Stance Toward Trade Talks. Available at: https://search.wikileaks.org/plusd/cables/06LAPAZ1565_a.html (accessed 20 March 2019).

US Embassy Bolivia La Paz (2006b) GOB Urges 'Creative' Approach to Bilateral Trade. Available at: https://search.wikileaks.org/plusd/cables/06LAPAZ2079_a.html (accessed 20 March 2019).

US Embassy Bolivia La Paz (2007) Andean Community Summit Preparations and EU Negotiations. Available at: https://search.wikileaks.org/plusd/cables/07LAPAZ1589_a.html (accessed 20 March 2019).

US Embassy Bolivia La Paz (2008a) Bolivia Burns More Trade Bridges. Available at: https://search.wikileaks.org/plusd/cables/08LAPAZ2442_a.html (accessed 20 March 2019).

US Embassy Bolivia La Paz (2008b) Harder European Line on Evo. Available at: https://search.wikileaks.org/plusd/cables/08LAPAZ1149_a.html (accessed 20 March 2019).

US Embassy Colombia Bogotá (2006) A/S SHANNON Meets with Foreign Minister Barco. Available at: https://wikileaks.org/plusd/cables/06BOGOTA5515_a.html (accessed 20 March 2019).

US Embassy Colombia Bogotá (2007) Colombia-Canada Trade Agreement Closing Fast. Available at: https://wikileaks.org/plusd/cables/07BOGOTA8002_a.html (accessed 20 March 2019).

US Embassy Colombia Bogotá (2008a) Colombia Signs FTA with EFTA. Available at: https://wikileaks.org/plusd/cables/08BOGOTA4234_a.html (accessed 20 March 2019).

US Embassy Colombia Bogotá (2008b) Colombia's Trade Agenda—Moving Ahead Without Us. Available at: https://wikileaks.org/plusd/cables/08BOGOTA1926_a.html (accessed 20 March 2019).

US Embassy Colombia Bogotá (2008c) EU to Initiate Trade Talks with Colombia and Peru: Will the CAN Get Canned? Available at: https://search.wikileaks.org/plusd/cables/08BOGOTA3705_a.html (accessed 20 March 2019).

US Embassy Colombia Bogotá (2009a) Colombia–EU Trade Talks Progress, Eyeing July Closure. Available at: https://search.wikileaks.org/plusd/cables/09BOGOTA1515_a.html (accessed 20 March 2019).

US Embassy Colombia Bogotá (2009b) EU–Andean FTA Talks Reawaken After Ten-Month Coma. Available at: www.wikileaks.org/plusd/cables/09BOGOTA558_a.html (accessed 20 March 2019).

US Embassy Colombia Bogotá (2010) 'FTA with US Is Blocking Colombia's Global Trade Policy,' Says Trade Minister. Available at: https://search.wikileaks.org/plusd/cables/10BOGOTA217_a.html (accessed 20 March 2019).

US Embassy Czech Republic Prague (2005) In-Depth Readout of EU's Cuba Compromise. Available at: https://search.wikileaks.org/plusd/cables/05PRAGUE1006_a.html (accessed 20 March 2019).

US Embassy Czech Republic Prague (2006) Czechs Express Concern for Future of Democracy in Venezuela, Cuba, and Latin America Generally. Available at: https://wikileaks.org/plusd/cables/06PRAGUE295_a.html (accessed 20 March 2019).

US Embassy Czech Republic Prague (2007) Czechs—Paying Attention to Developments in Venezuela. Available at: https://wikileaks.org/plusd/cables/07PRAGUE1219_a.html (accessed 20 March 2019).

US Embassy Ecuador Quito (2005) Ecuador Requests USG Action on WTO EU Banana Decision. Available at: https://search.wikileaks.org/plusd/cables/05QUITO2464_a.html (accessed 20 March 2019).

US Embassy Ecuador Quito (2006) CAN Leaders Meet in Quito. Available at: https://search.wikileaks.org/plusd/cables/06QUITO1477_a.html (accessed 20 March 2019).

US Embassy Ecuador Quito (2007a) Ecuador: Correa Appoints New Foreign Minister, Urging Trade Focus. Available at: https://search.wikileaks.org/plusd/cables/07QUITO2631_a.html (accessed 20 March 2019).

US Embassy Ecuador Quito (2007b) Ecuador Supports an EU–CAN Association Agrement. Available at: https://search.wikileaks.org/plusd/cables/07QUITO1478_a.html (accessed 20 March 2019).

US Embassy Ecuador Quito (2008a) CAN–EU Talks—Ecuador Will Negotiate Bilaterally. Available at: https://search.wikileaks.org/plusd/cables/08QUITO1126_a.html (accessed 20 March 2019).

US Embassy Ecuador Quito (2008b) Ecuador on CAN–EU Talks and Its Neighbors' FTAs. Available at: https://search.wikileaks.org/plusd/cables/08QUITO787_a.html (accessed 20 March 2019).

US Embassy Ecuador Quito (2008c) EU–CAN Negotiations—Not Dead Yet. Available at: https://search.wikileaks.org/plusd/cables/08QUITO482_a.html (accessed 20 March 2019).

US Embassy Italy Rome (2004) Italy Supports US Views on GAERC Agenda; FMs May Discuss ICC. Available at: https://wikileaks.org/plusd/cables/04ROME1898_a.html (accessed 20 March 2019).

US Embassy Nicaragua Managua (2009) Nicaragua Quite Trade Negotiations with Europeans. Available at: https://search.wikileaks.org/plusd/cables/09MANAGUA387_a.html (accessed 20 March 2019).

US Embassy Peru Lima (2005) EU Ambassador Provides Readout on South American Visit of EU External Relations Commissioner. Available at: https://search.wikileaks.org/plusd/cables/05LIMA3341_a.html (accessed 20 March 2019).

US Embassy Peru Lima (2006) EU Improves Peru's Trade Preferences but FTA Unlikely. Available at: https://search.wikileaks.org/plusd/cables/06LIMA469_a.html (accessed 20 March 2019).

US Embassy Peru Lima (2007) Peru's Fervour for Global Trade Marches Forward. Available at: https://search.wikileaks.org/plusd/cables/07LIMA826_a.html (accessed 20 March 2019).

US Embassy Peru Lima (2008) Peru Signs FTA with Canada and Moves Forward on Other Free Trade Agreements. Available at: https://search.wikileaks.org/plusd/cables/08LIMA150_a.html (accessed 20 March 2019).

US Embassy Spain Madrid (2005) Zapatero Venezuela Policy Perplexes Spanish MFA Officials. Available at: https://wikileaks.org/plusd/cables/05MADRID569_a.html (accessed 20 March 2019).

US Embassy Spain Madrid (2006a) Spain: Ambassador's Meeting with FM Moratinos. Available at: https://wikileaks.org/plusd/cables/06MADRID779_a.html (accessed 20 March 2019).

US Embassy Spain Madrid (2006b) Spain on EU–LAC Summit: 'It Could Have Been Worse'. Available at: https://wikileaks.org/plusd/cables/06MADRID1260_a.html (accessed 20 March 2019).

US Embassy Spain Madrid (2009) Spain's EU Presidency Priorities: Economic Reform, Summits, and the Lisbon Treaty. Available at: https://wikileaks.org/plusd/cables/09MADRID730_a.html (accessed 20 March 2019).

US Embassy Tegucigualpa (2009) TFH01: Honduran Coup: Political Wrap-Up 07/21/09. Available at: https://search.wikileaks.org/plusd/cables/09TEGUCIGALPA632_a.html (accessed 20 March 2019).

US Embassy Venezuela Caracas (2006) Implications of Venezuela's Leaving the CAN and Joining Mercosur: The Road Ahead. Available at: https://search.wikileaks.org/plusd/cables/06CARACAS2736_a.html (accessed 20 March 2019).

US Mission to the European Union (2007) U.S.–EU Meetings on Latin America. Available at: https://search.wikileaks.org/plusd/cables/07USEUBRUSSELS1276_a.html (accessed 20 March 2019).

US Mission to the European Union (2009) European Commission Suspends Aid to Nicaraguan Government. Available at: https://search.wikileaks.org/plusd/cables/09BRUSSELS30_a.html (accessed 20 March 2019).

Willis A (2009) EU–Andean Trade Talks to Restart (Ticker). *EUobserver*, 21 January. Brussels. Available at: http://euobserver.com/tickers/108614 (accessed 3 November 2018).

Woolcock S (2007) *European Union Policy Towards Free Trade Agreements*. ECIPE Working Paper 3/2007. Brussels: ECIPE. Available at: www.felixpena.com.ar/contenido/negociaciones/anexos/2010-09-european-union-policy-towards-free-trade-agreements.pdf (accessed 15 May 2019).

Woolcock S (2010) EU Trade and Investment Policymaking After the Lisbon Treaty. *Intereconomics* 45(1): 22–25.

Working Party on Latin America (2008) *Amendment to the Authorisation to Negotiate the Association Agreement Between the European Community and Its Member States, of the One Part, and the Andean Community and Its Member Countries, of the Other Part.* 'I/A' Item Note 17459/1/08, 22 December. Brussels: Council of the European Union.

6 Negotiations in the aftermath of the Lisbon Treaty's institutional turmoil

Integrative leaps in the evolution of the EU are bound to upset the delicate institutional balance of decision-making at the European level. This has been no different with the coming into force of the Treaty of Lisbon. This chapter sets out to trace the important effects of these changes on the EU's negotiations with the Latin American region since then. More so than before, the entry on the scene of an entirely new institutional actor, the EEAS, has challenged established ones and made cooperation on major foreign policy undertakings more difficult in the short to medium term. This is demonstrated through an analysis of the negotiation processes and outcomes of various negotiations with third actors in the region.

Ultimately, this chapter focuses on the challenge for a coordinated EU position on complex negotiations with the Latin American region that arose from the creation of a new EU-level institutional actor, as well as the associated decision-making turmoil in its wake. Given the absence of an overall EU strategy or a synchronized attempt to further relations with the region since the coming into force of the Lisbon Treaty, the chapter is loosely grouped around different kinds of negotiations with the region since then. While the initial sections on the EU's negotiations with Ecuador and Cuba outline the effects of the decision-making autonomy available to individual institutional actors in the early days of the new set-up, the latter ones are concerned with complex Association Agreement negotiations with Mexico and Chile and allow to demonstrate the gradual stratification of cooperation within the new institutional set-up.

The challenge of new institutions

In the eyes of many of the European officials working on Latin American dossiers in the aftermath of the Lisbon Treaty, the EU's policy towards the region has remained relatively constant. Nonetheless, it was possible to observe a weakening of the prior collective effort aimed to coordinate the EU's policy towards the region. This can be attributed, in large parts, to a divergence of perspectives between those institutional actors already involved in EU foreign policy-making prior to the new treaty and the new entrant, the EEAS.

While the latter has attempted to gain a foothold in the coordination of the EU's foreign policy, the others have naturally been keen to guard their institution's prior independence against what they perceived as an outside interference. The early days of the new set-up could thus be qualified as equating a free-for-all for most institutional actors on questions concerning their core competencies amidst a lack of political oversight. While this autonomy was possible given the early focus of the EEAS on becoming fully operational, recent developments have shown that much like in the past all actors involved have gradually evolved to once more cooperate closely in a gradually stratifying institutional environment.

In the early days of the EEAS, other institutions did not have to fear the institution making inroads either into their competencies or their policy priorities. Aside from the natural difficulties in setting up an entirely new institution out of a plethora of existing actors, its own challenge was to find a position on how it would approach the Latin American region in the first place. The choice of Catherine Ashton as the first High Representative in the post-Lisbon period and the interpretation of her role was the first issue for those officials working on Latin American affairs in the new institution. While the HRVP focused on shaping the new institution itself and interpreted her role as being closely tied to the preferences of the member states, guidance on political relations with the region was initially not forthcoming. This was perceived by officials tasked with formulating the EEAS position on Latin America as the HRVP's general lack of interest in it.[1] Pointedly, even outside observers noted that the position of the EEAS on Latin American matters at this time was mainly the result of ad hoc choices by individual EEAS officials, rather than emerging logically from top-down political guidance.[2]

While the original organizational structure for the units dealing with Latin American affairs was retained from the Commission's former DG RELEX in the EEAS' early years, the 2013 EEAS review redrew the institutional boundaries internally.[3] This was not explicitly addressed in the document outlining necessary changes to the institution's structure (EEAS, 2013), yet the geographical desks for EU–Latin American relations were nonetheless redrawn in the wake of the review, creating a new South America division (out of two previous ones), as well as merging two other divisions into a single one dealing with Mexico, Central America and the Caribbean.[4] This internal reorganization may have been beneficial in the longer run from an administrative perspective; however, in the short term, this further hampered the institution's perspective to develop political priorities for the region.

This restructuring occurred in a context where the administrative set-up of the other institutions remained largely unchanged. Unlike within the EEAS, the Commission officials working on the region in various DGs could therefore retain their previous priorities and strategies. Considering the functioning of the Council, the post-Lisbon set-up would see the EEAS win the role of the chair and therefore agenda-setting power in most relevant foreign policy configurations from the prior rotating chairmanship. Nonetheless, this was not the case across the board: While, on the one hand, COLAC changed chairmanship, on the other, the senior-level Working Party of Foreign Relations Counsellors, or the TPC (General Secretariat of the Council, 2019), did not follow suit. This further increased the risk of a lack of coordinated consideration of Latin American issues between these different bodies, particularly when it comes to cross-cutting issues such as Association Agreements.

Considering a true political leadership role for the EEAS as mandated by the Lisbon Treaty, this only truly became the case for the EU's Latin America policy once the second HRVP, Federica Mogherini, had entered office.[5] Much like her institutional preference to interpret the role more actively as that of a member of the European Commission (Morgenstern-Pomorski, 2018: 172), she has also taken a keen interest in the region itself.[6] Since then, the EEAS—with the support of a large coalition of member states—has been a keen advocate of showing its commitment to the region through a promise of negotiations for new agreements, or the upgrade of existing ones.[7]

In contrast, DG Trade has shown itself to be much more reluctant to alter its positions. This is due to the fact that the latter institution is lacking the necessary human resources to undertake a large number of parallel FTA negotiations at any given point in time.[8] In the initial period after Mogherini took over from Ashton, DG Trade officials have thus been keen to stress that negotiating further agreements in Latin America would divert from its own priorities which then focused on finalizing EU–Canada trade negotiations (CETA) and progressing on the later abandoned talks for TTIP with the US.

Going it alone: DG Trade and the EU–Ecuador FTA

The EU's negotiations for a Free Trade Agreement with Ecuador can be considered the first significant development in EU–Latin American relations since the full entry into force of the Treaty of Lisbon. However, rather than representing a case demonstrating the merits of the EU's foreign policy set-up under the new treaty, it is a crucial example for the policy autonomy of individual institutional actors in its aftermath, and particularly that of the Commission's DG Trade. The case thus illustrates how an individual institutional actor's autonomy can foster its resistance to policy change.

Aside from Bolivia, Ecuador was the other CAN country that initially did not conclude a FTA with the EU after the negotiations for a region-to-region EU–Andean Community Association Agreement had failed. The conclusion of the EU–Ecuador FTA in 2014 then essentially amounted to the country joining the existing EU–Colombia–Peru FTA, rather than an entirely new negotiation endeavour. This was made possible by the continued validity of the European Commission's negotiation mandate from the period predating the Treaty of Lisbon. While the role which the new treaty attributed to the EEAS would have given the institution the overall political oversight of relations with CAN as a regional organization—and therefore of those with Ecuador as one of its constituent members—its lack of political activity and guidance at the time, and the existing negotiation mandate meant that DG Trade could operate largely as if nothing had changed. It thereby set an initial precedent for the autonomy of the European Commission on this core competency of the EU in the post-Lisbon set-up.

What is striking about these negotiations is the fact that while Ecuador had initially left negotiations for the EU–Andean Community Association Agreement shortly after Bolivia, they were relaunched in 2013, not too long after negotiations had concluded with Colombia and Peru. Instead of leading entirely novel nego-tiations with the country, however, DG Trade then negotiated on the assumption that Ecuador would join the existing agreement, meaning that these negotiations could conclude by July 2014 (European Commission, 2014a) and therefore much more quickly than is the norm for such kinds of agreements. The pace of the pro-cess once more made it much more difficult for the EEAS to gain a foothold as these negotiations occurred. This willingness of Ecuador to alter its stance is an indication that circumstances had changed substantially for the country, which, as the remainder of this section shows, DG Trade could then capitalize on given its central role in the negotiation process.

The autonomy of the Commission in negotiating the FTA with Ecuador was enabled, in part, by the fact that the immediate post-Lisbon context made it impos-sible to develop substantial political strategy documents on the EU's relations with third countries. In fact, while the last political declaration on the EU's ties with the Andean region goes back to the immediate aftermath of the Lisbon-in-duced changes, the EEAS was not yet fully operational at that time. The meeting of the European Union-Andean Community Joint Committee which developed said document still operated under the terms of an original political agreement dating back to 1996. While a successor had been found afterwards, it has yet to be ratified to this date. In consequence, the meeting between representatives from the Andean region and those of the EU was largely staffed by European Commission personnel and merely restated the obvious with regard to EU–Andean Community ties:

> The European Union underlined that it did not renounce the reopening of negotiations for an Association Agreement when [political] conditions would allow for it to occur. It is and will continue to be its political priority in the Andean region to aim for a profound relaunch of region-to-region relations without exceptions and without a weakening of the Andean integration process.
> (Comisión mixta Comunidad Andina-Union Europea, 2010: 5, translation mine)

With the exception of a meeting of a structured High-Level Dialogue on drugs matters between both regions in 2012 (EU–CAN High Level Meeting on Drugs, 2012), no other political meetings were held that could have defined political priorities for relations with the regional grouping or its members ahead of the conclusion of the EU–Ecuador FTA. Similarly, there do not appear to have been internal discussions within the EEAS on such matters during its initial build-up phase. This could in turn explain the lack of discussions on establishing political dialogues in bilateral discussions with Peru and Colombia.

In the absence of political guidance from the institutional actor now tasked with this, DG Trade was thus able to develop ties with the region within its policy port-folio as it saw fit. What helped motivate Ecuador to return to the negotiation table in the first place was a reform of the EU's GSP, a scheme allowing for beneficial trade access to the EU's single market for developing countries. Ecuador had been a constant beneficiary of the GSP over time and initially still stood to benefit under reforms that came into force at the beginning of 2014 (DG Trade, 2012).

As one out of only 10 countries, it even gained immediate access to a specific scheme entitled GSP+, offering wide-ranging unilateral market access by the EU due to the country's signature of certain human rights-related international treaties and conventions (European Commission, 2013a). Given the country's economic growth and the changed criteria of eligibility for the GSP scheme, it nonetheless risked losing access to the EU's market as of 2015. While these developments to redefine the policy within DG Trade were unrelated to the negotiations with CAN, this provided a welcome opportunity for the officials in DG Trade's Latin America unit to try and relaunch negotiations with the country.

This is due to the fact that for Ecuador access to the EU's market is important in economic terms. In 2014, the EU was the country's second most important recipient for its goods exports, second only to the US. These exports amounted to a total value of 2.2 billion euros in 2014, mainly in agricultural goods, with the country additionally exporting services amounting to 400 million euros (DG Trade, 2015). These exports were facilitated in large part through the country's access to the European market under GSP+ conditions, which meant that in 2013 the country's exports to the EU were facing duties of only 253 million US dollars, as opposed to 606 million in the absence of GSP and GSP+ (Enríquez, 2014b).

Despite the lack of a FTA with the EU, Ecuador hence benefitted significantly from preferential access to the EU's market without having to reciprocally open up its own. This relative comfort of being able to trade with the EU added an important economic element to the country's reluctance to continue to negotiate with the EU in 2008. Ecuador's comfortable situation was due to change, however, as the country had been classified as an upper-middle-income country by the World Bank in 2011, 2012, and 2013. This meant that under the EU's technical GSP rules it would lose eligibility to both schemes one year later, on 1 January 2015 (European Commission, 2013b). This immediately put a large amount of Ecuador's exports to the EU at risk, in turn threatening to negatively impact the country's economy.

The problem was exacerbated by the provisional application of the EU's FTA with Peru and Colombia as of March and August of 2013, respectively, as well as the provisional entry into force of the trade chapter of the EU's agreement with Central American countries throughout 2013. This meant that these countries, which share partially similar (agricultural) export patterns to the EU, would not only continue to be able to export to the European market at rates similar to GSP, but at even lower ones for some of their exports.

As one interviewee familiar with the trade negotiations noted, Ecuador was facing not one, but two interrelated problems at the same time: firstly, the aforementioned risk to the competitivity of its exports to the EU if GSP conditions were to lapse, and secondly, the risk of trade diversion with EU importers turning to Colombia, Peru, and Central America amidst the lowering of tariffs for trade with these countries.[9] For Ecuador, the desire or even necessity to return to negotiations with the EU at this point thus appears clear.

DG Trade was aware of the fact that from an economic standpoint Ecuador had little choice but to entertain negotiations that would allow it to secure its exports to the EU. When the decision was made to negotiate an FTA only with willing members of the Andean Community in 2008, the associated negotiation mandate stated that either Bolivia or Ecuador could join the process later on. This was further emphasized in the text of the FTA between the EU, Colombia, and Peru, which recognizes the right of the other Andean countries to join it and mentions the importance of the Andean Community integration process in its Article 10 (see Official Journal of the European Union, 2012).

This meant that DG Trade could rely both on its pre-existing mandate and on the FTA to structure negotiations with Ecuador. What had changed, however, was that the EU's negotiation position towards Ecuador was significantly improved given the GSP's cut-off date and the fact that the country would merely join an existing FTA, rather than partaking in the negotiations on its substance. This path dependence also made it more difficult to consider the political elements of ties to the country on the EU's side.

The dominance of DG Trade in those negotiations is a particularly relevant motivating factor as the size of the Ecuadorean market is largely insignificant for the EU, and given that—unlike Colombia and Peru—the country had not concluded or planned to conclude a competing FTA with the US. The EU's fears of losing market access to Ecuador thus did not provide an overall incentive for DG Trade to suggest a change of the EU's position and to invest human resources in the conclusion of a fully fledged new agreement. Rather, it was the ease with which the country could be included within the existing agreement which provided an opportunity for DG Trade to become active.

A closer look at the institutional set-up also underlines the beneficial structural position of this institutional actor ahead of the start of negotiations in 2013. While the EEAS holds the overall authority over Association Agreements in the post-Lisbon set-up, this is not the case for pure FTAs as the existing one with Colombia and Peru. Furthermore, given that the EEAS lacked clear political priorities towards the Andean region, it initially welcomed any renewed EU activity towards Ecuador.[10] Additionally, DG Trade's activity could not clash with the preferences of DG DEVCO as development cooperation funding for the Andean region would shrink significantly in the period starting in 2014 and would exclude direct cooperation with the Andean Community's institutions,[11]

Lastly, DG Trade did not have to return to talks with the Council for a new mandate given that the old one was still valid and member states favoured the conclusion of new EU FTAs in the region amidst lobbying by Spain.[12] Overall, this political vacuum significantly reduced the necessity for DG Trade to resort to internal policy coordination, increased its policy autonomy, and thus reduced its overall workload required for an agreement that was to bring only little economic benefit otherwise.

The risk that the costs of negotiating the agreement would ultimately outweigh its benefits was further reduced as no new FTA would be on offer for Ecuador.

This is due to Article 329 of the existing EU–Colombia–Peru FTA which outlines a process under which the remaining Andean countries can join the existing agreement (see Official Journal of the European Union, 2012). These provisions foresee that it is the EU's sole responsibility to undertake such negotiations, which are limited by treaty to technical elements such as tariff schedules. Only once such negotiations have concluded do these need to be approved by representatives from all of the FTA's members, namely Colombia and Peru, in its dedicated trade committee.

Whereas Ecuador would have been able to shape the trade agreement itself had it remained part of the initial negotiations, the possibilities to alter the existing agreement were much more constrained once the country negotiated its accession to the previous deal. This reduced DG Trade's political risk of investing resources into complex negotiations that could be bound to fail. In reality, the actual negotiations would only involve relatively minor changes and require little work for EU trade officials amidst DG Trade's ongoing human resources constraints. This also distinguishes the Ecuador agreement from other negotiations in the post-Lisbon context, for which the likely benefits have always been carefully considered given the necessary investment of human resources by DG Trade (see the sections below).

Due to all of the above, it is thus unsurprising that DG Trade showed leadership on the issue, driving the process forward at a remarkable pace and by making use of all the trade policy tools at its disposal. The first element to consider is Ecuador's loss of GSP preferences. While the criteria used to determine GSP eligibility under the EU's reformed scheme outlined above are seemingly objective at first glance, a look at the debates that took place when the reform was debated in 2011 and 2012 reveals that there was some controversy related to these. A usual row over offering market access to former colonies of some EU member states aside, it was the usage of the World Bank classification of a country's level of development that came under some scrutiny. A working document for the European Parliament's Committee on International Trade acknowledged some of the objectivity problems related to the World Bank's classification, while also pointing out that for cases where the EU is aiming for a FTA with countries about to lose access to GSP "this proposal could of course lead to increased leverage for the EU in these negotiations" (Fjellner, 2011: 3).

That GSP reform was used as a means of pressure by the Commission even before its adoption can be seen when looking at a number of leaked diplomatic cables from Ecuador's embassy to the EU from 2011 and 2012. On 22 November 2011, the Ecuadorean Vice-Foreign Minister for Commercial Affairs, Francisco Rivadeneira, was informed of the EU's intent to reform its GSP and GSP+ schemes by DG Trade official Peter Thompson. Said official revealed that if the reform went ahead as planned, Ecuador would lose its preferential access. Given the general nature of the proposed criteria to determine GSP status, it was also pointed out that chances of gaining an exception were rather slim and that the country should hence aim for a speedy accession to the existing FTA with Colombia and Peru (Yépez Lasso, 2011a).

This take-it-or-leave-it offer was immediately accompanied by the potential of a figurative carrot, namely the possible extension of GSP preferences once an agreement had been signed. This would mean that no gap in terms of trade would occur between the country's loss of GSP status and its accession to the existing FTA. This offer was made despite the fact that member states did not want to formally politicize the GSP process by introducing exceptions and thereby potentially violate WTO provisions.[13]

The definitive nature of the EU's offer could be seen in a number of meetings between Ecuador's ambassador to the EU and different EU officials on the matter. While the Commission officials in question showed different levels of understanding for Ecuador's position, they nevertheless emphasized that Ecuador only had the chance to join the existing FTA, or risk losing preferential access to the European market altogether (Yépez Lasso, 2011b).

Given the previous failure to conclude an agreement with the EU, some officials also insisted that a formal relaunch of negotiations would have to be preceded by a declaration from Ecuador's President Correa stating his favourable position towards their speedy conclusion (Yépez Lasso, 2012c). When asked about the rather strong position of the EU on the matter, several DG Trade officials interviewed volunteered that the end of Ecuador's GSP status was merely coincidental.[14] However, they similarly acknowledged that the country's loss of GSP preference proved to be the perfect opportunity to invite the country back to the negotiation table amidst the otherwise uncertain post-Lisbon set-up.[15]

At first, Ecuador seems to have used a two-tier strategy in reaction to these revelations. While undertaking preliminary talks with the EU that could eventually lead to the relaunch of negotiations, Ecuador's diplomatic representatives have aimed to lobby EU member states and the European Parliament so as to introduce a possibility for middle-income economies (such as Ecuador) to continue benefitting from GSP+ if they kept fulfilling all political conditions beyond the initial deadline (Yépez Lasso, 2012b). This attempt to bypass DG Trade's central role in the process proved to be unsuccessful in the end, and the country was left with little choice but to join the negotiations or lose preferential access to the European market.

In the words of Ecuador's ambassador to the EU at the time, Fernando Yépez Lasso,

> the possibility of our country's exclusion from GSP+ is an element of pressure by the European Commission and certain business interests for Ecuador to join the FTA that the EU has concluded with Colombia and Peru as our only alternative to avoid a loss of market access and the eventual economic, commercial and social repercussions.
>
> (Yépez Lasso, 2011a: 4, translation mine)

While possibly exaggerating the intentionality and the political component of DG Trade's move, his assessment nonetheless accurately described the country's options ahead of its scheduled exclusion from GSP+ at the end of 2014.

The limited nature of Ecuador's influence over the agreement it would eventually join can be seen in the negotiation phase. As already mentioned, the official phase of negotiations was very brief, which can be explained in part by time playing to DG Trade's hand, as Ecuador was facing the deadline of losing GSP preferences as of the end of December 2014, but also by the limited number of adjustments that DG Trade was willing and able to offer to Ecuador. Ultimately, substantial negotiations were limited to tariff schedules and lines (Enríquez, 2014a, 2014c) rather than actual changes to the nature of the agreement.

This relatively harsh negotiation outcome was nevertheless flanked by the prospect of significant benefits that the country would receive in case of agreeing to accede to the existing agreement. By continuing to offer a piece of bridging legislation that would provide provisional GSP-like market access until the FTA could enter into force, the economic shock that the country would have faced on 1 January 2015 would not have to occur. However, DG Trade's conditions to discuss such a bridging measure were clear from the outset and dependent on the country's signature and launch of the ratification process of its accession to the FTA, as can be seen in some of the leaked diplomatic cables (Yépez Lasso, 2011a, 2012a) and in public declarations from EU diplomats in Quito, who were keen to stress that measures to prevent the country's loss of GSP status would only be studied once the negotiations had concluded (Enríquez, 2014c).

The proposal for the bridging legislation, while unique, was not a completely novel idea. Its political significance should nevertheless not be underestimated. While the EP'S INTA Committee floated the idea of an automatic extension of GSP preferences in case of a concluded but not yet applied FTA at the time the GSP reform was debated (Fjellner, 2012: 9), this did not find its way into the final piece of legislation. Furthermore, the end of negotiations by July 2014 only meant that any possible bridging legislation would have to pass through the EU's legislative process more rapidly than is the norm, so that it could apply from January 2015 onwards.

Ultimately, the legislative act was introduced by the Commission at the beginning of October 2014, with the votes taking place in the Council and Parliament on the same day in mid-December. This meant that it took less than two and a half months for the proposal to pass through the entirety of the EU's legislative process. This shows that ultimately DG Trade's choices in these negotiations were left largely unchallenged by any of the other institutions technically capable of doing so, as the conclusion of new EU FTAs had become part of the political mainstream within both the Council and the Parliament.

So as not to ease pressure on ratification by Ecuador, the proposal for the bridging legislation ultimately continued to contain a mix of figurative carrots and sticks. While offering Ecuador the much-needed GSP+ extension, it made the country's continued eligibility dependent on—amongst other things—"Ecuador conducting continuous efforts to sign and ratify the Protocol of Accession [to the FTA]" (European Union, 2014), thus introducing conditionality, in addition to a maximum timeframe of application of 2 years.

Despite the fact that it was ultimately passed, the proposal for the bridging legislation—rather than the FTA—was not without problems. These were not specific to the case of Ecuador, but rather concerning what this would mean for the EU's trade policy: On the one hand, some member states feared that this would create a precedent that would hollow out the technical nature of the EU's GSP scheme, while running counter to the EU's WTO obligations.[16] On the other, some MEPs feared a loss of influence given that the Commission alone would determine whether to suspend the preferences.[17] Lastly, the bridging legislation could lead to a problem where different Andean countries were treated differently, possibly weakening the EU's human rights conditionality towards the region.[18]

The existence of a tension over the problematic nature of the EU's use of its trade position for its own benefit equally became clear in Parliament, where the legislative proposal's rapporteur, Helmut Scholz from the GUE/NGL Group, mentioned the dilemma that Ecuador was finding itself in, even anticipating some of the upheaval in Ecuadorean civil society on the agreement that would take place over the course of 2015 (European Parliament, 2014). In any case, an interviewee reported heavy Ecuadorean lobbying ahead of the relevant legislative decisions. This was not only limited to Ecuador's diplomatic representation but also done through larger pro-trade networks.[19] Ultimately, the bridging legislation passed the EU's legislative process in time, and Ecuador's GSP+ preferences were upheld beyond the 2015 cut-off date.

At this point, other Commission DGs also became involved in the process. Rather than providing evidence for DG Trade attempting to coordinate its position with other DGs in the absence of EEAS leadership, however, the behaviour of DG DEVCO underscores the considerable autonomy of individual DGs: The EU's Commissioner for Development, Andris Piebalgs, travelled to the Andean region shortly after the conclusion of negotiations with Ecuador and announced that the country would continue to benefit from further EU development funding between 2014 and 2017 to the amount of 67 million euros (European Commission, 2014c) to prepare the country for its FTA accession, and despite the EU's overall move to end bilateral cooperation along the lines that the country received previously.

DG DEVCO officials have pointed out that this occurred independently of DG Trade's activity or EEAS guidance and in line with its own analysis of the needs of the country.[20] This mirrors similar adjustments of the EU's development cooperation funding in the context of the EU's FTA negotiations with Colombia and Peru. The interviews with DG DEVCO officials once more revealed the autonomy of Commission DGs in the aftermath of the Treaty of Lisbon, as DG Trade had not extensively consulted with DG DEVCO officials on the progress of FTA negotiations, nor did DG DEVCO officials want to involve DG Trade in the decision to alter the allocation of its development cooperation funding. Finally, one official estimated that about 90% of the decisions for the allocation of EU development funding in the 2014–2020 period were done within DG DEVCO itself, rather than in consultation with the newly created EEAS.[21]

Ultimately, DG Trade has made significant use of its trade policy instruments to influence Ecuador through a strategy of figurative carrots and sticks into its accession to the existing FTA with Colombia and Peru. While it would have been unlikely for the EU to show any interest in the country's loss of GSP and GSP+ status in the absence of previous FTA negotiations with the country, the precedent and its policy autonomy gave DG Trade the necessary opportunity to add one more of the Andean Community countries to an existing trade agreement, thereby getting closer to the initial aim of reaching an international agreement with all of the Andean Community's countries.

Nonetheless, that this negotiation process was ultimately steered by DG Trade only demonstrates the weaknesses of the EU's foreign policy decision-making system in the immediate post-Lisbon period. Given that the negotiations with the country coincided with a lack of political priorities for the region in the EEAS alongside the beginning of a new development cooperation funding period, this lack of internal policy coordination was less visible than it could have otherwise been. In that light, DG DEVCO's adjustment of the development cooperation money earmarked for Ecuador only appears to be the result of internal policy coordination, but was in reality done independently from DG Trade's negotiations.

The example of negotiations for Ecuador's accession to the existing EU–Colombia–Peru FTA therefore shows that the Treaty of Lisbon has once more disrupted established coordination mechanisms in the EU's foreign policy and increased the autonomy of individual actors to continue policy-making as they see fit, all while simultaneously increasing the potential for these holding diverging views on important foreign policy issues. These insights are rendered even more relevant as in this instance no compelling argument can be made as to what would have constituted a larger political aim spanning multiple policy areas for separately negotiating a limited FTA with Ecuador.

Flexing its muscle: The EEAS and political ties to Latin America

While DG Trade was able to demonstrate its continued control of EU trade negotiations through the process leading to the EU's FTA with Ecuador, the EEAS was keen to demonstrate its new leadership over issues mainly concerned with political ties to the region. This meant that after its initial set-up the EEAS oversaw the signature of sector-specific agreements with actors in the region. These were meant to complement existing ones, while also demonstrating its negotiating prowess in the conclusion of a political agreement with Cuba, which established the EEAS and the EU's HRVP as actors involved in processes of geopolitical relevance. Nonetheless, it shows that political ties remained largely separate from trade concerns in the initial period after the Treaty of Lisbon.

At the regional level, the EEAS was keen to take over the responsibility for the preparation of regular EU–Latin American summits from the prior rotating Council presidency.[22] This would theoretically allow the EEAS to develop long-term plans on what should be on the agenda at these high-level fora involving heads of state and government. The institution's interest in influencing region-wide developments could be seen in it taking over leadership in the process to set-up the European Union–Latin America and Caribbean Foundation (EU–LAC). This relatively small body is an institution designed to facilitate thinking on the evolution of ties between both regions which would ultimately transform itself into an international organization in its own right.[23] The process for the set-up of the foundation was started in the pre-Lisbon period almost as an after-thought at the EU–LAC Lima summit in 2008[24] and as the result of a thought process between the attending French, German, and Spanish heads of state and government.[25]

The decision to establish the foundation was then taken at the 2010 EU–LAC Madrid summit (Council of the European Union, 2010: 9), once more as a low-priority item, as discussions on this did not even feature in documents by Spain's rotating Council presidency which outlined proposed priorities for the sum-mit's agenda.[26] The language in the summit's declaration was sufficiently vague and specifically made further Senior Official Meetings (SOMs) responsible for the details, thus allowing the EEAS to step in on the EU's side,[27] all while the preparatory work prior to the Treaty of Lisbon had been the responsibility of the Commission.[28]

While the foundation was provisionally set up in Hamburg in November 2011, its creation was marred by funding issues and disagreements as to its underlying statute and political ownership.[29] This was reflected in the status of its relations with the EU's institutions. While the EEAS was meant to provide political guid-ance for the foundation a large part of its funding was, at one point, adminis-tered through DG DEVCO, creating important problems of oversight[30] and further demonstrating the autonomy of individual institutional actors in the EU's deci-sion-making system since Lisbon.

Furthermore, a treaty that would establish the foundation as an international organization was signed at 2015 EU–LAC summit in Brussels after important pre-paratory work done by the EEAS.[31] However, progress on its ratification has been slow given the low priority that it holds for most actors involved, including inter-nal divisions within the EEAS bureaucracy.[32] Despite the difficulties in setting it up, the issue of the EU–LAC Foundation demonstrates that in areas where the EEAS holds the overall competency it has been able to appropriate plans initiated before its inception by other institutional actors.

A similar development could also be seen in the EU's response to the crea-tion of the Pacific Alliance,[33] a relatively loose bloc of Latin American countries favouring free trade. Despite its focus on trade relations, the EEAS was keen to be seen as representing the EU at its meetings, and so EEAS, rather than DG Trade officials have attended its summits given the institution's overall responsibility for the political elements of the EU's external relations.[34]

The EEAS has also been fundamental in the process leading to two Latin American countries, Chile and Colombia signing Framework Participation Agreements to be able to take part in the EU's CSDP,[35] thus side-lining other issues in the relationship with the countries, such as the upcoming upgrade of the EU–Chile Association Agreement or the initial implementation phase of the EU–Colombia–Peru FTA.

As a last largely political element, the Lisbon change has also allowed for the 2014–2020 Multiannual Indicative Regional Programme for EU development funding for Latin America to be developed jointly between the EEAS and DG DEVCO. Under this new guidance, the previous programmes targeted at regional organizations have disappeared and were replaced with region-wide ones (DG Development and Cooperation, 2014). Nonetheless, while the EEAS tried to see its policy preferences being included in the document, the technical expertise of DG DEVCO and the ultimately general nature of its provisions have meant that the latter institution has been able to guard a large part of its autonomy on the matter[36] as was already outlined above when considering the FTA negotiations with Ecuador.

A major element for the EEAS to prove its new-found role, however, was the negotiations for a PDCA with Cuba, which began in 2014 and with the agreement entering provisionally into force on 1 November 2017. These negotiations show that institutional autonomy in the aftermath of the Treaty of Lisbon was not limited to Commission DGs, but could similarly be utilized by the EEAS to underscore its own role.

While the negotiations were dominated by the EEAS under the role attributed to it by the Lisbon Treaty, this was only possible given the gradually shifting and ultimately benign position of the Council towards Cuba. Ultimately, the member states—as the key actors in the non-communitarized aspects of the EU's foreign policy—therefore provided the EEAS with an opportunity to shape the EU's political relations with the country in the absence of a consideration of other policies. Here, the negotiation process represents an instance during which the autonomy of the EEAS as only one EU-level institution has played a key role in shaping the EU's overall stance. Mirroring the case of negotiations with Ecuador, the negotiations' limitation to the political realm meant that this time it was the EEAS that did not need to resort to extensive coordination with the European Commission. This made it possible to proceed with the negotiations despite possible diverging views on the matter within DG Trade or DG DEVCO.

The overall backdrop for these negotiations is Cuba's long-standing political outlier status in Latin America and consequently from the EU's policy towards the region. While part of the ACP countries, the Spanish-speaking island is a signatory neither of the Cotonou Agreement nor of an Economic Partnership Agreement (EPA) with the EU. It has also not seen a return of democracy or significant economic growth as experienced elsewhere, having been continually ruled by the Castro family ever since the Cuban Revolution of 1959 and until 2018.

As a consequence of the island's special status, the EU decided on a Common Position with regard to Cuba in 1996 which was based on a Spanish initiative. The document makes the intensification of the EU's and member state ties with the island dependent on its progress towards democracy and the rule of law (Council of the European Union, 1996). While relations with Cuba evolved slowly based on this consensus between 1996 and 2003 (Hare, 2008: 2–5), including the opening of a Commission delegation in the country, this would soon change. In 2003, Fidel Castro set in motion a clampdown against opposition leaders, and the EU in a review of its Common Position reacted by limiting political contacts with the country (Hare, 2008: 5–8). Castro in turn retaliated by unilaterally rejecting EU development cooperation funding.[37]

The 2003 decision was once more taken based on an initiative from Spain under its conservative Prime Minister José María Aznar, though supported by other countries favouring a hard line towards Cuba. The strongest supporters of this line were the Central and Eastern European states that would accede to the EU in 2004. The position of Spain changed slowly after the social democrat José Luis Rodríguez Zapatero became the country's prime minister in 2004. Nonetheless, the opposition of some hardliners, such as the Czech Republic (being suspicious of any government declaring itself to be Communist) meant that the EU could not agree on attenuating its position towards the country even after realizing that the 2003 position was not showing any effects.

The Council thus ultimately resisted policy change on the matter, much as would be expected from other institutional actors. Instead, "the EU's desire for a common position dominated the debate more than events in Cuba itself" (US Embassy Czech Republic Prague, 2005). This, taken together with the fact that the Czech Republic regularly leaked details of internal discussions to the US (US Embassy Czech Republic Prague, 2005, 2008) meant that any coherent EU policy towards the country would be very hard to achieve. This was mainly due to a lack of policy coherence between the member states and the difficulty to alter the Council's previously agreed Common Position.

This problem of policy coherence increased over time as more member states became unhappy about the impossibility of altering the Common Position at the EU level. Given the unanimity requirement for changing the EU's official stance, more and more member states resorted to modifying their national foreign policies towards the country independently. By 2013—when negotiations were officially suggested by the EEAS—16 of the EU's then 27 member states had established structured bilateral relations with the country (European Commission, 2013c: 3). By 2007, Spain then became increasingly vocal about its desire to alter or abandon the Common Position—a move which was enthusiastically supported by the EU's Development Policy Commissioner Louis Michel later on. To underline this point, Spain increased its own bilateral ties with the country (Hare, 2008: 2–5). Gradually, Eastern European states also changed their position towards it, with first timid Czech-Cuban meetings taking place in 2008.[38] Since then, the Czech Republic has become a strong supporter of a policy of engagement.[39]

This slow shift of member states' positions could also be seen in the evolution of the annual review of the Common Position and the actions by the Union's institutions. Already, in 2007, first meetings at the ministerial level occurred between EU and Cuban officials.[40] After the Common Position's 2008 review and a visit by Louis Michel to the island, the EU resumed its development cooperation.[41] By 2009, internal Council discussions were largely limited to debates over the language to use in the annual review of the Common Position, while there was a general agreement that EU engagement with Cuba should continue despite ongoing concerns as to the state of human rights, the rule of law, freedom, and democracy in the country.[42] Paul Hare, a former British ambassador to Cuba, sees 2008 as the year in which EU–Cuban relations returned to business as usual (Hare, 2008: 1). Nonetheless, the prospect of concluding an agreement with the country was still not on the horizon.

By 2010, in the immediate aftermath of the entry into force of the Treaty of Lisbon, the positions of the member states had converged so far that the HRVP was invited to develop proposals as to how to structure EU–Cuban relations going forward. The EEAS then recommended the opening of negotiations for the future PDCA by 2012 (European Commission, 2013c: 3). The 2010 policy change was made possible in part by Spain holding the rotating Council presidency in the first half of that year and being the host of the 2010 Madrid EU–Latin America and the Caribbean summit.[43] Where the idea for an EU–Cuba agreement originated is unclear, but an official interviewed stressed that, given the underlying shift of member state positions, the idea was developed within the EEAS bureaucracy despite a lack of political guidance from the HRVP herself.[44]

In any case by 2013, a recommendation was made to the Council to grant a negotiation mandate, outlining the rationale to do so as follows:

> The proposed EU-Republic of Cuba Political Dialogue and Cooperation Agreement aims at codifying, in a bilateral framework, the existing political, cooperation and trade relations between the two sides. It should create a coherent, legally binding overall framework for the EU's relations with the Republic of Cuba.
>
> (European Commission, 2013c: 3)

Rather than proposing a radically novel approach towards the country, the aim that was stated internally was to formalize existing relations and thus prioritize political over trade concerns.

Consequently, this would grant the EEAS negotiation autonomy as the Council's negotiation mandate would be solely addressed to this institution. The ultimate negotiation mandate agreed by the FAC on 10 February 2014 (Council of the European Union, 2014: 2) indeed provides for a central role of the HRVP, with COLAC overseeing the process in the Council, though assisted by the TPC for the limited number of trade issues. The preponderance of political concerns is also evidenced by the fact that the EP's INTA Committee has not been kept informed about the progress of negotiations,[45] which would have been necessary otherwise.

The EEAS seized this opportunity to demonstrate its new institutional role by prominently negotiating with a country that became ever more present in public reporting given a gradual shift of the historic position of the US towards it and its regime's attempt to use this opportunity for developing closer ties to the rest of the world.[46] While the EU's aim of developing closer ties with Cuba predates similar developments in the US, the historic handshake between Barack Obama and Raúl Castro and ensuing developments have only increased the EEAS' resolve to be seen as leaders, rather than simple followers of US-led developments.[47]

Under these circumstances, negotiations progressed rather quickly, coming to a close in the autumn of 2016. Throughout the process and ever since, the HRVP has remained very present, such as at the ceremonies surrounding the agreement's signature or ensuing political meetings, thereby emphasizing the institution's role in ensuring the success of the negotiations. The preponderant autonomous role of the EEAS was also confirmed by DG Trade officials who emphasized that given the limited trade elements contained in the mandate and the ensuing final agreement, there was no objection on this institution's part to leave the negotiations to the EEAS.[48]

The focus on political elements in the mandate helped the EEAS as a new actor to cement its position. Unlike in the trade realm, however, it made sure that other EU policy areas that it could influence would operate in sync with its political priorities for the agreement. For instance, 86 million euros in EU development funding were set aside for the country in the 2014–2020 financial framework despite Cuba's earlier unilateral refusal to accept funding from the EU. This linkage with the EU's development policy was possible given the timeline of the current financial framework and the new EEAS' role in shaping the overall allocation of the EU's development cooperation funding under it (European Commission, 2014b). Nonetheless, given the absence of an influence of the EEAS on other parts of the 2014–2020 development budget, the case of the negotiations with Cuba ought to be seen as an early exceptional imposition of the EEAS' position, rather than the illustration of how relations between the EEAS and DG DEVCO have played out over time.

Given the absence of inter-institutional rivalry and the broad support of member states for this endeavour led by the EEAS, the ratification process has been rather smooth so far. The Council gave its approval on 6 December 2016 for the EEAS to sign the agreement in a public ceremony, agreement by the European Parliament by a large majority followed on 5 July 2017 (European Parliament, 2017). This means that the agreement could provisionally enter into force while the member states complete the ratification process. National ratification was necessitated by the agreement being largely political in nature and therefore being mixed in nature. This process is not yet complete, though some initially critical member states such as the Czech Republic and Poland ratified the agreement relatively early on.

The EU's negotiations with Cuba once more demonstrate the autonomy of an individual institution at the EU level to conduct complex negotiations with a third party; however, only once certain conditions had been in place at the member state level. The requirement for unanimous decision-making in the realm of the CFSP meant that DG RELEX and later the EEAS could not alter positions at the EU level, thus precluding the risk of a Cuba policy where political relations would diverge from say, trade ties, for a long time. Nonetheless, this led to a considerable incoherence between the EU's Cuba policy and that of some of its member states. After all, the impossibility to alter the Common Position made it difficult for the EU to shift towards a policy of engagement and incentivized individual member states to alter their Cuba policy bilaterally.

It was only once member state positions started to align that the EEAS could become active and launch the initiative for the PDCA. Rather than representing a policy change across the board, the political nature of the agreement meant that the EEAS was autonomous in its actions and very little coordination had to occur with DG Trade. On the other hand, the EEAS' role in the EU's development policy meant that it could set aside funding for the country in the EU's 2014–2020 financial framework.

The premise of these bureaucratic explanations of the EU's Cuba policy contrasts with approaches that would see fundamental changes in Cuba at the core of this policy shift, as very little has changed in Cuba and given that the developments described here initially occurred independently of the US' efforts to normalize its relations with the country. The activity of the EEAS in this realm, especially in the light of its prominent public presentation, can thus be interpreted as a demonstration of its independent negotiation capacity and political capital within the post-Lisbon set-up of the EU's institutions.

Association Agreement negotiations amidst institutional divisions

The examples outlined above represented instances in which both DG Trade and the EEAS were able to act largely autonomously despite the new set-up of the Treaty of Lisbon. This was due to the fact that the negotiations covered so far were not spanning multiple policy areas and therefore cannot immediately be considered as complex negotiations. This is not the case for negotiations for Association Agreements, however, as these require inputs from different EU-level institutional actors and cover a multitude of policy areas on the EU's side. In consequence, the challenge for the EU's complex negotiations in the post-Lisbon context related to the creation of a new institutional actor can best be seen in such negotiations with the Latin American region. These are notably the EU's attempts to upgrade existing Association Agreements with Mexico and Chile.

The core underlying issue for both the Commission and the EEAS in this regard is their differing political priorities given their position within the EU's institutional system. Once the set-up of the EEAS had stabilized internally, its desire to continue developing closer political ties with the Latin American region became obvious. This can be explained, on the one hand, by there being more and more areas of mutual interest between the EU and the region, and by the fact that the piecemeal set-up of the EU's ties to Latin America has created a varying landscape of political relations that render the format and intensity of cooperation highly irregular between different kinds of partners.[49]

While the existing Association Agreements with actors in the region make for highly structured and dense economic and political ties, this is not the case for other kinds of partners such as Colombia, Peru, and Ecuador, with whom only an FTA has been signed. Furthermore, other political cooperation formats such as the strategic partnerships with Mexico and Brazil have proven largely ineffective[50] and have contributed to a rhetorical hierarchization of the EU's ties with the region (Schade, 2019). As a consequence, the EEAS has favoured the rapid upgrade of existing Association Agreements and the conclusion of new ones as a means to continue the development of political ties with the region.

DG Trade, on the other hand, has been a lot more reluctant to further its trade ties with the region given its lack of resources[51] amidst numerous other ongoing EU trade negotiations.[52] This is due to the fact that for DG Trade every individual trade negotiation ultimately represents a trade-off between potential economic gains and the human resources invested in it. For instance, there are only 10 officials working permanently in its Latin America unit,[53] with the detailed work necessary for trade negotiations relying primarily on specialists who are needed for the successful conduct of each and every EU FTA negotiation.[54] Given the scarcity of this expertise, DG Trade's scope for multiple simultaneous negotiations is limited[55] and requires careful prioritization.

Therefore, DG Trade was not opposed in principle to further trade negotiations with Latin American partners, but rather to the way in which the EEAS envisioned these. In the October 2015 EU trade strategy "Trade for all," DG Trade even specifically acknowledges the necessity to ultimately negotiate with Mercosur, Mexico, and Chile (European Commission, 2015: 33). However, no timeline was offered in the document. While DG Trade was thus not strictly opposed to negotiations with the Latin American region, it did not attach any particular priority to it given a number of other ongoing negotiations.

These differences of views between the two institutions played out in a setting in which some of the EU's Latin American partners became increasingly keen to upgrade their existing ties with the European Union. This is the case for Mexico and Chile, the two countries with which the EU had signed its first Association Agreements in the region. Both desired to modernize their existing relationship in line with the contents of some of the other EU agreements concluded with entities in the region since then. Furthermore, while the EU had begun negotiations with Mercosur on multiple occasions and then frozen these again, the political conditions within the countries making up the latter regional organization also changed sufficiently for them to desire returning to the negotiation table by the mid-2010s.

The EEAS has been keen to show its support for these initiatives from the start, signalling its interest to negotiate with both Chile and Mexico on the occasions of both the 2013 and 2015 EU–Latin America summit. In the case of Mexico, this once more represented an opportunity to take ownership of a position previously voiced by other institutional actors as initial discussions on upgrading the existing agreement with Mexico date back to 2008 in the pre-Lisbon period[56] when the country was declared a "strategic partner" of the EU.

The EEAS then desired to turn the general commitments under the strategic partnership into a binding legal framework, as would be possible to achieve through Association Agreement negotiations.[57] Consequently, the institution was not opposed to formally make its intent visible on the occasion of the 2013 summit, with the summit's final declaration stating that both sides had reached an "agreement to explore the options for a comprehensive update of the Economic Partnership, Political Coordination and Cooperation Agreement" (Council of the

European Union, 2013: 6). This was rendered more precise at the summit two years later: The Joint Statement of the EU–Mexico summit that was held in the margins of the 2015 EU–Latin America summit in Brussels acknowledges the necessity and willingness of both sides to upgrade the existing Global Agreement. Nonetheless, the language that had to be chosen reveals the political differences between the EEAS and DG Trade, as the final document only agreed to "a willingness to launch, in 2015, the process of starting negotiations [...] to modernise our Global Agreement and to reinforce our Strategic Partnership" (EU–Mexico Summit, 2015: 1), rather than deciding on an actual timeframe for negotiations.

When the first round of negotiations for the upgrade took place in June 2016, no matters of substance were discussed (EEAS, 2016) given that DG Trade was not ready to enter into technical talks with the country. Nonetheless, by April 2018, an agreement in principle had been found between both sides, with the agreement still undergoing technical revisions. While there was some political pressure that the agreement should be completed before the next EP elections in May 2019 so as to demonstrate the achievements of the Juncker Commission and out of fear over possible changed majorities in the next European Parliament,[58] this has ultimately proven impossible.

Underlying these institutional tensions were continued demands by the Mexican side to swiftly upgrade the agreement, which are supported by a coalition of member states led by Spain. Others, however, shared DG Trade's specific concerns about the complexity of the ensuing negotiations, questioning that this should be prioritized ahead of others.[59] These differences of opinion initially hindered the progression of the process, despite interviewees repeatedly mentioning the desire of both Mexico and the EEAS to press ahead.

A Mexican official interviewed furthermore voiced concerns that from the country's perspective it was incredibly difficult to identify the correct counterpart in the EU's institutions for different kinds of discussions, citing frustration that the EU would not move forward in renegotiating its ties with its "closest partner in the region despite repeated assurances by the EEAS."[60] Similarly, a Spanish official was concerned ahead of the start of negotiations that relations with the country would deteriorate if no progress was achieved soon.[61] The differing priorities of both institutions thus ultimately contributed to a setting in which the EEAS was keen to begin negotiations so as to please their Mexican counterparts, all while DG Trade had initially been more cautious.[62]

These difficulties were only overcome gradually as negotiations had officially begun. On the one hand, EEAS officials increasingly recognized the resource constraints of the other institution,[63] becoming more cautious in their approach towards the promise of negotiations with other third countries. DG Trade, on the other hand, ultimately translated the prior political commitment into practice by preparing a negotiation mandate for the trade part, which was adopted relatively swiftly by the Council in 2016.[64] The actual negotiations have then been conducted largely separately, with the EEAS coordinating the necessary activity of all Commission DGs except for DG Trade. The ultimate task of creating a single agreement under a unified legal framework was rendered more difficult by the fact that there was no exchange of drafts between both entities on the matter given DG Trade's fear that its negotiation hand might be revealed.[65]

The initial case for an upgrade of the EU's existing Association Agreement with Chile is largely similar, however this time around the differing views between both institutions led to a more gradual approach in negotiations with the country. In sync with Mexico, the country has lobbied the EU to upgrade the existing agreement ever since the 2013 EU–Latin America summit, the final declaration of which recognized that talks had taken place "to explore the options to modernise the Association Agreement after 10 years of Association" (Council of the European Union, 2013: 6). While the 2015 EU–Mexico summit was clear in that the existing agreement would be upgraded despite the lack of a timeline, the language adopted at the Brussels summit for the modernization of the Chile agreement two years later was more cautious, stating that both sides "agree to move forward in the process towards the modernisation of the bilateral Association Agreement through the establishment of a Joint Working Group" (EU–CELAC Summit, 2015: 17).

Chile is pro-FTA leaning, a member of the Pacific Alliance and the Trans-Pacific Partnership Agreement (TPP), which should make the country an obvious choice for an upgrade of the existing agreement. Nonetheless, the same DG Trade resource constraints remained,[66] while concluding the EEAS part of the negotiations (it is once more the lead institution overall) would once more be significantly easier.[67]

In this case, however, DG Trade was able to slow the process citing the ongoing negotiations with Mexico and has ultimately been more open about its preferences with the EEAS.[68] As a consequence, the negotiation mandate for a trade agreement was only transferred to the Council for deliberation in 2018,[69] with detailed negotiations starting shortly thereafter and having reached their fourth round by mid-2019 (European Commission, 2019).

If one also considers the renewed negotiations for the EU's Association Agreement with Mercosur (see Chapter 4), then the examples of the Association Agreement negotiations in the post-Lisbon set-up clearly show that the treaty has established a setting within which the priorities of different institutional actors at the EU level are bound to clash. While the EEAS has managed to establish its authority over coordinating negotiations including work by individual Commission DGs in most domains,[70] this is not the case for the trade part of such negotiations. Instead, DG Trade has continued to remain in control of this largely separate part of any negotiation, which is cemented by the distinct negotiation mandate given to it. As opposed to the initial years of the post-Lisbon set-up, however, both institutions have gradually grown to accept the others' role, with the EEAS recognizing that it is trade concerns which ultimately drive the relationship with Latin America, thus requiring it to follow the timing suggested by DG Trade given its resource constraints.[71]

Conclusion

Despite the stated aim of the Treaty of Lisbon to increase foreign policy coordination in the European Union, the institutional changes to the EU's foreign policy established with it have led to a situation in which existing EU-level institutional actors and a new one, the EEAS, had to establish a renewed role for themselves, as well as establish ways to cooperate with one another. The results of this institutional turmoil can be seen in the way in which negotiations with actors in Latin America have progressed since the treaty's entry into force.

On the one hand, each actor and particularly DG Trade and the EEAS as the entities holding core responsibilities for EU treaty negotiations have been keen to demonstrate their autonomy in cases where proposed agreements would largely fall within their exclusive competencies. While DG Trade was able to demonstrate its capacities in FTA negotiations with Ecuador, the EEAS could use the PDCA with Cuba as an example for its own negotiation prowess.

Where responsibilities are shared between both, such as when negotiating for Association Agreements, instances of bureaucratic infighting could be observed at first. It is only over time that both institutions' positions have once more stratified and cooperation between them became part of a routine and thus normalized. This ultimately reduced both institutions' desire for autonomy and should contribute to rendering inter-institutional ties between the Commission and the EEAS closer to those seen between different Commission DGs prior to the Lisbon Treaty. Nonetheless, these initial episodes of internal turmoil have not escaped the EU's negotiation partners in the region and demonstrate once more that even well-intended attempts at administrative reorganization do not necessarily translate into better policy outcomes in the short term.

Notes

1 EEAS officials, Brussels (Interview 8).
2 Member state diplomat, Brussels (Interview 29).
3 EEAS officials, Brussels (Interview 8).
4 EEAS officials, Brussels (Interview 8).
5 Member state diplomat, Brussels (Interview 29); Latin American diplomats, Brussels (Interview 7).
6 Member state diplomat, Brussels (Interview 29); Latin American diplomats, Brussels (Interview 7); EEAS desk officer, Brussels (Interview 34).
7 Member state diplomat, Brussels (Interview 9).
8 Member state diplomat, Brussels (Interview 9); DG Trade official, Brussels (Interview 32).
9 Member state diplomat, Brussels (Interview 29).
10 Senior EEAS official, Brussels (Interview 13).
11 DG DEVCO officials, Brussels (Interview 24).
12 Member state diplomat, Brussels (Interview 9).
13 Former EU official, Brussels (Interview 17); Member state diplomat, Brussels (Interview 19).
14 Former EU official, Brussels (Interview 17).
15 Member state diplomat, Brussels (Interview 29).
16 Member state diplomat, Brussels, 17.6.2015 (Interview 9). The legality of GSP schemes depends in large parts on the objective nature of the criteria used to determine eligibility.
17 This was agreed to despite the European Parliament's legal services questioning the legality of such a formulation.
18 The concern was primarily related to the fact that the EP had insisted on creating a human rights "road map" in the case of Colombia, but not in the case of Ecuador.

19 European Parliament official, Brussels (Interview 25).
20 DG DEVCO officials, Brussels (Interview 24; 35).
21 DG DEVCO official, Brussels (Interview 35).
22 Senior EEAS official, Brussels (Interview 13).
23 Senior EEAS official, Brussels (Interview 33).
24 Former EU official, Brussels (Interview 17).
25 Former Commission official, Hamburg (Interview 2).
26 Internal Council CFSP document dated 2009.
27 Internal Council CFSP document dated January 2011.
28 Internal Council CFSP document dated November 2009.
29 Latin American diplomat, Brussels (Interview 26).
30 Former Commission official, Hamburg (Interview 2).
31 Former Commission official, Hamburg (Interview 2).
32 Senior EEAS official, Brussels (Interview 33); Latin American diplomat, Brussels (Interview 26).
33 An informal intergovernmental organization based on free trade between its members. Currently, it is composed of Chile, Colombia, Peru, and Mexico.
34 Commission officials, Brussels (Interview 24).
35 Commission officials, Brussels (Interview 24).
36 DG DEVCO official, Brussels (Interview 35); Senior EEAS official, Brussels (Interview 33).
37 Internal Council CFSP document dated June 2008.
38 Former EU official, Brussels (Interview 17).
39 Member state diplomat, Brussels (Interview 29).
40 Internal Council CFSP document dated June 2008.
41 Internal Council CFSP document dated April 2009.
42 Internal Council CFSP document dated June 2009.
43 Member state diplomat, Brussels (Interview 29).
44 Senior EEAS official, Brussels (Interview 13).
45 European Parliament official, Brussels (Interview 14).
46 Senior EEAS official, Brussels (Interview 13).
47 European Parliament official, Brussels (Interview 25).
48 DG Trade official, Brussels (Interview 32).
49 EEAS official, Brussels (Interview 33).
50 EEAS official, Brussels (Interview 33); EEAS official, Brussels (Interview 34).
51 Member state diplomat, Brussels (Interview 9).
52 DG Trade official, Brussels (Interview 12).
53 DG Trade official, Brussels (Interview 32).
54 DG Trade official, Brussels (Interview 32).
55 DG Trade official, Brussels (Interview 32).
56 DG Trade official, Brussels (Interview 12).
57 EEAS official, Brussels (Interview 34).
58 EEAS official, Brussels (Interview 33); DG DEVCO official, Brussels (Interview 35).
59 Member state diplomat, Brussels (Interview 9).
60 Latin American diplomat, Brussels (Interview 26).
61 Member state diplomat, Brussels (Interview 29).
62 EEAS officials, Brussels (Interview 8).
63 EEAS officials, Brussels (Interview 8).
64 DG Trade official, Brussels (Interview 32).
65 EEAS official, Brussels (Interview 34).
66 European Parliament official, Brussels (Interview 14).
67 Member state diplomat, Brussels (Interview 29).
68 Senior EEAS official, Brussels (Interview 34).

69 DG Trade official, Brussels (Interview 32).
70 EEAS official, Brussels (Interview 34).
71 Senior EEAS official, Brussels (Interview 33).

Bibliography

Comisión mixta Comunidad Andina—Union Europea (2010) *Acta de la XI reunión de la Comisión mixta Comunidad Andina—Unión Europea.* Available at: http://eeas.europa.eu/andean/docs/joint_comm_050310_es.pdf (accessed 5 January 2016).

Council of the European Union (1996) *Common Position of 2 December 1996 on Cuba.* 96/697/CFSP. Brussels: Council of the European Union. Available at: http://eur-lex.europa.eu/legal-content/EN/TXT/PDF/?uri=CELEX:31996E0697&from=EN (accessed 14 January 2016).

Council of the European Union (2010) *Madrid Declaration.* Madrid: Council of the European Union. Available at: www.consilium.europa.eu/uedocs/cms_Data/docs/pressdata/en/er/114535.pdf (accessed 12 June 2018).

Council of the European Union (2013) *Santiago Declaration.* Santiago de Chile: Council of the European Union. Available at: www.eeas.europa.eu/la/summits/docs/2013_santiago_summit_declaration_en.pdf (accessed 12 June 2016).

Council of the European Union (2014) *List of 'A' Items 3291st meeting of the Council of the European Union (Foreign Affairs).* 6123/14, 10 February. Brussels: Council of the European Union. Available at: http://data.consilium.europa.eu/doc/document/ST-6123-2014-INIT/en/pdf.

DG Development and Cooperation (2014) *Multiannual Indicative Regional Programme for Latin America.* Development Cooperation Instrument (DCI) 2014–2020. Brussels: European Commission. Available at: https://ec.europa.eu/europeaid/sites/devco/files/dci-multindicativeprogramme-latinamerica-07082014_en.pdf.

DG Trade (2012) *The EU's New Generalised Scheme of Preferences (GSP).* December. Available at: http://trade.ec.europa.eu/doclib/docs/2012/december/tradoc_150164.pdf (accessed 4 December 2018).

DG Trade (2015) *EU Ecuador Trade.* Available at: http://trade.ec.europa.eu/doclib/docs/2006/september/tradoc_111501.pdf (accessed 12 January 2016).

EEAS (2013) *EEAS Review.* Brussels: European External Action Service. Available at: http://eeas.europa.eu/library/publications/2013/3/2013_eeas_review_en.pdf (accessed 15 January 2016).

EEAS (2016) *Joint Press Release on the First Round of EU–Mexico Negotiations of the Global Agreement.* Press Release 60614_03_en, 14 June. Brussels: European External Action Service. Available at: http://eeas.europa.eu/statements-eeas/2016/160614_03_en.htm (accessed 16 June 2016).

Enríquez C (2014a) El acuerdo con la Unión Europea depende de dos temas. *El Comercio*, 7 July. Quito. Available at: Factiva Document COMCIO0020140707ea770000b (accessed 29 April 2019).

Enríquez C (2014b) El Régimen ya planea nueva cita con la Unión Europea. *El Comercio*, 28 March. Quito. Available at: Factiva Document COMCIO0020140328ea3s00007 (accessed 29 April 2019).

Enríquez C (2014c) Un mes para cerrar el acuerdo con la Unión Europea. *El Comercio*, 9 May. Quito. Available at: Factiva Document COMCIO0020140509ea5900008 (accessed 29 April 2019).

EU–CAN High Level Meeting on Drugs (2012) *XI Reunión de diálogo especializado de alto nivel sobre drogas Comunidad Andina—Unión Europea Quito—Ecuador Comunicado Conjunto.* Available at: http://eeas.europa.eu/andean/docs/xi_reunion_de_dialogo_comunicado_conjunto_es.pdf (accessed 1 October 2016).

EU–CELAC Summit (2015) *Brussels Declaration.* Brussels: European Council. Available at: www.consilium.europa.eu/en/meetings/international-summit/2015/06/EU-CEL-AC-Brussels-declaration_pdf/ (accessed 1 August 2015).

EU–Mexico Summit (2015) *VII EU–Mexico Summit Joint Statement,* 12 June. Brussels: Council of the European Union.

European Commission (2013a) *Commission Delegated Regulation No 1/2014 of 28 August 2013 Establishing Annex III to Regulation (EU) No 978/2012 of the European Parliament and of the Council Applying a Scheme of Generalised Tariff Preferences,* 28 August. Brussels: Official Journal of the European Union. Available at: http://trade.ec.europa.eu/doclib/docs/2014/january/tradoc_152057.pdf (accessed 4 December 2016).

European Commission (2013b) *Commission Delegated Regulation No 1421/2013 of 30 October 2013 Amending Annexes I, II and IV to Regulation (EU) No 978/2012 of the European Parliament and of the Council Applying a Scheme of Generalised Tariff Preferences,* 31 December. Brussels: Official Journal of the European Union. Available at: http://trade.ec.europa.eu/doclib/docs/2014/january/tradoc_152057.pdf (accessed 4 December 2016).

European Commission (2013c) *Recommendation from the Commission to the Council to Authorise the European Commission and the High Representative of the Union for Foreign Affairs and Security Policy to Open Negotiations and Negotiate, on Behalf of the European Union, the Provisions of a Political Dialogue and Cooperation Agreement Between the European Union, of the One Part, and the Republic of Cuba, of the Other Part.* COM(2013) 221 Final, 18 April. Brussels: European Commission. Available at: http://data.consilium.europa.eu/doc/document/ST-8702-2013-EXT-1/en/pdf (accessed 1 May 2016).

European Commission (2014a) *EU and Ecuador Conclude Negotiations for Trade and Development Agreement.* Press Release, 17 July. Brussels: European Commission. Available at: http://europa.eu/rapid/press-release_IP-14-845_en.htm (accessed 4 December 2018).

European Commission (2014b) *Multiannual Indicative Programme (MIP) for Cuba 2014–2020.* Available at: https://eulacfoundation.org/en/system/files/Multiannual%20Indicative%20Programme%20%28MIP%29%20for%20Cuba%202014-2020.pdf (accessed 2 January 2016).

European Commission (2014c) *New Funding for Ecuador Announced by Commissioner Piebalgs During Visit.* Press Release, 23 July. Brussels: European Commission. Available at: http://europa.eu/rapid/press-release_IP-14-874_en.htm (accessed 4 December 2018).

European Commission (2015) *Trade for All: Towards a More Responsible Trade and Investment Policy.* Brussels: European Commission. Available at: http://trade.ec.europa.eu/doclib/docs/2015/october/tradoc_153846.pdf (accessed 1 May 2016).

European Commission (2019) *Report on the 4th Round of Negotiations Between the EU and Chile for Modernisign the Trade Part of the EU–Chile Association Agreement.* Brussels: European Commission. Available at: http://trade.ec.europa.eu/doclib/docs/2019/april/tradoc_157867.pdf (accessed 30 May 2019).

European Parliament (2014) *European Parliament Plenary Debate Protocol 16 December 2014.* European Parliament. Available at: www.europarl.europa.eu/sides/getDoc.do?pubRef=-//EP//TEXT+CRE+20141216+ITEM-017+DOC+XML+V0//EN (accessed 21 June 2015).

European Parliament (2017) *MEPs Back First Ever EU–Cuba Deal*. Press Release, 5 July. Strasbourg: European Parliament. Available at: www.europarl.europa.eu/news/en/press-room/20170629IPR78654/meps-back-first-ever-eu-cuba-deal.

European Union (2014) *Regulation (EU) No 1384/2014 of the European Parliament and of the Council of 18 December 2014 on the Tariff Treatment for Goods Originating in Ecuador*, 30 December. Brussels: Official Journal of the European Union. Available at: http://eur-lex.europa.eu/legal-content/EN/TXT/PDF/?uri=CELEX:32014R1384&-from=EN (accessed 4 January 2015).

Fjellner C (2011) *Working Document on a Proposal for a Regulation of the European Parliament and the Council Applying a Scheme of Generalised Tariff Preferences*. PE472.115v01-00, 28 September. Brussels: Committee on International Trade.

Fjellner C (2012) *Report on the Proposal for a Regulation of the European Parliament and of the Council Applying a Scheme of Generalised Tariff Preferences*. A7-0054/2012, 8 March. Brussels: Committee on International Trade.

General Secretariat of the Council (2019) *List of Council Preparatory Bodies*. Available at: http://data.consilium.europa.eu/doc/document/ST-10075-2017-INIT/en/pdf (accessed 25 May 2019).

Hare P (2008) *The Odd Couple: The EU and Cuba 1996–2008*. September. Washington, DC: Brookings Institution. Available at: https://eulacfoundation.org/en/system/files/The%20Odd%20Couple%20The%20EU%20and%20Cuba%201996–2008.pdf (accessed 14 January 2016).

Morgenstern-Pomorski J-H (2018) *The Contested Diplomacy of the European External Action Service: Inception, Establishment and Consolidation*. Abingdon: Routledge.

Official Journal of the European Union (2012) *Trade Agreement Between the European Union and Its Member States, of the One Part, and Colombia and Peru, or the Other Part*. Available at: http://eur-lex.europa.eu/legal-content/EN/TXT/PDF/?uri=O-J:L:2012:354:FULL&from=EN (accessed 10 November 2015).

Schade D (2019) Of Insiders and Outsiders: Assessing EU Strategic Partnerships in Their Regional Context. *International Politics* 56(3): 375–394. DOI: 10.1057/s41311-017-0132-y.

US Embassy Czech Republic Prague (2005) *In-depth Readout of EU's Cuba Compromise*. Available at: https://search.wikileaks.org/plusd/cables/05PRAGUE1006_a.html (accessed 20 March 2019).

US Embassy Czech Republic Prague (2008) *Czech Comments on Draft U.S.–EU Summit Declaration*. Available at: https://wikileaks.org/plusd/cables/08PRAGUE328_a.html (accessed 20 March 2019).

Yépez Lasso F (2011a) *Entrevista de viceministro de comercio con director adjunto de comercio de la Comision*. Diplomatic Cable 1556-BRU/2011, 22 November. Brussels: Ecuadorian Embassy to the European Union.

Yépez Lasso F (2011b) *TLC con la Union Europea*. Diplomatic Cable 1635-BRU/2011, 7 December. Brussels: Ecuadorian Embassy to the European Union.

Yépez Lasso F (2012a) *Gestiones SGP+, TLC con la Union Europea y adhesion al Mercosur*. Diplomatic Cable 4-BRU/2012, 4 January. Brussels: Ecuadorian Embassy to the European Union.

Yépez Lasso F (2012b) *Gestiones sobre SGP+ con Consejo de la UE y Parlamento Europeo*. Diplomatic Cable 38-BRU/2012, 10 January. Brussels: Ecuadorian Embassy to the European Union.

Yépez Lasso F (2012c) *TLC con la Union Europea. Adhesion al Mercosur*. Diplomatic Cable 80-BRU/2012, 16 January. Brussels: Ecuadorian Embassy to the European Union.

Part III

Understanding the wider dynamics of complex EU negotiations

7 Negotiations with the rest of the world

Introduction

Having tested this book's analytical framework in a context which allowed to study the effect of institutional changes over time, this chapter sets out to explore the model's relevance for the analysis of the EU's behaviour in other recent complex Association Agreement negotiations where key elements may differ from those relevant in the negotiations in the Latin American context explored beforehand. Whereas the scope and political relevance of the negotiations considered in the main empirical part of this book were relatively similar, this is not necessarily the case in other kinds of complex EU negotiations. In consequence, this chapter analyses two cases where economic, geographic, political, or security aspects altered both the aims to be achieved with complex negotiations as well as the political background conditions.

Firstly, an analysis of the Ukraine–EU Association Agreement serves to illustrate cases in which the eventual prospect of EU membership and wider political and security considerations played a major role. Secondly, a consideration of the EU–Japan FTA and the parallel Strategic Partnership Agreement (SPA) outlines a case of complex EU negotiations with a major global economy. Ultimately, these serve to exemplify that factors of bureaucratic politics still help to understand the dynamics of negotiations in such other contexts, thereby demonstrating the utility of the analytical framework beyond the main geographic scope of the book's core empirical part. While the analysis of the negotiations considered in the latter was detailed and based on a wide array of sources, the two negotiations outlined here merely serve as an illustration and are less detailed in consequence.

The Ukraine–EU Association Agreement

Although the negotiations for the Ukraine–EU Association Agreement differed importantly from those for other complex EU agreements, similar issues of bureaucratic politics could nonetheless be observed throughout the negotiation process. What makes this particular agreement so unique is its integration focus and the politicization that has occurred as negotiations progressed.

The Ukraine–EU Association Agreement stands apart from similar kinds of agreements as it is "integration-oriented" (Van der Loo et al., 2014: 2), meaning that its provisions ultimately contribute to Ukraine's integration with the EU and its single market without the country becoming an EU member state. The specific setting of EU–Ukraine relations as embedded in the evolution of EU–Russia relations has also meant that the agreement has become heavily politicized. This was not so much the case given the political contents of the actual AA, but due to the country's choice for closer alignment with the EU and away from Russia that the agreement represented. It was Ukraine's then President Viktor Yanukovych's refusal to sign the negotiated agreement which helped spark the Euromaidan protests in early 2014 (Dragneva and Wolczuk, 2014: 214) and the ensuing Russia–Ukraine conflict in Crimea and Eastern Ukraine which continues to this date.

Initially, the EU's ties with the country were structured by a PCA concluded in the late 1990s as it was not part of group of countries that would join the EU in its Eastern enlargement rounds. The incomplete and inflexible nature of this type of agreement which was also applied to other countries in the EU's new Eastern neighbourhood created demands on the Ukrainian side to deepen EU–Ukraine ties through further agreements (Dragneva and Wolczuk, 2014: 215–7), including an eventual membership perspective.

While the EU's ties with the country were then gradually altered through a number of specific EU commitments, it wasn't until the mid-2000s, and therefore in the pre-Lisbon period, that the eventual prospect of an Association Agreement with the country became part of the EU's approach towards the country. Ultimately, the promise of negotiations with Ukraine was then tied to normative concerns over it's democratic development and the EU's evolving economic interests (Smith, 2014).

It is in this context of the EU increasingly using the prospect of negotiations with the country to help achieve certain political reform aims in Ukraine, and especially reforms related to the rule of law and democratization, that disagreements between key EU actors on the EU's policy towards the country could first be observed (Dragneva and Wolczuk, 2014: 220). While it soon became clear that what was on offer for Ukraine would be a type of complex agreement that would reflect the necessary density of the EU's ties to a state within its neighbourhood, there was considerable disagreement within the EU as to whether the ultimate agreement would emphasize Ukraine's eventual EU enlargement prospects.

These debates included disagreement over whether the eventual agreement should be named Association Agreement, as some more critical EU member states felt that giving the agreement such a name would go too far in emphasizing the country's ultimate accession perspective. At the same time, other countries and the EU's then External Relations Commissioner Benita Ferrero-Waldner felt that emphasizing the country's EU perspective was precisely the kind of strong message that should be sent to Ukraine (Agence Europe, 2008b, 2008c).

While the issue of the agreement's name was ultimately resolved, the mandate given by the Council in 2007 reflected differing views between the member states and ultimately called for a relatively restricted agreement to be negotiated primarily by the Commission, with only little input by the EU's CFSP structures (Gehring et al., 2017: 734–5). This emphasis on the primary role of the Commission was not unusual at the time, as the EU's pre-Lisbon set-up meant that this institution still played a larger role in the EU's external relations than it does today.

This restricted mandate by the Council contrasted with the Commission's attempts to develop an extensive partnership with Ukraine in the negotiations, which ultimately limited the Commission's room for manoeuvre (Dragneva and Wolczuk, 2014: 221–2). Within the Commission key responsibilities were then shared between DG Trade, which would be responsible for the key FTA part of the agreement, as well as DG Enlargement and European Neighbourhood Policy (Gehring et al., 2017: 234–5) for aspects relating to the country's de facto European integration. As the original negotiation mandate survived the institutional change only a small role was attributed to CFSP structures throughout the entire process. Both the differing positions between the Council and the Commission and the split responsibilities within the latter institution ultimately show the influence that different aspects of bureaucratic politics had on these negotiations.

Aside from the envisioned language on Ukraine's EU accession prospects, initially progress during the negotiation period relied on Ukraine joining the WTO in 2008, as the political elements of the agreement were easier to resolve (Agence Europe, 2008a, 2009). Nonetheless, in addition to these economic aspects, Ukrainian concerns over security and territorial sovereignty—which would come to the forefront after the beginning of the Ukraine crisis in 2014—already rendered initial negotiations relatively complex (Agence Europe, 2010a).

Political conditionality between different of the policy areas touched by the negotiations also increasingly rendered these more difficult: Whereas the EU used the negotiations as a means to pressure the country into improving its human rights and rule of law track record, Ukraine hoped that FTA concessions with negative economic impact in Ukraine would be rewarded with increased financial aid towards the country (Agence Europe, 2010b). Divergences between the EU's trade preferences and its concerns over the rule of law in the country became ever more prevalent once Ukraine's former Prime Minister Yulia Tymoshenko received a prison sentence in the country.

By this time, the EU's institutional set-up had changed to its post-Lisbon state which meant that the EU's concerns over the matter were communicated by Catherine Ashton in association with Commission President José Manuel Barroso (Agence Europe, 2011c), despite the fact that the key negotiation responsibility continued to reside within the Commission. Simultaneously, the newly emboldened EP started to be more actively involved in the negotiations, with MEPs who would have to ratify the final agreement by consent becoming increasingly sceptical of the merits of an EU–Ukraine Association Agreement amidst similar concerns (Agence Europe, 2011a).

While technical negotiations in the realm of trade indeed made rapid progress so that the agreement negotiations were technically finished by the end of 2011, in the end, these concerns meant that the EU proved unwilling to officially close them amidst the increasing criticism of some member states on the remaining political issues (Agence Europe, 2011d). The EU in the person of the Council President Herman van Rompuy then used this element to pressure the country into further reforms to its justice system (Agence Europe, 2011e).

While progress on such matters meant that the agreement could be initialled in 2012, thereby signifying an end to the technical negotiation process, this did not end the increasingly political process ahead of the agreement's conclusion. This is due to the fact that continued political concerns of the EU's member states meant that it was unlikely for the Council to accept signing the agreement, and in consequence, political pressure for reforms in Ukraine was upheld by key European decision-makers (Agence Europe, 2013d). It would then take until 2013 for the Commission to conclude that the political environment had changed sufficiently to formally suggest the agreement's conclusion to the Council ahead of the beginning of ratification proceedings (Agence Europe, 2013b).

While the process of EU–Ukraine negotiations had remained a largely bilateral matter between the EU And Ukraine until then, the signature of the agreement by Ukraine was put increasingly in doubt by increased Russian criticism as to what the AA would mean for Russia–Ukraine ties (Agence Europe, 2013c; Dragneva and Wolczuk, 2014). While the Euromaidan movement and the ensuing political revolution in the country were ultimately born out of the refusal by Ukraine's President Viktor Yanukovych to sign the agreement, the EU initially aimed to address Russian concerns by entering into a series of trilateral discussions between all parties (Agence Europe, 2014a) ahead of the Crimean crisis.

It was in this format that ultimately a promise was made by the EU that the implementation of the FTA part of the Association Agreement would be delayed (Agence Europe, 2014b), all while the ratification process could get underway after Ukraine's new President Petro Poroshenko signed the agreement in March 2014. Despite continued criticism in the EP, it was then ratified in September 2014 at the same time as in the Ukrainian Parliament (Agence Europe, 2014c). After this, national ratification within all EU member states still remained a necessity.

It is at this stage of the process that the complexity of decision-making on complex EU agreements and the long duration of such processes once more influenced the overall dynamics in an important manner. Twenty-seven of the EU's member states ratified the agreement relatively quickly given that overarching political concerns that had arisen in the Ukraine crisis gradually aligned member states' preferences. The emerging consensus around supporting Ukraine's position in the conflict by committing to the Association Agreement is also exemplified in the EU's capacity to find a consensus on sanctions against Russia in the aftermath of the annexation of Crimea (Sjursen and Rosén, 2017).

However, a non-binding referendum on the domestic ratification of the Association Agreement in the Netherlands altered the political conditions for the process in the country (Van der Loo, 2017) as 64% of participants in the referendum voted against it (Agence Europe, 2016). Ultimately, a political decision in the Council providing a certain clarification on some of the agreement's provisions then proved sufficient for the Netherlands to ratify the agreement, which fully entered into force on 1 September 2017 (Agence Europe, 2017d).

Given the exceptional circumstances surrounding the agreement's signature and eventual ratification amidst a rising geopolitical crisis—aside from attempts to ratify the Association Agreement rapidly—the EU also used a number of other measures to support Ukraine. In line with the nature of most EU policy-making, and given continued disagreements on the wider geopolitical implications of the Ukraine crisis amongst the member states, the response of the EU's institutions was largely technocratic in nature (Dragneva and Wolczuk, 2015: 119–20). Nonetheless, the technical measures taken still represent an exceptional use of the policy tools at the EU's disposal and which can be attributed to a permissive consensus amongst EU-level institutions on supporting Ukraine.

While EU development, neighbourhood, and cooperation funding were made available to the country (Agence Europe, 2015), the most important exceptional measures occurred in the realm of EU–Ukraine trade relations. Firstly, the delay in the ratification of the agreement led the EU to extend unilateral trade preferences to Ukraine (Agence Europe, 2014d; Van der Loo et al., 2014: 5–6) akin to the Ecuadorean case explored earlier in this book. Furthermore, once the agreement had been concluded but not ratified yet, the scope for its provisional application was made exceptionally large (Van der Loo, 2017: 341–2; Van der Loo et al., 2014: 6–7). Lastly, a number of additional trade facilitations were approved in addition to the measures contained in the AAs FTA component (Agence Europe, 2017c). All of this required to reach a widespread consensus between the Commission, Council, and of the European Parliament.

Negotiating the Japan–EU Free Trade Agreement

In contrast to the EU's Association Agreement with Ukraine, the negotiations for the EU–Japan EPA—also known as Japan–EU Free Trade Agreement (JEFTA)—have received considerably less public scrutiny. This is despite the fact that Japan is a major global economy and a relatively important trading partner for the EU. While the EPA is an advanced FTA without significant political commitments, the parallel negotiation of an EU–Japan SPA has meant that the overarching negotiation dynamics were still those for a complex agreement similar to Association Agreement negotiations. Ultimately, the case of JEFTA can thus help illustrate how even in absence of a single negotiation framework interlinkages between different external policy areas shape the negotiation process. This is particularly relevant as splitting a cross-cutting negotiation into separate legal agreements has become a more regular feature of complex EU negotiations in cases such as the EU's agreements with South Korea or Canada (D'Ambrogio, 2019: 3–4).

What distinguishes the EU–Japan negotiations from the ones considered in the main empirical part of this book is that EU–Japan ties are economically more salient than those with partners in the Latin American region. Together, the economies of the EU and those of Japan account for more than a quarter of world GDP and Japan is a more relevant trade partner for the EU overall (Frenkel and Walter, 2017: 359).

Nonetheless, similar factors have shaped the negotiations as were considered earlier in the book. A first element of note increasing the possible influence of bureaucratic politics, and particularly a combination of bureaucratic inertia and parallel institutional change, is the long duration of the negotiations at hand, which was in line with some of the negotiations explored in more detail earlier on. Once more, the process involved three consecutive European Commissions and European Parliament sessions, including the major change of the set-up of the EU's foreign policy apparatus with the Lisbon Treaty. This meant that these negotiations were shaped again by changes to the very structure of the EU's institutions and decision-making as well as changing majorities and political actors involved.

While initial talks for the EPA began in 2011 in the wake of the Tsunami and nuclear disaster (Suzuki, 2017: 879–80), the potential for an FTA was first discussed within the confines of existing EU–Japan dialogue bodies in 2009 (de Prado, 2014: 15). In consequence, while initial discussions on the negotiations predate the implementation of the changes to the EU's foreign policy system with the Lisbon Treaty, they were formally launched by José Manuel Barroso as Commission President and by Herman van Rompuy as the Council President in 2011. This occurred at a point in time when the EEAS had barely begun to be operational under the leadership of HRVP Catherine Ashton.

The beginning of negotiations with Japan thus fell into a time period of important bureaucratic change within the EU's institutions and allowed administrative divisions to take root on the matter (Agence Europe, 2011b). This contributed to a considerable delay in launching the procedure to formally agree a negotiation mandate for both agreements, with the Commission under the leadership of Trade Commissioner Karel De Gucht only formally requesting a mandate from the Council one year later (Agence Europe, 2012). This meant that the formal launch of both parallel negotiations only occurred in 2013 (Agence Europe, 2013a).

The process leading to the eventual EPA and SPA with Japan had not finished by mid-2019. While the split of the talks into two separate legal agreements has facilitated the ratification process for its trade component, the ratification of the SPA is more complex given the mixity of the agreement. In consequence, it was possible for the EPA to fully enter into force on 1 February 2019 after both the Council and the EP had given their consent. While both institutions also approved the SPA in parallel, the necessity for national ratification of this agreement has meant that only parts of it have been provisionally applied.

Considering the presence of bureaucratic divisions irrespective of the specific timeline of the negotiations, it is important to note that contemporary EU–Japan ties date back to the Hague Declaration of 1991. This document set out institutional formats for dialogues between the two sides, which were reemphasized in a 2001 Declaration (Gilson, 2016: 795). A number of smaller and very specific agreements on particular policy issues then further helped to structure the EU's ties to Japan (Ueta, 2018: 107). Nonetheless, any dialogue activity occurring within these frameworks was ultimately marred by the fact that few resources or energy were put into these relations by either side (de Prado, 2014: 14; Gilson,

2016: 792) and that there was very little internal EU coordination between the differing actors involved in maintaining the dialogue (Gilson, 2016: 792).

Unlike for some of the negotiations considered earlier in this book, the idea to separate the trade parts of the agreement from the negotiation of other ties with the country was part of the EU's negotiation strategy from the outset (Gilson, 2016: 792). Aside from the EPA and the SPA, another aim of the negotiations was to go beyond the two agreements, as it was also planned to conclude a Framework Participation Agreement for Japan to partake in the CSDP (Berkofsky, 2019: 18–26), which has not proven to be successful so far.

The division of the negotiations into separate agreements can ultimately be attributed to competency struggles between the Commission, and DG Trade in particular, on one side, and the EEAS, on the other. This is exemplified by the fact that throughout the negotiations no regular dialogue format existed between both institutions to coordinate various parts of their Japan policy throughout the process (Berkofsky, 2019: 18). These difficulties may also have contributed to the initially slow pace of the negotiations (de Prado, 2017: 437). Despite this, the negotiation directives that DG Trade received from the Commission called for the set-up of legal and institutional links between both agreements so that a "clear legal and institutional link should be established between the Agreement and the Framework Agreement to be concluded" (Council of the European Union, 2012: 14).

Considering the actual negotiation process, its pace and development were shaped by a number of external developments which helped create a permissive consensus of all relevant actors internal to the EU, particularly as negotiations came to a close. Initially, the EPA has to be considered in the context of other complex EU negotiations in the region, such as the precedent set by the EU's complex negotiations with South Korea (de Prado, 2014: 31; Gilson, 2016: 799; Nelson, 2012: 340–2).

Nonetheless, it was ultimately the failure of the EU's negotiations on TTIP with the US and the Trump administration's opposition to FTA's that created the political conditions necessary to find an agreement (Frenkel and Walter, 2017: 361; Söderberg et al., 2019: 243–4). This, together with the fact that the UK's decision on withdrawal from the European Union created a certain urgency to reach provisional application of the economic parts of an EU–Japan agreement before Brexit would occur (Agence Europe, 2018a), ultimately helped reach political agreement on both agreements ahead of the 2017 G20 summit in Hamburg (de Prado, 2017: 437).

While other EU negotiations that happened at the same time were rendered more difficult by increasing public scrutiny of them, those with Japan received considerably less attention (Suzuki, 2017) despite the fact that similar concerns on issues such as investor-state dispute settlement were initially present in the agreement, but then bracketed from the negotiation process (Agence Europe, 2017b). While the general increase in scrutiny led the Commission to publish the EPA negotiation mandates (Agence Europe, 2017a) as for other agreements, this did not further harm the negotiations themselves or indeed the ratification process.

What did impact the process though, were some debates between the Commission and groups of member states on whether the EPA and SPA would ultimately be exclusive EU agreements, leading to a simple ratification, or mixed agreements requiring national ratification (Berkofsky, 2019: 21; Gilson, 2016: 798). Ultimately, the EPA was deemed to be an exclusive EU agreement, while the SPA would require national ratification.

Lastly, while parts of the European Parliament were concerned over Japan's track record on human rights and its signature of international labour conventions, the EP did not stand in the way of ratification (D'Ambrogio, 2019: 5–6) with the EPA being ratified by a large majority within it (Agence Europe, 2018b) at the same time as the vote on the SPA in December 2018.

Conclusion

Whereas the analytical model has previously only been tested for complex EU negotiations in the Latin American context, the examples of the EU–Ukraine Association Agreement and both agreements with Japan illustrate that similar factors of bureaucratic politics shape the dynamics of EU negotiations in radically different contexts. While the analysis in this chapter is somewhat more superficial than that for some of the negotiations considered previously, certain elements of bureaucratic politics could nonetheless be observed in both negotiations here.

Firstly, both processes were shaped by the institutional autonomy of bureaucratic actors within the European Commission or between the Commission and the EEAS. Secondly, both negotiations were of a considerable duration, thus altering the structure of key political actors as negotiations progressed. Whereas the process for an EU–Ukraine Association Agreement was initiated already prior to the Treaty of Lisbon and only concluded thereafter, the negotiation briefs for the EU–Japan agreements were adopted by the Council at the time of the EU's institutional transition to its post-Lisbon set-up. The increasing politicization of EU–Ukraine ties then led to a relatively rapid conclusion, provisional application, and ratification process for the Association Agreement. In the case of the EU's negotiations with Japan, something similar could be achieved for the EPA dimension given the split of the negotiations, but the lack of political urgency has meant that the ratification process for the SPA has progressed relatively slowly.

Where both negotiations differed substantially is on the evolution of the key actors' positions towards the negotiations. While there was an overall permissive consensus on the necessity to conclude the agreements with Japan between all key institutional actors involved, the political developments surrounding the EU–Ukraine Association Agreement gradually led to a convergence of institutional positions on the matter—which then facilitated the latter stages of the ratification process. What also differed substantially between both cases is the degree of internal EU politicization which these have seen. In particular, the issue of the public referendum in the Netherlands once more serves to illustrate the influence that the complexity of such factors can have on complex EU negotiation processes.

Bibliography

Agence Europe (2008a) EU/UKRAINE: At Paris Summit, EU Confirms Will to Deepen Its Relations with Ukraine but Does Not Offer Accession Prospect. *Agence Europe*, 10 September. Brussels. Available at: Factiva Document AGEU000020080910e49a00003.

Agence Europe (2008b) EU/UKRAINE: Evian Summit Approaches but EU27 Still Seeking Common Position on Ukraine's "European Prospects". *Agence Europe*, 5 September. Brussels. Available at: Factiva Document AGEU000020080905e49500003.

Agence Europe (2008c) EU/UKRAINE: Member States Strongly Support "Association Agreement"—Differences Over Prospects for Joining Europe. *Agence Europe*, 23 July. Brussels. Available at: Factiva Document AGEU000020080723e47n00004.

Agence Europe (2009) EU/UKRAINE: Kiev Summit (4 December) May Mark Beginning of Final Phase of Negotiations for Association Agreement. *Agence Europe*, 29 September. Brussels. Available at: Factiva Document AGEU000020090929e59t00003.

Agence Europe (2010a) EP/UKRAINE: Negotiations on Association Agreement Should Be Concluded Within a Year. *Agence Europe*, 9 April. Brussels. Available at: Factiva Document AGEU000020100409e64900005.

Agence Europe (2010b) EU/UKRAINE: Some Member States Using "Pretexts" to Undermine Ukraine's European Integration, Regrets Ambassador Yelisieiev—"No Free Trade Area Without Appropriate EU Financial Aid". *Agence Europe*, 5 October. Brussels. Available at: Factiva Document AGEU000020101005e6a500004.

Agence Europe (2011a) EP/UKRAINE: Association Agreement—Ukraine Must Respect Rule of Law. *Agence Europe*, 19 November. Brussels. Available at: Factiva Document AGEU000020111119e7bj00005.

Agence Europe (2011b) EU/JAPAN: Towards Negotiation of Binding Cooperation Agreement. *Agence Europe*, 31 May. Brussels. Available at: Factiva Document AGEU000020110531e75v00003 (accessed 19 June 2019).

Agence Europe (2011c) EU/UKRAINE: EU Reflects on Its Relations with Kiev. *Agence Europe*, 12 October. Brussels. Available at: Factiva Document AGEU000020111012e7ac00007.

Agence Europe (2011d) EU/UKRAINE: Summit to Take Place but Doubts About Association Agreement. *Agence Europe*, 15 December. Brussels. Available at: Factiva Document AGEU000020111215e7cf0000r.

Agence Europe (2011e) UKRAINE: Association Agreement Signature Depends on Political Progress. *Agence Europe*, 20 December. Brussels. Available at: Factiva Document AGEU000020111220e7ck0000s.

Agence Europe (2012) JAPAN: Commission Proposes Negotiation of Free Trade Agreement. *Agence Europe*, 19 July. Brussels. Available at: Factiva Document AGEU000020120719e87j0000n (accessed 19 June 2019).

Agence Europe (2013a) JAPAN: Negotiations Launched on Cooperation and Free Trade. *Agence Europe*, 26 March. Brussels. Available at: Factiva Document AGEU000020130326e93q0000b (accessed 19 June 2019).

Agence Europe (2013b) UKRAINE: Adoption of Proposals for Signing Agreement. *Agence Europe*, 16 May. Brussels. Available at: Factiva Document AGEU000020130516e95g00005.

Agence Europe (2013c) UKRAINE: EU and Kiev Leave Door Open for Signing Agreement. *Agence Europe*, 30 November. Brussels. Available at: Factiva Document AGEU000020131130e9bu0000h.

Agence Europe (2013d) UKRAINE: EU Calls for Further Efforts from Kiev. *Agence Europe*, 26 June. Brussels. Available at: Factiva Document AGEU000020130626e96q0000f.

Agence Europe (2014a) RUSSIA: EU and Russia Ready to Discuss Association Agreement with Kiev. *Agence Europe*, 17 June. Brussels. Available at: Factiva Document AGEU000020140617ea6h0000l.

Agence Europe (2014b) UKRAINE: Entry into Force of Free Trade Agreement Postponed Until End 2015. *Agence Europe*, 16 September. Brussels. Available at: Factiva Document AGEU000020140916ea9g0000n.

Agence Europe (2014c) UKRAINE: European and Ukrainian Parliaments Ratify Association Agreement. *Agence Europe*, 17 September. Brussels. Available at: Factiva Document AGEU000020140917ea9h00003.

Agence Europe (2014d) UKRAINE: Parliament's Green Light to Extending Unilateral Preferences. *Agence Europe*, 24 October. Brussels. Available at: Factiva Document AGEU000020141024eaao0000e.

Agence Europe (2015) UKRAINE: €110 Million in EU Aid for Ukrainian SMEs. *Agence Europe*, 29 April. Brussels. Available at: Factiva Document AGEU000020150429eb4t0000m.

Agence Europe (2016) NETHERLANDS: Future of EU–Ukraine Association Agreement in Rutte's Hands. *Agence Europe*, 8 April. Brussels. Available at: Factiva Document AGEU000020160408ec4800006.

Agence Europe (2017a) JAPAN; EU Council Publishes Its Negotiation Directives for EU–Japan Trade Agreement. *Agence Europe*, 15 September. Brussels. Available at: Factiva Document AGEU000020170915ed9f0000z (accessed 19 June 2019).

Agence Europe (2017b) JAPAN; Political Agreement at Ministerial Level Provisionally Sealing EU–Japan Free Trade Agreement. *Agence Europe*, 6 July. Brussels. Available at: Factiva Document AGEU000020170706ed7600001 (accessed 19 June 2019).

Agence Europe (2017c) UKRAINE; Council Confirms Political Agreement on Further EU Trade Preferences. *Agence Europe*, 29 June. Brussels. Available at: Factiva Document AGEU000020170629ed6t0000j.

Agence Europe (2017d) UKRAINE; EU Council Concludes Ratification Process for Association Agreement. *Agence Europe*, 12 July. Brussels. Available at: Factiva Document AGEU000020170712ed7c0000m.

Agence Europe (2018a) JAPAN; EU and Japan Rush to Implement Their Trade Agreement Without Investment Chapter Before Brexit. *Agence Europe*, 2 March. Brussels. Available at: Factiva Document AGEU000020180302ee320000p (accessed 19 June 2019).

Agence Europe (2018b) JAPAN; MEPs Vote in Favour of "World's Most Important Trade Agreement". *Agence Europe*, 13 December. Brussels. Available at: Factiva Document AGEU000020181213eecd0000e (accessed 19 June 2019).

Berkofsky A (2019) The Strategic Partnership Agreement: New and Better or More of the Same EU–Japan Security Cooperation? In: Berkofsky A, Hughes CW, Midford P, et al. (eds) *The EU–Japan Partnership in the Shadow of China: The Crisis of Liberalism*. London: Routledge. Available at: https://www-1taylorfrancis-1com-1ssnxtmiy0505.hanserver.suub.uni-bremen.de/books/e/9781351172165 (accessed 18 June 2019).

Council of the European Union (2012) *Directives for the Negotiation of a Free Trade Agreement with Japan*. 15864/12, 29 November. Brussels: Council of the European Union.

D'Ambrogio E (2019) *The EU–Japan Strategic Partnership Agreement (SPA): A Framework to Promote Shared Values*. PE 630.323. Brussels: European Parliamentary Research Service. Available at: www.europarl.europa.eu/RegData/etudes/BRIE/2018/630323/EPRS_BRI(2018)630323_EN.pdf.

de Prado C (2014). *Prospects for the EU–Japan Strategic Partnership: A Global Multi-Level and Swot Analysis*. Florence: European University Institute. Available at: www.eu-japan. eu/sites/eu-japan.eu/files/EUJPStrategicPartnership.pdf.

de Prado C (2017) Towards a Substantial EU–Japan Partnership. *European Foreign Affairs Review* 22(4): 435–454.

Dragneva R and Wolczuk K (2014) The EU–Ukraine Association Agreement and the Challenges of Inter-Regionalism. *Review of Central and East European Law* 39: 213.

Dragneva R and Wolczuk K (2015) *Ukraine Between the EU and Russia: The Integration Challenge*. Houndmills, Basingstoke: Palgrave Macmillan.

Frenkel M and Walter B (2017) The EU–Japan Economic Partnership Agreement: Relevance: Content and Policy Implications. *Intereconomics* 52(6): 358–363. DOI: 10.1007/s10272-017-0704-5

Gehring T, Urbanski K, and Oberthür S (2017) The European Union as an Inadvertent Great Power: EU Actorness and the Ukraine Crisis. *JCMS: Journal of Common Market Studies* 55(4): 727–743. DOI: 10.1111/jcms.12530.

Gilson J (2016) The Strategic Partnership Agreement Between the EU and Japan: The Pitfalls of Path Dependency? *Journal of European Integration* 38(7): 791–806. DOI: 10.1080/07036337.2016.1176027.

Nelson PA (2012) The Lisbon Treaty Effect: Toward a New EU–Japan Economic and Trade Partnership? *Japan Forum* 24(3): 339–368. DOI: 10.1080/09555803.2012.699456.

Sjursen H and Rosén G (2017) Arguing Sanctions. On the EU's Response to the Crisis in Ukraine. *JCMS: Journal of Common Market Studies* 55(1): 20–36. DOI: 10.1111/jcms.12443.

Smith NR (2014) The Underpinning Realpolitik of the EU's Policies Towards Ukraine: An Analysis of Interests and Norms in the EU–Ukraine Association Agreement. *European Foreign Affairs Review* 19(4): 581–596.

Söderberg M, Berkofsky A, Hughes CW, et al. (2019) Conclusions: The Way forward. In: Berkofsky A, Hughes CW, Midford P, et al. (eds) *The EU–Japan Partnership in the Shadow of China: The Crisis of Liberalism*. London: Routledge, pp. 243–254. Available at: https://www-1taylorfrancis-1com-1ssnxtmiy0505.hanserver.suub.uni-bremen.de/books/e/9781351172165 (accessed 18 June 2019).

Suzuki H (2017) The New Politics of Trade: EU–Japan. *Journal of European Integration* 39(7): 875–889. DOI: 10.1080/07036337.2017.1371709.

Ueta T (2018) Japan's Relations with the EU in a Changing World. In: Vanoverbeke D, Suami T, Ueta T, et al. (eds) *Developing EU–Japan Relations in a Changing Regional Context: A Focus on Security, Law and Policies*. Abingdon: Routledge, pp. 103–121.

Van der Loo G (2017) The Dutch Referendum on the EU–Ukraine Association Agreement: Legal Implications and Solutions. In: Kuijer M and Werner W (eds) *Netherlands Yearbook of International Law 2016: The Changing Nature of Territoriality in International Law*. Netherlands Yearbook of International Law. The Hague: T.M.C. Asser Press, pp. 337–350. DOI: 10.1007/978-94-6265-207-1_14.

Van der Loo G, Van Elsuwege P, and Petrov R (2014) *The EU–Ukraine Association Agreement: Assessment of an Innovative Legal Instrument*. 2014/09. EUI Working Paper Law, 10 July. Florence: Social Science Research Network.

8 Reflections on the drivers of EU behaviour in complex international negotiations

This book has explored the EU's behaviour in international negotiations covering more than one of its policy areas with an external remit. In so doing, it has put the spotlight on how institutional dynamics internal to the European Union shape those complex negotiations which primarily aim at concluding Association Agreements. This enquiry was based on an obvious mismatch between the EU's increasing attempts to move away from concluding traditional bilateral Free Trade Agreements in favour of the conclusion of Association Agreements spanning multiple policy areas and partner countries, and the ultimate outcome of many such negotiations promoting trade ties to individual partners.

Research on such complex EU negotiations has, so far, often focused on grand dynamics: Some researchers are interested in their link to the EU's aim of supporting regional integration elsewhere (Börzel and Risse, 2009, 2015), in how these can be read as attempts to develop the EU's ties to emerging powers (Santander, 2013), or in how far they represent the EU's quest for economic influence on the world stage (Meissner, 2018). However, such views tend to conceptualize the EU as a unitary actor in its external relations and leave aside the underlying dynamics internal to the EU. While such approaches have proven very helpful for the study of the EU's international trade negotiations, this is not necessarily the case for the kinds of complex negotiations that involve more than one of the EU's policy areas and large parts of its external relations bureaucracy.

In contrast to the above approaches, this book therefore makes the case that the nature of today's complex negotiations fundamentally alters the institutional dynamics underlying the negotiation process within the EU. Its core theoretical contribution consists in developing an analytical framework to understand how the dynamics of interactions between the various actors involved in such negotiations on the EU's side influence its ultimate negotiation behaviour. This, in turn, is conceptualized not only as the relatively short timeframe of actual negotiations with outside partners, but also as a process beginning with a first consideration of an international negotiation in the EU's bureaucracy and ending in either the successful conclusion of an international agreement or the ultimate failure of the negotiation process. While Association Agreements bring the complexity of the EU's ties to third partners under a single treaty framework, the EU's complex negotiations may also occur in contexts where several kinds of agreements are negotiated in parallel.

So as to be able to study institutional dynamics within the EU's external relations bureaucracy, the analytical model outlined draws on a wide range of Foreign Policy Analysis scholarship going back to its roots with the seminal work by Allison and others (Allison and Halperin, 1972; Allison and Zelikow, 1999). It also considers its more recent application for diverse sets of foreign policy developments (Doeser, 2011; Gustavsson, 1998; such as Welch, 2005), including how it may inform our understanding of EU foreign policy-making (Carlsnaes et al., 2004; Dijkstra, 2009; Larsen, 2009; Smith, 2013; White, 1999). Ultimately, the book then adopts and adapts some of FPA's core tenets for the study of the EU's behaviour in complex international negotiations.

The major advantage of such an analytical perspective lies in FPA's ability to offer multifaceted and multifactored explanations of foreign policy behaviour (Hudson, 2015: 1), encouraging process tracing of foreign policy decision-making processes. In the case at hand, this has allowed to consider the international environment within which complex EU negotiations take place as an input into the institutional dynamics within the EU.

However, this is only regarded as one of the multiple factors that ultimately shape its positioning and behaviour in those negotiations. Simultaneously, it allows to gain insights at a more micro-level than existing grand theories on the EU's behaviour in negotiations. While principal-agent scholarship on the EU similarly allows for a consideration of institutional dynamics within the institutions' decision-making system (Delreux, 2015: 159–62; Pollack, 1997, 2003), its application is somewhat difficult in the context of the EU's complex international negotiations.

This is due to the fact that the complexity of divergent modes of decision-making across individual policy areas of the EU's external relations would require models considering a multitude of principals and agents and thereby limit the possibility for analytical insights. Ultimately, it is the particular application of FPA proposed here, that allows major developments in complex EU negotiations to be traced to individual bureaucratic actors or even individuals within the EU's foreign policy apparatus, and to make an assessment as to whether policy choices are based on broader policy considerations linked to external developments, or the dynamics of the bureaucratic process in and of itself. Furthermore, through the outline of this analytical framework and its empirical application, this book not only offers a new perspective on EU public policy or its behaviour in external relations, but also further demonstrates the applicability of International Relations scholarship on FPA for the study of a non-state entity such as the EU.

The following section of this chapter outlines how utilizing the conceptual framework has helped our understanding of the EU's behaviour in the negotiations covered in the empirical chapters. This is followed by an assessment as to how the individual determinants of the EU's stance in complex international negotiations interact and when each is particularly influential. The remaining sections then briefly discuss empirical insights going beyond the analytical scope of this book and offer suggestions for the continued study of the EU's behaviour in complex international negotiations.

Lessons from the empirical chapters

The empirical sections of this book have shown the utility of considering the institutional dynamics underlying the EU's stance in complex international negotiations. The empirical focus on the Latin American region allowed for the study of a particularly dense set of negotiation attempts for Association Agreements principally covering the EU's trade and development policy, as well as elements of political cooperation. At the same time, the focus on a region in which the economic and political interests of the EU's member states largely converge allowed to focus primarily on the institutional dynamics within the EU's external relations bureaucracy. In essence, this meant that the determinants of the EU's behaviour in complex negotiations could be analysed in what comes relatively close to a "standard" setting where core negotiation responsibilities lie within the Commission, or with the Commission and the EEAS, respectively.

Considering the EU's behaviour in the particular complex negotiation settings analysed, the empirical evidence in this book has pointed to the EU's difficulty in bringing together its preferences in different policy areas in a unified stance on negotiations with partners in the region from the outset. For instance, when considering initial negotiations with Mercosur in the late 1990s, the EU's then Latin America Commissioner aimed for opening negotiations on a comprehensive Association Agreement in line with the EU's previously agreed Latin America strategy. However, the preferences of other institutions meant that the goals and outcomes of the negotiations at the time were much more modest.

Similarly, while the aim was to reach a comprehensive Association Agreement in the case of Mexico, the development policy and political clauses of the agreement were concluded beforehand, and the linked FTA negotiated largely separately and only after the conclusion of the other parts of the agreement. The ensuing negotiations for a more comprehensive Association Agreement with Mercosur and Chile then once more demonstrated the propensity of the EU to alter its position, as this process ended in the conclusion of a separate Association Agreement with Chile only. At the same time, the negotiations with Mercosur originally ended unsuccessfully only to be revived at a later date.

The next chapter then discussed the simultaneous negotiations for Association Agreements with the Central American region and the Andean Community. Once more, the initial ambition of these negotiations did not match the outcome in the case of negotiations with the Andean Community, as this resulted in FTAs with two of its members, Colombia and Peru, only. The final empirical chapter in the second part of the book then provided further evidence for the EU's difficulties to link its preferences in different policy areas, as is evidenced in the mismatch between its apparent desire to negotiate upgraded Association Agreements with Mexico and Chile, while not being able to underpin this rhetoric with substantial negotiations given bureaucratic divisions.

The analytical perspective of this book has helped uncover how this EU behaviour in the complex negotiations covered was shaped by bureaucratic politics. The insights from the initial empirical chapter were particularly dense in this regard given the wide array of negotiations that it covered. The first relevant observation of a general nature for these negotiations is that the Commission DG responsible for the EU's ties with Latin America disposed of a considerable autonomy to shape the EU's approach towards the region in the mid to late 1990s, leading to the EU's first attempts to negotiate Association Agreements with regional partners.

This was due to the fact that Latin America was not of a primary economic importance to the EU at this point in time, while the member states ultimately were favourable of any policy emerging in the Commission that would embolden the EU as an international actor. Taking a look at the institutional dynamics within the Commission itself, its portfolios and DGs were organized around geographic portfolios at the time, meaning that an individual Commissioner held the responsibility for the entirety of the EU's ties with Latin America across all relevant policy areas. It is in this context that the numerous Commission suggestions for Association Agreement negotiations explored in the chapter can be understood.

Despite the lack of strong preferences by the member states or indeed other Commission DGs on the contents of the EU's approach towards Latin America, it nonetheless became clear that as actual negotiations with partners in the region approached, the preferences of all institutional actors were not aligned. For instance, the Commissioner and DG responsible for the EU's CAP, as well as member states with important agricultural interests, feared the attempts to conclude an Association Agreement with Mercosur given that this would have important effects on the EU's agricultural market. As a result of these divergent preferences between the different DGs and in absence of a clear decision-making hierarchy which could arbitrate between them, this goal was initially abandoned. In contrast, agricultural interests played less of a role in negotiations with Mexico, allowing for a first EU Association Agreement covering multiple policy areas to be successfully negotiated in 1997. Furthermore, the country's status as a member of NAFTA increased multiple institutional actors' desire to negotiate an FTA with the country. Nonetheless, the fact that the political component of the AA with the country was concluded separately from its trade part demonstrated that decision-making on the different elements of Association Agreements was largely separated between different DGs which acted largely autonomously on the EU's side. In particular, the responsibilities for the country in the Commission were split between the DGs responsible for ties with Latin America, and that covering trade ties with North America.

Ensuing negotiations for more extensive agreements with Mercosur and Chile in the aftermath of the successful negotiation with Mexico were then once more aided by the geographically defined position of a DG and Commissioner responsible for Latin American affairs. However, what was proposed for an overall Latin America strategy by this particular DG became more difficult once encroaching on the autonomous responsibilities of others, such as agriculture, which feared the results of negotiating with the major agricultural exporters in Mercosur.

Such particular agricultural interests also garnered support from member state agricultural officials in the Council, pointing to similar institutional dynamics playing out within its different preparatory bodies and working groups. Once more, the divergent positions of individual actors within the Commission then determined the EU's stance in negotiations and contributed to the protracted and continuing process of EU–Mercosur negotiations which were halted repeatedly only to be relaunched afterwards. These efforts have only paid off very recently after a 20-year negotiation period. The case of the successful negotiation and conclusion of an Association Agreement with Chile then showed that in cases where no important divergence of views existed, however, the EU was able to develop a negotiation position that was unified across different policy areas and ultimately helped the successful conclusion of an agreement.

However, this success can be attributed not only to the smaller difference in underlying positions of individual DGs, but also to an altered organizational logic of the Commission: Romano Prodi, the Commission's president from 1999–2004, favoured a policy-centred division of portfolios and underlying DGs, increasing the oversight over the Commission's activity so as to ensure that institutional actors in the Commission coordinate their activities and thereby reducing their autonomy.

The empirical chapter focusing on the two parallel negotiations with the Andean Community and Central America showed once again how the divergent views of institutional actors within the EU can alter the rationale behind negotiations at different phases. In this case, it was particularly the reaction of DG Trade to the altered international environment in which several CAN countries were negotiating FTAs with the US, which led this institution to prefer negotiating bilateral trade agreements over an Association Agreement with all Andean Community countries. The latter, however, was preferred by DG RELEX and conflict between the two institutional actors ensued.

DG Trade's view ultimately prevailed in the Council as well, leading to a de facto abandonment of the regional, developmental, and political dimensions of the previous negotiations. In contrast, this divergence of preferences of these two key Commission actors did not occur in negotiations with Central America, as the EU's economic interests there were limited in that case. In this instance, DG Trade even preferred an approach which would see the EU negotiate with all Central American states in unison so as to reduce the workload placed on its officials. While both relevant Commission DGs thus retained their autonomy, the alignment of their interests led the EU to be able to present a unified position in the negotiations which ended in the successful conclusion of an AA.

What is most interesting in the consideration of these agreements is the factor of a changed institutional and political environment when it came to the agreements' ratification phase. Between the conclusion of negotiations and their ratification, the Lisbon Treaty reforms had come into place, a new EP was elected, and the composition of the Commission changed. This meant that the agreements' negotiations which had largely preceded the EU's Lisbon era now had to be ratified following the new rules, thus leading to some political divergences over the agreements' contents between the Commission, the European Parliament, and the EU's negotiation partners in the Andean region.

The last empirical chapter was able to offer further insights into how the Lisbon Treaty has changed the dynamics of the EU's stance in complex international negotiations. Once more, the important influence of individual institutions' autonomy in the policy process could be observed. This was particularly the case when it came to the largely independent DG Trade negotiations for an FTA with Ecuador and the efforts of the EEAS to conclude a largely political agreement with Cuba. Here, once again, the duration of such negotiation processes from their initial consideration to the ultimate ratification increased institutional autonomy in the case of negotiations with Ecuador. While the Lisbon changes would have required for an entirely novel negotiation position to be coordinated between the EEAS and DG Trade, the survival of a negotiation mandate for DG Trade from the period preceding Lisbon allowed this institutional actor to take largely autonomous action. Similarly, DG Trade's pre-existing mandate for negotiations with Mercosur has enabled this actor to relaunch the negotiation process relatively independently when the Mercosur countries signalled their willingness to return to the negotiation table.

The extent to which both the EEAS and DG Trade were able to act largely autonomously in the aftermath of the Lisbon Treaty, as well as their usage of these circumstances, is astonishing and has also influenced the processes leading to negotiations for upgraded Association Agreements with both Mexico and Chile. The different positions of both DG Trade and the EEAS were even noticeable to the EU's negotiation partners and thereby visibly threatened the EU's position. It is only as both institutions gradually adapted to new realities that these issues of autonomy and coordination have come to be less relevant, and the negotiation processes more streamlined. This was ultimately also helped by the change of tenure of the position of the HRVP from Catherine Ashton to Federica Mogherini.

Key factors determining the EU's stance in complex negotiations

The confrontation of the analytical framework with the empirical reality of the EU's complex international negotiations in the Latin American region has allowed to gain some more fine-grained insights into how mechanisms of bureaucratic politics play out in conjunction and over time. The EU's institutional set-up has, much like is the case in any other complex administration, created the potential for individual parts of its bureaucracy to have divergent preferences and hold differing views on the best course of action. These are largely determined by the official function of each institutional actor, its position in the decision-making system, and the maturity of the institutional actor in and of itself.

In line with established FPA literature on bureaucratic politics in general, and on its applicability to the EU (Delreux, 2015: 154–5), a perspective emphasizing the diversity of views within individual institutional actors such as DG Trade or DG DEVCO within the Commission is just as important as the diverging views between the Commission, the Council, and the European Parliament. In the case at hand, the above entities have developed a distinct identity and sense of purpose within the EU's institutional set-up. While the former's preferences are largely driven by its interest to increase the EU's clout in global trade, the latter's interests are based on achieving certain developmental goals in third countries.

Similarly, the interests of DG RELEX and its successor the relatively novel EEAS, an institution now wholly separate from the Commission, are based mainly on the development of good relations with outside partners. While not at the heart of the analysis in this book, sometimes similarly divergent preferences could be observed within various of the Council's preparatory bodies and working groups which are staffed by member state officials from different ministries.

Lastly, in addition to these identities, all of the actors mentioned above also have a distinct set of interests revolving around maintaining or increasing their influence in the existing institutional set-up. This leads them to be keen to defend the status quo of the EU's bureaucratic set-up against proposed changes, or even try to augment their influence in the policy process. The observed divergences of interests and views thus mirror the conflict lines outlined by others for the EU's foreign and security policy since the Treaty of Lisbon (Smith, 2013), which see bureaucratic actors and different conceptions of EU external relations compete with one another.

Considering the preferences of individual institutional actors within the Commission involved in the EU's complex international negotiations, it became clear that the institutional logic of the Commission at any given point in time had a key influence on the preferences of its constituent Commissioners and DGs. This is in line with existing research outlining links between bureaucratic structure and actual policy-making (Egeberg, 1999). While at times, its external relations-related DGs have been organized around a geographic logic, giving individual Commissioners a responsibility for specific geographic regions of the globe, this has contrasted with a Commission structure in place up to today which emphasizes a policy logic, organizing portfolios and DGs around policy areas such as trade or development.

The former set-up has been beneficial for an EU stance towards complex negotiations which linked its preferences in different policy areas towards a specific geographic area. At the same time, it created tensions with Commissioners and DGs with portfolios related to other world regions or concerned with internal EU policies such as agriculture which are influenced by the EU's ties to the rest of the world. The latter set-up then has been beneficial for streamlining the EU's expertise in specific policy areas and prioritizing the use of its resources in line with policy-specific goals, all while rendering it more complex to develop a stance in complex international organizations which considers the EU's policy preferences across all areas of its external relations to a similar degree. The influence of such organizational changes on policy preferences could be observed not only in Commission reorganization rounds in the past, but also when the EEAS has altered its set-up at a more micro-level such as when reorganizing its internal institutional structure when country desks were moved from one organizational unit to another.

The preferences of institutions in the EU's political system are not always shaped by mere bureaucratic interests alone, but as the empirical analysis has shown, there is a genuine room for individuals to play a role in determining the preferences and activities of Commission DGs. This has was particularly important in the pre-Lisbon days when it came to defining certain policy preferences, as could be seen in the empirical chapter focusing on initial complex negotiations with Latin American partners. Nonetheless, the differing behaviour of the EEAS between the tenure of Catherine Ashton as HRVP and that of her successor Federica Mogherini shows that individuals are still capable to play a large role in the positioning of the institutions that they lead. This is particularly relevant in cases where these are relatively autonomous in their activity, as is explored below.

While such phenomena can be found in any complex bureaucracy, the extent to which this influences policy outcomes, or in this case the EU's stance in complex international negotiations, depends on each institution's role and autonomy within the EU's decision-making system. This factor has played a relatively more important role in shaping the EU's negotiation stance than could be expected in most national political systems. This is due to the fact that the Commission's bureaucracy is a uniquely multifaceted institution, the oversight of which is complex given its "multiple political masters" (Ellinas and Suleiman, 2012: 196).

Chapter 3 shows that individual European Commissioners and their respective DGs have indeed been relatively independent from central oversight in the past due to the modalities of Commissioner selection, their institutional position, tradition, and the personality of past Commission presidents. This has only begun to change in substance more recently with attempts by the Juncker Commission to reach a more hierarchical logic within the Commission, including attempts to coordinate its external relations portfolios under the guidance of the HRVP who also serves as a vice-president of the Commission.

However, the insights that could be gained in this regard mainly concern autonomy within the Commission's bureaucracy itself. This is due to the fact that the nature of the cases studied meant that they revealed somewhat less about particular institutional relationship between the Commission, on one side, and the Council and the European Parliament on the other. After all, for most of the negotiations considered here, the member states gave the Commission a relatively large room of manoeuvre, and the European Parliament's powers in the area of international negotiations were curtailed in the period prior to the Lisbon Treaty. Nonetheless, the examples of the EU's negotiations with Cuba—which were rendered possible by a gradual shift of the majority view in the Council—as well as some difficulties in the Parliamentary ratification of certain of the agreements studied, show that this factor should not be underestimated and will necessitate closer scrutiny for negotiations where the EP or the Council may be more interested in curtailing the Commission's autonomy.

Another factor influencing the autonomy of the above institutional actors at least temporarily is reorganization rounds of the Commission's bureaucracy, or indeed the radical change of introducing the EEAS as a new institution in its external relations universe. In the aftermath of such bureaucratic restructuring, the autonomy of institutional actors, and particularly of those which have been left untouched by the reforms, tends to increase until the others can adapt and regain the capacity to make their views heard (Schade, 2019). This is particularly relevant in a setting where changes are made to an existing system of institutional oversight. The autonomy of individual Commissioners and DGs has often temporarily increased through the frequent reorganization of portfolio divisions up to the Lisbon Treaty. This is due to the fact that individual institutional actors require time to adapt to new settings and regain the capacity to interoperate and coordinate with other institutional actors. Once more, this phenomenon can be observed in any bureaucratic organization (March and Olson, 1983) and has also been observed for the EU's external relations in the past (Peterson and Sjursen, 1998: 179). Here, the set-up of the EEAS and the related fundamental reform to the functioning of the EU's foreign affairs bureaucracy was perhaps one of the largest bureaucratic reorganizations of such kind in the history of the EU and has thus temporarily increased the autonomy of individual external relations DGs in the Commission, all while creating incentives for the new EEAS to autonomously prove its utility for the EU's external relations bureaucracy. The gradual renewed emergence of cooperation between relevant Commission DGs and the EEAS observed in Chapter 6 then shows that adaptation to cooperation as a factor reducing autonomy should not be underestimated, and the absence of large-scale institutional innovations in the EU's foreign affairs bureaucracy since the Lisbon Treaty reforms is a positive sign in this regard.

Another crucial factor determining the EU's stance in complex international negotiations beyond elements that are usually considered in FPA scholarship is the effects on the EU's negotiation stance associated with the long duration of complex EU negotiations from their initial consideration to the ultimate conclusion of an international agreement. This contributes, to policy inertia exhibited by individual institutional actors and further enables the development of diverging policy preferences by individual institutional actors over time.

If an institutional actor has heavily invested in a negotiation process—such as through the development of the EU's initial stance and leading the negotiations in a later phase—then this institutional actor will be much less willing to alter its position when faced with the policy preferences of other institutions at a later negotiation phase. It is also then able to justify a continuation of a previous policy stance based on the long duration during which this has informed its policy-making. Conversely, new entrants to a negotiation process such as through administrative reorganization lack such prior commitments and will be more willing to consider alternative courses of action.

Such dynamics play out particularly strongly in protracted negotiations, such as the ones with Mercosur, or when an institutional change happens between distinct negotiation phases. Such an issue of path dependence has already been observed specifically for the case of the EU's Association Agreement negotiation with Chile (García, 2008, 2011). The importance of this phenomenon could be additionally observed in the dynamics surrounding the negotiations for the agreements in the Andean region and Central America, as well as the ensuing difficulties in the ratification process under a newly emboldened EP. A similar dynamic was at play when the EEAS negotiated the agreement with Cuba and

DG Trade that with Ecuador while attempting to avoid policy coordination with the other.

The long timeframe of the overall negotiation processes also justifies a view which emphasizes bureaucratic politics as a continuously occurring phenomenon, rather than a one-off event. This allows for a consideration of not only bureaucratic reorganization as factors shaping the EU's stance in international negotiations, but also the effect of political change such as through European Parliament elections or a change of majority in the Council. Once more, while such factors were not the focus of the cases under consideration here, the potential influence on the EU's positioning in negotiations could nonetheless be seen on multiple occasions in the empirical chapters and needs to be emphasized as a possibly relevant factor when analysing the EU's stance in any complex negotiation.

Insights into EU–Latin American relations

Moving away from its core focus on how institutional dynamics within the EU shape its behaviour in complex international negotiations, this book also offers insights contributing to the literature on the EU's relations with Latin America and its pursuit of interregional ties. Its findings resonate directly with research into why the EU's interregionalism policies appear to have waned (García, 2015; Hardacre and Smith, 2009, 2014; Meissner, 2018), with existing explanations ranging from a weakening of regional integration mechanisms elsewhere, to the EU's attempts at defending its core trade interests. This book offers a further analytical perspective to accompany those existing insights, and provides empirical material to support views underlining the importance of the EU's trade preferences in the negotiation processes, albeit moderated by the underpinning institutional dynamics.

This was particularly relevant in cases where the EU has attempted to negotiate interregional Association Agreements, only to ultimately revert to bilateral trade ties on many occasions. The empirical insights from this book indeed support the view that for initial complex negotiations with Mercosur and Chile, the EU's pursuit of interregionalism and normative concerns were a key motivating factor as is argued in parts of the existing literature (Börzel and Risse, 2009, 2015; Dominguez, 2015: 172). Nonetheless, the analysis of the later negotiations partially confirms other perspectives emphasizing the EU's increasing return to bilateralism and pure trade agreements amidst political difficulties in the EU's partner countries (Dominguez, 2015: 173–5; Meissner, 2018; Santander, 2010, 2013), all while upholding the initial rhetoric of interregionalism. Therefore, the findings of this book can also partially support the idea of the existence of the EU's pursuit of "complex interregionalism" that would see the EU making use of what it deems to be the most appropriate venues for the development of ties with different third actors (Hardacre and Smith, 2009, 2014). Nonetheless, as the analytical framework developed for the EU's behaviour in complex negotiation cautions, this is not necessarily the result of a strategic consideration on the part of the EU, but largely influenced by its bureaucratic politics.

Through its use of internal EU documents and interviews, this book has also provided novel empirical insights into particular EU agreements with partners in the Latin American region. While some of these agreements, such as the initial ones with Chile and Mexico, have been analysed in great detail in the existing literature (see, for instance, García, 2011; Szymanski and Smith, 2005), this is not the case for some of the more recent negotiations discussed in this book. Its empirical insights into the EU's complex negotiations with Central America and the Andean Community beyond the underlying bureaucratic politics offer an outlook on the importance of developments in the global economy in determining the trade preferences of the EU and its relevant institutional actors. Chapter 5 elaborates how the trade strategy of the US influenced the EU's views on this matter and ultimately led it to opt for bilateral trade negotiations with Colombia and Peru, while an absence of strong economic preferences and competition in the case of Central America helped the EU's determination to conclude a biregional Association Agreement going beyond mere trade policy. This mirrors similar perspectives which see competition between the EU and the US as an important factor determining the EU's trade policy (Meissner, 2018: 180–4; Sbragia, 2010). Similarly, the last empirical chapter in Part II was able to uncover how the economic isolation of Ecuador contributed to the EU's negotiation success in concluding an FTA with the country, as well as pointing to the fact that the change of the EU's Cuba policy precedes the much more public change of policy by the US during the Obama administration.

The EU in complex international negotiations beyond Latin America

The findings of this book underline the relevance of internal institutional dynamics for the study of the EU's behaviour in external relations, and in complex international negotiations, in particular. The application of the analytical framework to the empirical cases in the Latin American region has shown the merits of using insights from FPA to conceptualize the EU's behaviour in such negotiations. Nonetheless, both the analytical framework developed and its empirical verification in Part II of the book are obviously limited in scope. Therefore, the tentative analysis of other complex EU negotiations in the previous chapter demonstrates the analytical framework's validity beyond the Latin American context and offers cues as to avenues for future research.

This study's core empirical work was limited to negotiations in which future EU membership, security concerns, and other traditional "high politics" domains did not play a significant role. This choice was deliberate as the focus on negotiations with Latin America allowed for the study of EU negotiations under "standard" conditions, meaning that institutional dynamics within the Commission and between the Commission and the EEAS could be highlighted, while a permissive consensus on such negotiations was generally present in the Council.

The brief consideration of the EU's negotiations for an EU–Ukraine Association Agreement and for the two agreements with Japan in the previous chapter then demonstrated that the analytical framework can similarly be applied to other complex EU negotiations where different kinds of policy concerns are primordial. While the analysis of these two negotiations was somewhat more limited in scope, it nonetheless showed that even for negotiations where larger economic or political concerns are at stake factors such as institutional autonomy, the complexity of the EU's decision-making system until an international agreement is concluded, and the sheer duration of negotiations similarly affect negotiation dynamics.

Nonetheless, a closer analysis of such other negotiations may ultimately necessitate adapting the analytical framework somewhat to consider the different roles played by individual EU institutions in such "high politics" contexts. Particularly, when such negotiations are paired with important security concerns, it can be assumed that the influence of individual EU member states will be more relevant than was the case for the Latin American negotiations considered. This could be done through, for instance, incorporating insights from FPA literature as to the centrality of different actors in foreign policy decision-making processes in addition to the factors considered here and thus allow for a further generalization of this book's findings.

Furthermore, research anchored in the principal-agent tradition suggests that the Council has tried to increase its influence on the EU's position in trade negotiations vis-à-vis the Commission from the early phase of the negotiations onwards (Gastinger, 2016). Such insights should be considered carefully when considering to apply the model to complex negotiations outside of the standard setting discussed here given that they can provide clues as to what kind of control is exercised by one actor over another.

Given its extensive focus on institutional behaviour, this book was able to identify the relatively regular reorganization of the EU's foreign affairs bureaucracy as a major factor contributing to the development and deepening of divergent preferences amongst individual institutional actors involved in the EU's foreign policy process, and in its international negotiations, in particular. The changes introduced with the Lisbon Treaty and the set-up of the EEAS, have once more been a challenge for ensuring that the EU is able to define a coordinated position in complex negotiations across policy areas. This is primarily due to the hybrid nature of the post of the HRVP as a simultaneous member of the Commission and the head of the independent EEAS. At the same time, the emergence of this new bureaucracy has transferred policy coordination problems that had previously been resolved within the Commission's bureaucracy to an inter-institutional context, and united officials from different bureaucratic origins in a new entity.

Past experience from reforms of the EU's treaties and the Commission's organization shows that it can take time until administrative innovations truly become effective and new modes of operation have been found for the interaction between the different institutions. Indeed, as the EU's relatively recent preparations for negotiations with Mexico and Chile demonstrate, some of these initial difficulties appear to have been at least partially resolved by now. However, as was noted elsewhere (Morgenstern-Pomorski, 2018: 195), it is presently unclear whether this relative drop of conflict between the EEAS and the Commission is genuinely down to their adaptation towards the other and the development of functioning coordination mechanisms, or whether this merely reflects the approach of the EU's second HRVP Federica Mogherini who prioritized interactions with the European Commission. The future development of policy coordination between the EEAS and the Commission in various areas of the EU's external relations, including its security policy (Smith, 2013), therefore offers ample room for enquiries into the EU's behaviour in complex negotiations.

Relatedly, this book has, at times, also unearthed conflict between individual DGs of the Commission arising from their particular division of competencies at any given point in time. The set-up of clearer chains of responsibilities and the introduction of several posts for Commission vice-presidents to streamline its operation are an interesting development in this regard. Here as well, a closer analysis of the effects that this altered set-up has had on the autonomy of individual Commission DGs in various areas of the EU's external relations would warrant a closer study. This is particularly relevant as the ongoing crisis of the EU's political system has seen the Commission's autonomy in complex negotiations being questioned more and more (Gastinger, 2016).

Lastly, given the interest by researchers in determining what kind of actor the EU is in the international system (Börzel and Risse, 2015; Damro, 2012, 2015; Meunier and Nicolaïdis, 2006; Toje, 2011), it would also be valuable to explore how the internal dynamics of the EU's foreign policy decision-making system have shaped the EU's capacity to exercise influence in the rest of the world. The insights from this book certainly point to the EU's difficulty in behaving uniformly and coherently in complex international negotiations, which has not gone unnoticed by its negotiation partners. The EU's capacity to translate its continued economic importance into international influence through its complex international negotiations will thus ultimately be shaped by its capacity to coordinate the activity of its foreign affairs bureaucracy. If this problem is gradually resolving itself as the EEAS and the Commission continue to adapt their activity despite prior bureaucratic reorganization, or whether ultimately only further reforms to the EU's institutional system can help in this regard remains to be seen.

Bibliography

Allison GT and Halperin MH (1972) Bureaucratic Politics: A Paradigm and Some Policy Implications. *World Politics* 24(Supplement: Theory and Policy in International Relations): 40–79. DOI: 10.2307/2010559.

Allison GT and Zelikow P (1999) *Essence of Decision: Explaining the Cuban Missile Crisis*. 2nd ed. New York, NY: Longman.

Börzel T and Risse T (2009) *The Rise of (Inter-)Regionalism: The EU as a Model of Regional Integration*. APSA 2009 Toronto Meeting Paper, 13 August. SSRN. Available at: http://papers.ssrn.com/abstract=1450391 (accessed 15 January 2018).

Börzel TA and Risse T (2015) The EU and the Diffusion of Regionalism. In: Telò M, Fawcett L, and Ponjaert F (eds) *Interregionalism and the European Union: A Post-Revisionist Approach to Europe's Place in a Changing World*. Farnham: Ashgate, pp. 51–65.

Carlsnaes W, Sjursen H, and White B (eds) (2004) *Contemporary European Foreign Policy*. London: SAGE.

Damro C (2012) Market Power Europe. *Journal of European Public Policy* 19(5): 682–699. DOI: 10.1080/13501763.2011.646779.

Damro C (2015) Market Power Europe: Exploring a Dynamic Conceptual Framework. *Journal of European Public Policy* 22(9): 1336–1354. DOI: 10.1080/13501763.2015. 1046903.

Delreux T (2015) Bureaucratic Politics, New Institutionalism and Principal-Agent Models. In: Jørgensen KE, Aarstad ÅK, Drieskens E, et al. (eds) *The SAGE Handbook of European Foreign Policy*. London: SAGE, pp. 152–165.

Dijkstra H (2009) Commission Versus Council Secretariat: An Analysis of Bureaucratic Rivalry in European Foreign Policy. *European Foreign Affairs Review* 14(3): 431–450.

Doeser F (2011) Domestic Politics and Foreign Policy Change in Small States: The Fall of the Danish 'Footnote Policy'. *Cooperation and Conflict* 46(2): 222–241. DOI: 10.1177/0010836711406417.

Dominguez R (2015) *EU Foreign Policy Towards Latin America*. New York, NY: Palgrave MacMillan.

Egeberg M (1999) The Impact of Bureaucratic Structure on Policy Making. *Public Administration* 77(1): 155–170. DOI: 10.1111/1467-9299.00148.

Ellinas AA and Suleiman E (2012) *The European Commission and Bureaucratic Autonomy: Europe's Custodians*. Cambridge: Cambridge University Press.

García M (2008) *The Path to the 2002 Association Agreement Between the European Union and Chile: A Case Study in Successful Political Negotiation*. Lewiston, NY: Edwin Mellen.

García M (2011) Incidents Along the Path: Understanding the Rationale Behind the EU–Chile Association Agreement. *JCMS: Journal of Common Market Studies* 49(3): 501–524. DOI: 10.1111/j.1468-5965.2010.02149.x.

García M (2015) The European Union and Latin America: 'Transformative Power Europe' Versus the Realities of Economic Interests. *Cambridge Review of International Affairs* 28(4): 621–640. DOI: 10.1080/09557571.2011.647762.

Gastinger M (2016) The Tables Have Turned on the European Commission: The Changing Nature of the Pre-negotiation Phase in EU Bilateral Trade Agreements. *Journal of European Public Policy* 23(9): 1367–1385. DOI: 10.1080/13501763.2015.1079233.

Gustavsson J (1998) *The Politics of Foreign Policy Change: Explaining the Swedish Reorientation on EC Membership*. PhD Dissertation. Lund University, Lund. Available at: www.svet.lu.se/Fulltext/Jakob_G.pdf.

Hardacre A and Smith M (2009) The EU and the Diplomacy of Complex Interregionalism. *The Hague Journal of Diplomacy* 4(2): 167–188. DOI: 10.1163/187119109X440898.

Hardacre A and Smith M (2014) The European Union and the Contradictions of Complex Interregionalism. In: *Intersecting Interregionalism: Regions, Global Governance and the EU*. Dordrecht: Springer, pp. 91–106.

Hudson VM (2015) Foreign Policy Analysis Beyond North America. In: Brummer K and Hudson VM (eds) *Foreign Policy Analysis Beyond North America*. London: Lynne Rienner, pp. 1–14.

Larsen H (2009) A Distinct FPA for Europe? Towards a Comprehensive Framework for Analysing the Foreign Policy of EU Member States. *European Journal of International Relations* 15(3): 537–566. DOI: 10.1177/1354066109388247.

March JG and Olson JP (1983) Organizing Political Life: What Administrative Reorganization Tells Us About Government. *American Political Science Review* 77(2): 281–296. DOI: 10.2307/1958916.

Meissner KL (2018) *Commercial Realism and EU Trade Policy: Competing for Economic Power in Asia and the Americas*. Abingdon: Routledge.

Meunier S and Nicolaïdis K (2006) The European Union as a Conflicted Trade Power. *Journal of European Public Policy* 13(6): 906–925. DOI: 10.1080/13501760600838623.

Morgenstern-Pomorski J-H (2018) *The Contested Diplomacy of the European External Action Service: Inception, Establishment and Consolidation*. Abingdon: Routledge.

Peterson J and Sjursen H (1998) Conclusion: The Myth of the CFSP? In: Peterson J and Sjursen H (eds) *A Common Foreign Policy for Europe? Competing Visions of the CFSP*. London: Routledge, pp. 169–184.

Pollack MA (1997) Delegation, Agency, and Agenda Setting in the European Community. *International Organization* 51(1): 99–134.

Pollack MA (2003) *The Engines of European Integration: Delegation, Agency, and Agenda Setting in the EU*. Oxford: OUP.

Santander S (2010) The Ups and Downs of Interregionalism in Latin America. In: Söderbaum F and Stålgren P (eds) *The European Union and the Global South*. Boulder, CO: Lynne Rienner, pp. 89–114.

Santander S (2013) L'Union européenne, l'interrégionalisme et les puissances émergentes. *Politique européenne* 39(1): 106–135.

Sbragia A (2010) The EU, the US, and Trade Policy: Competitive Interdependence in the Management of Globalization. *Journal of European Public Policy* 17(3): 368–382. DOI: 10.1080/13501761003662016.

Schade D (2019) Fuzzy Roles in EU External Relations Governance: The Difficult Construction of Informal Policy Coordination Frameworks. In: van Heumen L and Roos M (eds) *The Informal Construction of Europe*. Routledge, pp. 199–216.

Smith ME (2013) The European External Action Service and the Security–Development Nexus: Organizing for Effectiveness or Incoherence? *Journal of European Public Policy* 20(9): 1299–1315.

Szymanski M and Smith ME (2005) Coherence and Conditionality in European Foreign Policy: Negotiating the EU–Mexico Global Agreement. *JCMS: Journal of Common Market Studies* 43(1): 171–192. DOI: 10.1111/j.0021-9886.2005.00551.x.

Toje A (2011) The European Union as a Small Power. *JCMS: Journal of Common Market Studies* 49(1): 43–60. DOI: 10.1111/j.1468-5965.2010.02128.x.

Welch DA (2005) *Painful Choices: A Theory of Foreign Policy Change*. Princeton, NJ: Princeton University Press.

White B (1999) The European Challenge to Foreign Policy Analysis. *European Journal of International Relations* 5(1): 37–66. DOI: 10.1177/1354066199005001002.

Appendix
List of interviews

#	Interviewee description	Place	Other
1	Former Commission official	Hamburg	
2	Former Latin American diplomat		Via telephone
3	Former member of the Barroso cabinet	London	
4	German official	Brussels	
5	Former Commission official	Brussels	Follow-up (Interview 1)
6	Senior DG Trade official	Brussels	
7	Senior Latin American diplomat	Brussels	Group interview
	Latin American diplomat 1		
	Latin American diplomat 2		
8	Senior EEAS official	Brussels	Group interview
	EEAS official		
9	Member state diplomat	Brussels	
10	Member of the European Parliament	Brussels	
11	Senior EU official	Brussels	Group interview
	EU official		
12	DG Trade official	Brussels	
13	Senior EEAS official	Brussels	
14	European Parliament official	Brussels	
15	NGO official	Brussels	
16	EEAS official	Brussels	Group interview
	EEAS official		
17	Former EU official	Brussels	
18	Former DG RELEX official	Brussels	
19	Member state diplomat	Brussels	
20	European Parliament official	Brussels	
21	European Parliament official	Brussels	
22	EEAS official	Brussels	
23	NGO official	Brussels	
24	Senior DG DEVCO official	Brussels	Group interview
	DG DEVCO official 1		
	DG DEVCO official 2		
25	European Parliament official	Brussels	
26	Latin American diplomat	Brussels	
27	Latin American diplomat	Brussels	
28	Latin American diplomat	Brussels	

(*Continued*)

Appendix (Continued)

#	Interviewee description	Place	Other
29	Member state diplomat	Brussels	
30	Member state diplomat 1	Brussels	Group interview
	Member state diplomat 2		
	Member state diplomat 3		
31	Former EU official	Brussels	Follow-up (Interview 17)
32	DG Trade official	Brussels	
33	Senior EEAS official	Brussels	
34	EEAS official	Brussels	
35	DG DEVCO official		

Index

Note: Entries in bold refer to tables. Entries followed by "n" refer to endnotes.

ALBA 131, 136, 162n26, 162n38
Andean Community 7, 126, 135–7, 173–4, 176; preparing negotiations with 129, 133–9; negotiations with 140–50; change of negotiation approach 144–50; ratification of FTAs 155–60; *see also* Ecuador
Ashton, Catherine 67–8, 146, 172
Association Agreement 3–5, **8**, 7–9; decision-making 58–60; *see also* Andean Community, Central America, Chile, Mercosur, Mexico, Ukraine
autonomy: in the Commission 60, 171–3; of institutions 26–8, **33**

Barroso, José Manuel 67–8, 127–8
Bolivia 136–7, 141–3, 147–9
Brazil 90, 108, 111; *see also* Mercosur
bureaucratic politics 10–11, 22–4, 33, 49–51, 60–1, 215–19; *see also* FPA

Cablegate *see* WikiLeaks
CAN *see* Andean Community
CAP 97, 99–100, 102–3
Central America 124–7; preparing negotiations with 127–30, 133–5, 137–8; negotiations with 150–4; ratification of AA 155, 157–60
CFSP 57–8, 67–8, 79–80, 200–1
Chile 9, 95–9, 104, 111–13, 188, 190
coherence *see* foreign policy coherence
Colombia 155; road map 156–7, 159; *see also* Andean Community
Common Foreign and Security Policy *see* CFSP
complex negotiations 3–7, **8**, 9–10, 19–20, 210–11, 220–2; determinants of EU position 215–19
Common Agricultural Policy *see* CAP

Common Commercial Policy 50–4, 155
coordination 5, 27–8, 59–62, 64–7, 69
COREPER 138–9
Council of the EU 76–7, 101–6, 109–10, 137–9; presidency 57, 77, 93, 104, 131–2, 150
CSDP 182, 205
Cuba 183–7; Common Position 134, 183–4

decision-making: complexity 28–9; rationality 21–3, 30; *see also* Association Agreement, FTA, negotiations
democracy clause 93–4
development cooperation 141–2, 180–1, 183–4; decision-making 54–7
DG Trade 28, 51–4, 110–11, 130, 132, 173–81
Directorate-General (DG): organization 69, **70–3**, 74–5; *see also* DG Trade
Doha Development Agenda 124, 131–4

economy: competition 135, 145, 176, 220; interests 124–7
Ecuador 131, 141–3, 148–9; FTA 173–81; *see also* Andean Community
EEAS 56–7, 67–8, 75, 80–2, 172–3, 218, 221–2; in negotiations 181–90
EU Delegation 74
EU–Latin America relations 89–90, 219–20; 1999 Rio summit 99–100, 102–5; 2004 Guadalajara summit 109; 2002 Madrid summit 111–12, 128; 2006 Vienna summit 131, 133, 135–7; 2008 Lima summit 143; 2010 Madrid summit 149–50, 182; 2013/2015 summits 188–9; EU–LAC Foundation 181–2
EU Trade Policy *see* Common Commercial Policy

European Commission: portfolios **63–4**; organisation 60–2, 64–8; *see also* Directorate-General, DG Trade
European External Action Service *see* EEAS
European Parliament 94, 154–7, 177–80, 186, 206; decision-making 51–3, 59
European Union Latin America and the Caribbean Foundation *see* EU–Latin American relations

Ferrero-Waldner, Benita 67–8, 128–9
Foreign Policy Analysis *see* FPA
foreign policy change 21–2, 24; *see also* FPA
foreign policy coherence 5, 15–18, 40–1, 78, 81
FPA 10, 18–19, 211; and the EU 17–21, 211, 215, 218; *see also* bureaucratic politics
Free Trade Agreement *see* FTA
Free Trade Area of the Americas (FTAA) 98
FTA: decision-making 50–4; *see also* DG Trade

Generalised System of Preferences (GSP) 158, 174–5, 177–80

historical institutionalism 31; *see also* institutionalism
Honduras 151–2
human rights 79–80, 94, 142, 156–7, 159, 201

institutionalism 29–32
institutional change: EU Commission 62, **63–4**, 64–8; Council of the EU 76–7; DGs 69, **70–3** 74–5
institutions: autonomy 26–8; interests 25–6
interregionalism 37–40, 219

Japan 203–6
Juncker Commission 68, 217

Latin America strategy 90, 103, 133–4, 149,
lobbying 99, 103–4, 107, 109, 144, 156–7, 178

Marín, Manuel 64–5, 90, 92–3, 96, 99, 100–1, 103
member states 51–4, 57–8, 76–8; permissive consensus 134, 220
Mexico: Global Agreement 90–5; Association Agreement 187–90
Mercosur 95–101; negotiation mandate approval 101–6; negotiations 106–11
mixed agreement 51–2, 59, 158, 186, 206
Mogherini, Federica 173, 217, 221–2

NAFTA 91–2, 94
negotiation mandate 9, 51–3, 58–9
negotiations: decision-making 50–4, 57–60, *see also* complex negotiations
Nicaragua 151–3

Ordinary Legislative Procedure (OLP) 55, 155

Pacific Alliance 182, 190
path dependence 31, 176, 218–19
Peru *see* Andean Community
policy inertia 23–5, **33**, 204, 218
political dialogue 57–8, 90, 126, 204–6
principal-agent analysis 29–31
process tracing 32
provisional application 157–9, 175, 203

ratification 51–2, 59, 155
regional integration 7, 37–9, 89–90, 95–8, 219–20
research methods 32–4
safeguards legislation 155, 157
sources 34–7
strategic partnership 8–9, 187–88

Trade Policy Committee 52, 54, 76
Treaty of Lisbon 49, 80–2, 154–5, 171–3

Ukraine 199–203; AA referendum 202–3
United States (US) 91–2, 98, 132–3, 220

Venezuela 131, 134–6

WikiLeaks 36
World Trade Organization (WTO) 50–1, 97, 100, 105, 108, 131–2; banana dispute 131, 138–9, 149